Arnold Wesker (FRSL, Litt.D.), born in Stepney in 1932, was taught at Upton House School in Hackney. His education came mainly from reading books and listening to BBC Radio. Between 1948 and 1958 he pursued many trades from furniture-maker to pastry-cook. His career began when Lindsay Anderson, who had read *The Kitchen* and *Chicken Soup with Barley*, brought Wesker to the attention of George Devine at the Royal Court Theatre; Devine, uncertain about *Chicken Soup with Barley*, sent it to the Belgrade Theatre in Coventry, where it was first produced in 1958, directed by John Dexter. A year later, having been turned down by the Royal Court, *Roots* was directed by Dexter, again at the Belgrade, and in the following months he directed *The Kitchen* at the Court for two Sunday night experimental performances 'without decor'. Later in 1959 *I'm Talking about Jerusalem* was added to make up *The Wesker Trilogy*, which created an enormous impact when produced in its entirety at the Royal Court in 1960 and again at the Shaw Theatre in 1978. In 1979 the National Film Development Board commissioned a film script of the three plays, which, because Wesker made many cuts and additions, is a new work – *The Trilogy* twenty years on! Over 350,000 copies of the Penguin edition have been sold. The hardback is in its fifth printing.

His other plays include *Chips With Everything* (1962, voted 'Play of the Year'), *Their Very Own and Golden City* (1965, winner of the Italian Premio Marzotto Drama Award in 1964), *The Four Seasons* (1965), *The Friends* (1970), *The Old Ones* (1972), *The Journalists* (1972), *The Wedding Feast* (1974), *Shylock* (1976), *Love Letters on Blue Paper* (1977), *One More Ride on the Merry-go-round* (1978), *Caritas* (1980); *Annie Wobbler* (1981), *Four Portraits – of Mothers* (1982), *Yardsale* (1984), *Whatever Happened to Betty Lemon?* (1986), *The Mistress* (1988), these last five forming the cycle of *One-Woman Plays*; *Bluey* (1984, European Radio Commission), *Sullied Hand* (1985), *When God Wanted a Son* (1986), *Shoeshine* and *Little Old Lady* (1987; one-act plays for young people), *Lady Othello* (1987) and the six plays collected here.

In addition to plays for the stage Arnold Wesker has written television and film scripts, poems, short stories and numerous essays and lectures. He has published two collections of essays, *Fears of Fragmentation* (1970) and *Distinctions* (1985), and three volumes of stories, *Six Sundays in January* (1971), *Love Letters on Blue Paper* (1974) and *Said the Old Man to the Young Man* (1978). In 1974 he wrote the text for a book of primitive paintings of the East End by John Allin, *Say Goodbye You May Never See Them Again*. In 1977, after a brief stay in the offices of the *Sunday Times* to gather material for *The Journalists*, he published an account of his visit called 'Journey into Journalism'. In 1978 came *Fatlips*, his only book for young people. Penguin have published seven volumes of his plays and a collection of short stories under the title *Love Letters on Blue Paper*.

From 1961 to 1970 Arnold Wesker was artistic director of Centre 42, a cultural movement for popularizing the arts primarily through trade-union support. From 1981 to 1983 he was President of the International Playwrights' Committee. He is a grandfather and lives in Wales. His recently completed autobiography, *As Much as I Dare*, is due to be published in late 1994.

ARNOLD WESKER

WILD SPRING
AND OTHER PLAYS

Badenheim 1939
Beorhtel's Hill
Three Women Talking
Letter to a Daughter
Blood Libel
Wild Spring

VOLUME 7

PENGUIN BOOKS

PENGUIN BOOKS

Published by the Penguin Group
Penguin Books Ltd, 27 Wrights Lane, London w8 5tz, England
Penguin Books USA Inc., 375 Hudson Street, New York, New York 10014, USA
Penguin Books Australia Ltd, Ringwood, Victoria, Australia
Penguin Books Canada Ltd, 10 Alcorn Avenue, Toronto, Ontario, Canada m4v 3b2
Penguin Books (NZ) Ltd, 182–190 Wairau Road, Auckland 10, New Zealand

Penguin Books Ltd, Registered Offices: Harmondsworth, Middlesex, England

This collection published in Penguin Books 1994
1 3 5 7 9 10 8 6 4 2

The extract on pp. 64–5 from 'For Frau Johanna Von Kunesch' in *Poems: 1906 to 1926* by
Rainer Maria Rilke, translated by J. B. Leishman, appears by permission of the Estate of Rainer
Maria Rilke, the Estate of J. B. Leishman and the Hogarth Press

Badenheim 1939 is an adaptation of Aharon Appelfeld's novel *Badenheim 1939* and is published
by permission of Aharon Appelfeld and Wylie, Aitken & Stone, Inc.

The epigraph to *Wild Spring* by George Bernard Shaw appears by permission of the Society
of Authors on behalf of the George Bernard Shaw Estate

The moral right of the author has been asserted

Set in 10½/12½ pt Monophoto Bembo

Printed in England by Clays Ltd, St Ives plc

CONTENTS

BADENHEIM 1939

a play in five parts
no interval

with music needing to be composed

adapted by *Arnold Wesker*
from the novel by *Aharon Appelfeld*

Blaendigeddi
September 1987

CHARACTERS
(in order of appearance)

Much doubling of characters is of course possible.

SIX SANITATION INSPECTORS
MARTIN, the chemist
TRUDE, his wife
HEADWAITER
WAITRESS
PASTRY-SHOP OWNER
SALLY, a local ex-whore
GERTIE, the same
KARL
LOTTE, his girlfriend
GUESTS, as many as
    affordable
PORTERS
SIX-MAN BAND including
    SAMITZKY and
    CONDUCTOR
DR SHUTZ
SCHOOLGIRL
DR PAPPENHEIM
FRAU ZAUBERBLIT
PROFESSOR RAINER
    FUSSHOLDT

FRAU MITZI FUSSHOLDT, his
    wife
PRINCESS MILBAUM
THE TWINS, her protégés
DR LANGMAN
OLD MAN
TELEGRAPH ASSISTANT
THE YANUKA, a wunderkind
TOWNSWOMAN
THE MANDELBAUM TRIO
STRANGERS: parents and
    children; middle aged and
    well dressed
THE MAJOR
FRAU ZAUBERBLIT'S
    DAUGHTER
HOTEL OWNER
CHEF, from pastry shop
SALO, the salesman
TWO SANATORIUM MEN
HELENA, Trude's daughter
OLD RABBI in wheelchair

NOTES

Badenheim is an Austrian spa. The guests are mostly middle-class, bohemian Jews.

Settings and action centre round the town square.

As a general principle dialogue and movement are concurrent: that is to say, exchanges take place while there is movement elsewhere.

Occasionally certain areas will need to come into focus; then all else freezes. This is necessary not only to intrude, say, on THE MANDELBAUM TRIO or THE TWINS rehearsing, but to facilitate the technical effect of the settings deteriorating.

MUSIC

Original music is called for. Namely:

five dances: waltz, polka, tango, Hasidic dance, jazz dance
band music
a work for trio and brass band
songs for THE YANUKA
incidental music

BREAKDOWN OF SCENES AND MUSIC

PART ONE
: The town square — *waltz*
The chemist's shop
The café tables
The chemist's shop — *band music*
The town square

PART TWO
: The municipal notice-board
The café tables
A hotel room
Telegraph office
Hotel lobby
Professor Fussholdt's room
The town square — *polka*
The café tables — *Hasidic dance*

PART THREE
: The town square — *chamber music*
The chemist's shop
A corner of the square
Frau Zauberblit's room
Telegraph office
Sanitation Department
Frau Zauberblit's room
Sanitation Department
Hotel lounge
The concert hall — THE YANUKA'S SONGS

PART FOUR
: Hotel front door
The pastry shop
Hotel bar — *jazz dance* and *work for trio and brass band*

Frau Zauberblit's room
The chemist's shop
Hotel lobby
The town square
The hotel cellar — *tango*

} Silent scenes
except for
*work for trio
and brass band*

The café tables and town square — *tango*
The chemist's shop
Hotel dining-room
Gertie's and Sally's front-room — music from old
    horn gramophone

PART FIVE   The hotel steps — *a fierce violin cadenza*
Road to the station
The station

PART ONE

THE TOWN SQUARE

Something impending. What?

We are uncertain if it is spring into summer, the town blossoming into holiday spa or —

— something else.

The first two events are ominous, dark, at variance with the setting's poised promise of gaiety.

But to begin —

the stage is shrouded in spring's shadows.

Slowly they withdraw, leaving the stage bathed in the cheerful light of an early summer sun.

Before this movement of light is completed, two men arrive in the distinctive uniform of SANITATION INSPECTORS.

They prise open the heavy metal lid of first one sewer, then another, checking.

They are more than what they seem to be.

Before they leave, a woman peers out of the window over the chemist's shop. TRUDE: *a disturbed soul.*

She watches them as they leave.

They register her.

A man passes them, carrying packages from the station: MARTIN, *the chemist,* TRUDE's *husband.*

The SANITATION INSPECTORS *register him too.*

MARTIN [*to* TRUDE, *indicating his packages*]: The train arrived on time.

TRUDE: And the mail?

MARTIN: A summer's supply of medication.

TRUDE: Where is the mail?

MARTIN: The holiday-makers can over-indulge. Food, drink, passion — I have a remedy.

9

TRUDE: No mail?

MARTIN [*patient and sad*]: No mail, Trude. It's Monday, the mail only comes in the afternoon.

[*She withdraws. He enters.*

The shadows have been moving away all this time. The growing light is — tingling!

Perhaps some of the town's inhabitants cross the square.

The HEADWAITER *to his hotel?*

The WAITRESS *to her café?*

The PASTRY-SHOP OWNER *to open his shop?*

SALLY *and* GERTIE, *the local ex-whores, admiring each other's new summer frocks?*

One couple arrive, just off the train. Guests for the hotel: KARL *pulls* LOTTE, *his reluctant partner for the holiday. They enter.*

Life slowly burgeons. Light grows. The air is full of church-bells and a sense of — arrival!

The spa bursts into life.

GUESTS *emerge from the hotel on their way to walks.*

Other GUESTS *take their places in the café.*

PASTRY-SHOP OWNER *decorates his shop with flowers.*

PORTERS *carry bags into the hotel.*

Activity around the souvenir shop.

The SIX-MAN BAND, *dressed in blue, take their places in the bandstand under their* CONDUCTOR.

When the different areas of life at the spa have been established, there is a sudden hush. Something is about to happen. Gaiety held in check. Suppressed giggles. Stifled squeals of delight. The CONDUCTOR *raises his baton. Anticipation!*

The BAND *play a waltz! The square is alive with* WALTZ-ING COUPLES.

When it is over, applause, laughter.

A young man, DR SHUTZ, *emerges from the pastry shop with a tray of cream cakes. He seems anxious not to be observed. They are for* SALLY *and* GERTIE, *who are delighted.*]

SALLY: Forbidden cakes!

GERTIE: Which *we* are forbidden!

DR SHUTZ: He'll never know.

[*But the* PASTRY-SHOP OWNER *has seen him.*]

PASTRY-SHOP OWNER: No cakes for whores! No cakes for whores! They have disgraced the town. Never again, Dr Shutz. You will not enter my shop ever again.

[*Mixed laughter, scandalized cries.*]

DR SHUTZ: He'll forget and forgive. Eat and enjoy.

[*Suddenly — an apparition! A young woman arrives. She is stunningly beautiful but anxious, as though she should not be there and fears being caught. She is the* SCHOOLGIRL.

DR SHUTZ *is struck. Cannot take his eyes off her. Hypnotized, he moves to her, takes her cases and helps her into the hotel, out of which comes —*

DR PAPPENHEIM, *a most important man, Artistic Director of Badenheim's central event: the Music Festival. There is even a little applause as he appears.*

He approaches SALLY *and* GERTIE.]

DR PAPPENHEIM: And how are the ladies?

GERTIE: Ah! Dr Pappenheim, if only everyone thought us ladies.

DR PAPPENHEIM: The past is the past. We must all be allowed to change our views, our styles, our friends, our husbands, our wives, our skins, our very lives!

GERTIE: A gentleman!

SALLY: A gentleman!

GERTIE: A real gentleman!

SALLY: And what has been happening out there in the big wide world?

GERTIE: The spa in winter is a very isolated place for women like us.

SALLY: For all the townspeople.

GERTIE: For all the townspeople.

DR PAPPENHEIM: Happening? Out there? Oh, nothing out of the ordinary.

GERTIE: But it was a strange winter.

SALLY: You must agree, a strange winter.

DR PAPPENHEIM: Not to worry! My festival's full of surprises this year.

SALLY [*delighted*]: Oh! Surprises!

DR PAPPENHEIM: A yanuka.

SALLY [*to* GERTIE, *maternally*]: A yanuka.

DR PAPPENHEIM: A child prodigy.

GERTIE [*to* SALLY]: A child prodigy.

DR PAPPENHEIM: With a voice to bring back paradise and all our lost innocence.

SALLY: All our lost innocence.

[*The* HEADWAITER *brings a telegram for* DR PAPPEN-HEIM.]

DR PAPPENHEIM [*opening it*]: Discovered him in Vienna. In the winter.

[*He reads telegram.*]

Catastrophe!

[*One of the bandsmen,* SAMITZKY, *strolls up.*]

SAMITZKY: Telegrams are always catastrophe.

DR PAPPENHEIM: Mandelbaum!

SAMITZKY [*impressed*]: Mandelbaum?

DR PAPPENHEIM: He's ill!

SAMITZKY: Mandelbaum here?

DR PAPPENHEIM: He's cancelled.

SAMITZKY: You managed to persuade the Mandelbaum Trio to come here?

DR PAPPENHEIM: After years and years of begging.

SAMITZKY: The Mandelbaum Trio!

DR PAPPENHEIM: The crowning glory!

SAMITZKY: Don't despair. At least you have us.

[DR PAPPENHEIM, *never having had real respect for the band, rushes off.*]

DR PAPPENHEIM: Telegrams! I must send telegrams. My festival is falling apart.

[FRAU ZAUBERBLIT *greets* SAMITZKY.]

FRAU ZAUBERBLIT: There is a faraway look in your eye, Mr Samitzky.

SAMITZKY: Strange thing. I feel homesick for Poland.

FRAU ZAUBERBLIT: And why is that?

SAMITZKY: Who knows? I was seven when I left, but it seems only yesterday.

FRAU ZAUBERBLIT: Ah! Longings, longings. They come at you from nowhere. I was thinking about my grandfather's house. He was the Rabbi of Kirchenhaus, you know. A man of God. In the evenings he'd walk by the river. He loved nature.

[*A* BANDSMAN *calls to* SAMITZKY.]

BANDSMAN: Samitzky! Come and look at this pay cheque.

[FRAU ZAUBERBLIT *bows to* SAMITZKY *as he excuses himself.*
    She is deciding which way to go for her walk. Her gaze stops at a couple.
    It is LOTTE *and* KARL.]

LOTTE: All you know about me is that my husband was the head of a big firm and that he was killed in an avalanche. And all I know about you is that you're divorced and that your children live with their grandfather.

KARL: We'll learn more as the weeks go by. You'll see. Baden-heim gives one such a feeling of vitality. You'll be so happy you've decided to stay.

LOTTE: I *haven't* decided to stay.

[TRUDE, *sad, at her window.*]

TRUDE [*to* MARTIN *below*]: Why is everyone walking so slowly?

MARTIN: Because they're on vacation, silly woman, that's why.

TRUDE: They all look very pale to me.

MARTIN: They've just come from the city.

TRUDE: Isn't that man standing beside Frau Zauberblit her brother?

MARTIN: No, Trude. Her brother's been dead for years.

TRUDE: Has the mail come yet?

MARTIN: Yes, but there's nothing for us.

[*No one is standing beside* FRAU ZAUBERBLIT.
The SCHOOLGIRL *joins her and they go off, followed by a besotted* DR SHUTZ.]

FRAU ZAUBERBLIT: There's nothing like a holiday in Badenheim.

[*At the bandstand.*]

BANDSMAN [*to* SAMITZKY]: Is this what was agreed?

SAMITZKY [*impatiently*]: It was agreed, it was agreed!

BANDSMAN: Because Pappenheim is not to be trusted, you know.

SAMITZKY: Are your rooms satisfactory?

BANDSMAN: For a change!

SAMITZKY: Clean sheets, clean linen?

BANDSMAN: Because we nagged all these years.

SAMITZKY: And who keeps you supplied with sweets and beer?

BANDSMAN: No more than our due.

SAMITZKY: Our due! Our due! We're a third-rate band, we never rehearse, and we keep on and on and on about our due! Me? I don't care. We'll soon be going to Poland.

BANDSMAN: Poland?

SAMITZKY [*uncertain why he's said it*]: So you'd better brush up on your Yiddish.

[LOTTE *approaches.*]

LOTTE: Excuse me, is it possible to post a letter from here?

SAMITZKY: Of course.

LOTTE: That's strange. I thought the place was completely isolated.

[*She wanders off as though lost.*]

BANDSMAN: *She's* not a regular.
SAMITZKY: She's not the only one.

[*The* CONDUCTOR *raps his baton. Time to continue playing.*
As they play, it becomes evening.
Against the music all else freezes.]

THE CHEMIST'S SHOP

TRUDE *upstairs lying on the bed.*

  Downstairs MARTIN *is being questioned by a* SANITATION IN-SPECTOR, *who writes down the answers.*

SANITATION INSPECTOR: The business is yours?

MARTIN: Yes, sir.

SANITATION INSPECTOR: Under your name only?

MARTIN: Martin Kesselman, yes, sir.

SANITATION INSPECTOR: Did you inherit it?

MARTIN: Inherit? [*laughs*] My parents were penniless.

SANITATION INSPECTOR: Then how could you acquire such a prosperous concern?

MARTIN: When I bought this shop it was not prosperous. The natural beauty of Badenheim hadn't been discovered yet.

SANITATION INSPECTOR: It is worth how much now would you say?

MARTIN: Such strange questions. You're the Sanitation Department. Why aren't you asking when I last spring-cleaned and disinfected?

SANITATION INSPECTOR: When *was* that?

MARTIN: Funny people! A month ago.

  [*The* SANITATION INSPECTOR *puts away his papers. Takes out a measure and measures the room.*
  While he's doing that, TRUDE *calls:*]

TRUDE: Martin? Martin?

  [*He cannot go to her until the* SANITATION INSPECTOR *has finished measuring and leaves, which he does without a word.*]

MARTIN: Funny people.

[MARTIN *runs upstairs to* TRUDE.]

TRUDE: Helena doesn't write because Leopold won't let her. He beats her and he's afraid she'll complain to us.

MARTIN: These are delusions, Trude. Your daughter's well and your son-in-law is a good man.

TRUDE: I wish I had kept in contact with my brothers.

MARTIN: That's your problem! Your heart is still with the old world, with those peasant Jews up in the mountains. Finish with this nostalgia and melancholy. It's beginning to affect me.

THE CAFÉ TABLES

People strolling.

DR PAPPENHEIM, FRAU ZAUBERBLIT *and* FRAU MITZI FUSS-
HOLDT *sit at the café table.* DR PAPPENHEIM *is distressed.*

MITZI [*of* DR PAPPENHEIM]: He's inconsolable.

FRAU ZAUBERBLIT: I'll buy him his favourite French wine.

DR PAPPENHEIM: Who will save me from artists!

FRAU ZAUBERBLIT: Don't worry. If the Mandelbaum Trio
doesn't answer your telegrams, I'll get the Kraus Chamber
Ensemble for you. No unhappiness! I won't have it. I left the
sanatorium to holiday in Badenheim with old friends. I feel
young and happy –

MITZI: – and in love –

FRAU ZAUBERBLIT: – and in love. Isn't it absurd? At my age.
And with a drummer in a band who still speaks German with
a Polish accent.

[*At a nearby table* LOTTE *and* KARL: *a strained relationship.*]

LOTTE: What am I doing here? Why did you bring me?

KARL: Relax. Please.

LOTTE: What's so wonderful about this place?

KARL: A festival.

LOTTE: A festival?

KARL: A music festival.

LOTTE: You didn't say.

KARL: Everybody comes to Badenheim for the air and the
festival.

LOTTE [*momentarily interested*]: Where does it take place?

KARL: In the big hall.

LOTTE [*her interest evaporates*]: I must go.

[*Stands, moves away, restless.*]

KARL: You can't imagine how wonderful it is.
LOTTE: I've been trying to go for days.
KARL: The great artists —
LOTTE: Why won't you let me go?
KARL: — the atmosphere . . .
LOTTE: Just point me in the direction of the station.
KARL: It's night. There are no trains.

[*He reaches for her hand. She is unhappy, which —*
— contrasts to the happy laughter we hear from the SCHOOL-
GIRL *being chased by a wild* DR SHUTZ.]

FRAU ZAUBERBLIT [*calling*]: Dr Shutz! Join us! Intelligent com-
pany and intelligent conversation.
DR SHUTZ [*in flight*]: For to everything there is a season!
DR PAPPENHEIM: Wasted! The man has a great musical talent.
FRAU ZAUBERBLIT: The man also has a rich old mother who
pays his debts.
MITZI: Everyone spoils him. The darling of Badenheim. Besotted
by him.
FRAU ZAUBERBLIT: Though now I rather think he's besotted *by*.
MITZI: Who *is* she?
FRAU ZAUBERBLIT: A wild young thing! A runaway! From her
boarding-school.
DR PAPPENHEIM: Spring drives the young mad. Me — it makes
gloomy.
FRAU ZAUBERBLIT: No gloom! I've promised to cover your
losses. No gloom!

[LOTTE *still stands, wanting to go, somewhere, anywhere.*]

LOTTE: Why, *why* did you bring me here?
KARL: The festival! Believe me! No evil intentions! An artistic
experience.
LOTTE: I don't need an artistic experience!
KARL: Stay for one event.
LOTTE: I want to go back to the city.

KARL: Just one event. You can go back after that.

LOTTE [*unconvinced*]: I do not know what I am doing here.

KARL: Because it would be a loss. To miss such an impressive experience would be a loss.

> [*Suddenly a scream rends the air.*
> *Everyone freezes.*]

THE CHEMIST'S SHOP

TRUDE. *Her bedroom. She cannot stop screaming.*
  MARTIN *on his knees, his arms round her waist, his head clasped to her belly.*

MARTIN: Trude, please, Trude! Calm yourself. There's no forest here. There's no wolves here. There's only me. Martin. Your husband. Trude, please.

  [*Music from the band takes over from her screams.*
    The music is — strange.]

THE TOWN SQUARE

The atmosphere is equally strange.

The square is full of uncertain people, uncertain shadows.

As the light falls, DR SHUTZ *is drawing the shy* SCHOOLGIRL *back up the hotel steps and through its doors.*

Blackout.

PART TWO

THE MUNICIPAL NOTICE-BOARD

Days later.

GUESTS *cluster round the board. A buzz of concern rises from them, grows, and finally bursts as though from a pressure they had been enclosing.*

What they have been enclosing are five SANITATION INSPECTORS.

Two busy themselves measuring places — the café, the souvenir shop, the pastry shop — and writing in their books.

Three engage three separate persons or couples in questions, the answers to which are also written in their books.

The questioning is quiet, even friendly.

The first confrontation is with MITZI *and* PROFESSOR FUSSHOLDT.

1ST SANITATION INSPECTOR [*to* MITZI *and* PROFESSOR FUSSHOLDT]: Name?

PROFESSOR FUSSHOLDT: Professor Rainer and Frau Mitzi Fussholdt.

1ST SANITATION INSPECTOR: Ages?

PROFESSOR FUSSHOLDT: Forty-five and thirty-five. My wife that is, thirty-five. I'm forty-five.

1ST SANITATION INSPECTOR: Profession?

PROFESSOR FUSSHOLDT: University lecturer.

1ST SANITATION INSPECTOR: In what?

PROFESSOR FUSSHOLDT: Jewish history.

1ST SANITATION INSPECTOR: Purpose of visit?

PROFESSOR FUSSHOLDT: Holiday ostensibly, but in fact it will be my wife who enjoys the holiday. I'm here to work on the proofs of my last book. Five years' work. My best. The jewel in my crown.

1ST SANITATION INSPECTOR: It is about?

PROFESSOR FUSSHOLDT: I've lectured on Theodor Herzl, a hack writer with Messianic pretensions. It could be about that. I've lectured on Martin Buber, who couldn't make up his mind if he was a prophet or a professor. It could be about that. I've lectured about Karl Kraus, now *there* was a great Jew — though he didn't like Jews if the truth be known but — he revived satire! Very important! How can a society be healthy without satire? It could be a book about that. Hack journalists, Jewish art, opportunism — it could be about any of those things.

1ST SANITATION INSPECTOR: And which of those things *is* it about?

PROFESSOR FUSSHOLDT: Ha! Look at him! He writes everything down!

[2ND SANITATION INSPECTOR *questions the* WAITRESS.]

2ND SANITATION INSPECTOR: Married or single?

WAITRESS: Single.

2ND SANITATION INSPECTOR: Do you live here?

WAITRESS: Oh no, only for the season.

2ND SANITATION INSPECTOR: Permanent address?

WAITRESS: 29 Kaiser Strasse, Vienna.

2ND SANITATION INSPECTOR: Father's name?

WAITRESS: Same as mine. Rosenbaum. Theodore Rosenbaum.

2ND SANITATION INSPECTOR: Mother's maiden name?

WAITRESS: Schmidt. Eva Schmidt.

2ND SANITATION INSPECTOR: Father — Rosenbaum, mother — Schmidt? A curious mixture.

WAITRESS: And I'm the curious result!

[*She laughs gaily. Not so the* 2ND SANITATION INSPECTOR.

3RD SANITATION INSPECTOR *questions newly arrived guests,* PRINCESS MILBAUM *and* THE TWINS.]

3RD SANITATION INSPECTOR: And you are their **patroness**, Duchess?

PRINCESS MILBAUM: I have that honour.

3RD SANITATION INSPECTOR: Is this their first appearance at the festival?

PRINCESS MILBAUM: Good heavens, no! They have been coming every year for seven years.

3RD SANITATION INSPECTOR: And they have come to do what precisely?

PRINCESS MILBAUM: To give readings precisely.

3RD SANITATION INSPECTOR: And what do they read?

PRINCESS MILBAUM: Poetry, young man, poetry! Do you have many more of these questions?

3RD SANITATION INSPECTOR [*with quiet contempt*]: Poetry. The poetry of whom?

PRINCESS MILBAUM: The poetry of Rainer Maria Rilke.

3RD SANITATION INSPECTOR [*writing*]: Rainer Maria Rilke.

[*A* 6TH SANITATION INSPECTOR *has appeared during these interrogations and has been sticking up posters on the various municipal boards.*

We become aware of them. They read:

LABOUR IS LIFE.
THE AIR IN POLAND IS FRESH.
SAIL ON THE VISTULA.
THE DEVELOPMENT AREAS NEED YOU.
GET TO KNOW THE SLAVIC CULTURE.

GROUPS *gather to look at them.*

Sounds of knocking.

Renewed activity.

SANITATION INSPECTORS *walk through carrying rolls of barbed wire and cement pillars suggestive of prisoner compounds.*

The knocking stops.

Sounds of orders, instructions, barked.

In the distance we see poles rising and strange, unpleasant flags being hoisted.]

SAMITZKY: If you ask me, the Sanitation Department is going to all this trouble because the festival's going to be a big affair this year.

FRAU ZAUBERBLIT: Our dear Dr Pappenheim is making a name for himself at last.

SAMITZKY: There'll be more fun and games this year than ever.

MITZI: How can you be so sure?

[*A new guest emerges,* DR LANGMAN.]

DR LANGMAN: It could be that a health hazard has cropped up.

SAMITZKY: A health hazard? With such preparations?

DR LANGMAN: Or they could be Income Tax Inspectors. Disguised!

SAMITZKY: Income Tax Inspectors go looking for bigger fish, and the barriers are for a public celebration.

MITZI: I'm going for a swim in the pool, public celebration or no public celebration.

SAMITZKY: A really, really big affair.

[MITZI *leaves.*

We see her later, on the veranda overlooking the pool, in a swimsuit in which she stays for most of the season.

SAMITZKY *and* FRAU ZAUBERBLIT *take a seat in the café.*]

SAMITZKY [*to* FRAU ZAUBERBLIT, *shyly*]: I like your straw hat.

FRAU ZAUBERBLIT: One day, it was in the afternoon, after the doctors had taken my temperature, measured the amount of blood in my phlegm, written their little signs and notes on those utterly incomprehensible charts, I saw him. Death. Plain, undisguised. In the corridor, next to the basin. Like an old lover. Herr Death. And I decided. There and then. I dressed, made up this old, ravaged face you see before you, packed a bag, put on my straw hat and went to the railway station. Badenheim! I had to return to Badenheim.

I used to come here with my daughter and my ex-husband, you know. General Von Schmidt. She inherited his blond hair and pink cheeks. Attends a girls' *lycée* now. And the moment I arrived and saw familiar carriages, the faces of old friends, the pastry shop, the hotel, dear Dr Pappenheim — death left me. I feel no pain, I have appetite, I'm filled with an urge to go on long walks, and I want to laugh all the time.

[*reverie*] When I was young. When they were young. When the world was young.

[*reawakening*] But best of all, I've found my prince!

SAMITZKY: A prince who still speaks German with a Polish accent —

FRAU ZAUBERBLIT: But who speaks a wonderful musical Yiddish.

SAMITZKY: — who has these yearnings to go back to his little village in Poland?

FRAU ZAUBERBLIT: Poland is the most beautiful country in the world.

SAMITZKY: Most of the time I don't understand what you're saying, Frau Zauberblit. But I like you. I like you very much indeed. All these years I've played in the band, it's blunted me. I drink, sleep, beat my drum. That's my life. But now, you touch me. I don't understand what I can do for you but if I make you laugh – good! It's important to laugh.

[*An* OLD MAN *has been sitting eating a pastry in the café. Immaculately dressed.*

Suddenly he rises, half-eaten pastry in hand, clutches his heart, drops dead.

Commotion. He's carried off.

Two more SANITATION INSPECTORS *cross, carrying another roll of barbed wire.*

The CONDUCTOR *plays patience at a table.*

The WAITRESS *flirts with him.*]

WAITRESS: And last night someone dropped dead in the casino, and three weeks ago an old couple were found dead sitting in their armchairs. It's worrying. None of us stays young. Not even for a minute. So every death is a worry. Here, poppy-seed cake.

CONDUCTOR: Look, I can put a red queen on a black king and a black jack on the red queen. Now, what am *I*? A black king with a red queen laying on me or a black jack laying on a red queen?

[*He puts a hand up her skirt.*]

WAITRESS [*skipping away, pleased*]: Eat your poppy-seed cake. It's the last piece. There's no telling when the chef can make some more.

A HOTEL ROOM

THE TWINS, *the readers, rehearsing.*

PRINCESS MILBAUM, *enraptured, watches them.*

One is agitated in his delivery, the other is subdued. We see but do not hear them, as in a mime.

Their rehearsal is interrupted by the appearance of the HEAD-WAITER, *bringing a tray of pastries.*

PRINCESS MILBAUM *offers them to* THE TWINS, *who turn away. She pleads. No! She eats them herself.*

The rehearsal continues.

TELEGRAPH OFFICE

DR SHUTZ *has written a telegram, which the* TELEGRAPH ASSIST-
ANT *is checking by reading aloud. As he reads, he eats a pastry.*

TELEGRAPH ASSISTANT: DEAREST, DEAREST MOTHER. It's
cheaper to put one DEAREST.

    [*Contemptuous snort from* DR SHUTZ.]

    DEAREST, DEAREST MOTHER.
DR SHUTZ: You don't have to make a public performance out of
it.
TELEGRAPH ASSISTANT [*too softly*]: DEAREST, DEAREST MOTHER
STOP COST OF EVERYTHING IN BADENHEIM UP THIS YEAR
STOP DON'T KNOW WHERE MONEY IS GOING STOP YOUR
FAVOURITE SON EMBARRASSED WITH DEBTS STOP GENEROUS
LOAN WOULD HELP AND BE REPAID ON RETURN STOP THE
SWEET AIR IS DOING ME GOOD STOP WILL COME BACK
HEALTHY AND RENEWED STOP YOUR ADORING SON
RUDOLPH.

HOTEL LOBBY

A dark area in which an aquarium is illuminated.
    KARL, LOTTE *and* HEADWAITER *are looking at the fish.*

HEADWAITER: Last year a nature-lover persuaded the hotel owner to let him put some new fish into the tank. Blue Cambium they were called. First few days, perfect. They swam gaily back and forth. A very boring sort of life I've always thought, but no problem. Great harmony. Then, one morning, slaughtered! All the other fish. A massacre.

KARL: And are these the descendants of the murderers?

HEADWAITER: No, the hotel owner sentenced the murderers to death. These are new fish.

LOTTE: I see green ones and red ones.

HEADWAITER: I'm very fond of the red ones. There's something magnificent about them, don't you think?

KARL: Do they live in peace among themselves?

HEADWAITER: I think so. The green ones are very modest and retiring, not at all belligerent.

KARL: Shouldn't they be separated?

HEADWAITER: Perhaps. [*Beat.*] Come, I have some special pastries for you.

PROFESSOR FUSSHOLDT'S ROOM

PROFESSOR FUSSHOLDT, *absorbed in proof-reading. The room is filled with smoke from his pipe.*

His wife, MITZI, *enters with a plate of pastries.*

He takes one unheedingly.

She eats one. Lasciviously.

She is bored. He pays her no attention. She will try to attract his attention.

She reaches for a pot of cream, eases the strap of her swimsuit off her shoulder. Rubs cream into her skin.

Her husband continues with his work.

She takes cream in both hands, reaches into her swimsuit, rubs cream on her breasts.

In the distance — music. The SIX-MAN BAND.

The suggestive action is lost on PROFESSOR FUSSHOLDT. MITZI *gives up, irritated.*

The music explodes!

THE TOWN SQUARE

A polka! Dancing in the square.

Everybody who is not dancing eats pastries, which the WAITRESS *and* HEADWAITER *are serving relentlessly.*

When the dancing is over, there are cries of —

ASSORTED: Pastry! Pastry! I'm dying for a pastry! Cream! Strawberries! Chocolate! Marzipan!

> [*Out of the hubbub appears a baby-faced young man, almost a child, with a case in each hand:* THE YANUKA. *He wears a suit too big for him. He seems lost and out of place.*
>
> *His arrival brings the activity to a halt.*
>
> DR PAPPENHEIM *appears.*]

DR PAPPENHEIM: He's arrived! The Yanuka has arrived! Now you will hear a voice. *Now* will you hear a voice. I feel confident about my festival again and you will all feel proud and privileged to have been in Badenheim in 1939.

> [DR PAPPENHEIM *embraces the young man.*
>
> *The familiar circle gather round him, pull him to a café table, ply him with huge pastries.*
>
> *Most return to their activities.*
>
> *Two* SANITATION INSPECTORS *cross with another roll of barbed wire.*
>
> *A* 3RD SANITATION INSPECTOR *follows behind with two massive Dobermann dogs on heavy chains.*]

DR PAPPENHEIM: No more pastries. He needs a substantial meal first.

SALLY: One pastry won't harm.

GERTIE: Not one, surely.

DR PAPPENHEIM: Badenheim's gone mad. Everyone's eating pastries. They can't stop eating pastries. It's an illness.

SALLY: He's so young.

GERTIE: So sweet.

DR PAPPENHEIM: Everyone will love him.

FRAU ZAUBERBLIT: What's your name?

DR PAPPENHEIM: His name is Nahum Slotzker. Speak slowly. He doesn't understand German.

FRAU ZAUBERBLIT: Then what language will he sing in?

DR PAPPENHEIM: Yiddish of course! What a question. Yiddish! He'll sing in Yiddish.

SAMITZKY: Foen van ent bist Du? Lodz? (Where are you from? Lodz?)

THE YANUKA: Ich bin foen Kalashin. (I'm from Kalashin.)

SAMITZKY: Vos macht dein fater? (What does your father do?)

THE YANUKA: Erh reparirt shich. (He mends shoes.)

SAMITZKY: Uhn dein mamer hot a grinns gesheft! (And I'm sure your mother runs a vegetable store.)

THE YANUKA: Vee azoi hot ihr gevust? (How did you know?)

FRAU ZAUBERBLIT: Don't you love the way he speaks Yiddish?

GERTIE: But what does he say?

SALLY: We can't all speak Yiddish, you know.

SAMITZKY: He was born in Kalashin, his father's a cobbler and I guessed his mother ran a vegetable store.

FRAU ZAUBERBLIT [*with pride*]: He guessed.

SAMITZKY: I look at him and my youth comes back to me. We

came from different villages in Poland but I know everybody he knows.

DR PAPPENHEIM: Enough! He must rest. I'm making a banquet for him. You'll be able to ask him all the questions you want.

[DR PAPPENHEIM *departs with* THE YANUKA.

A buzz of whispers grows. ⋆ *It seems to be coming from a small group who are around one of the notice-boards.*

As each person leaves it, he seems to be handing on its message to someone else.

Others replace them by the board. The message spreads.

The words MUST ... JEWS ... ALL ... REGISTER ... *are heard disjointedly until gradually the full sentence is heard loud and clear and finally uttered by one very distressed person.*]

DR LANGMAN: All Jews must register?
SAMITZKY: That means me.

[*The refrain is picked up by others.*]

ASSORTED: And me ... and me ... and me ...

[*But not picked up by all. Some are confused. Some are angry, stern, aloof, silent.*]

SALLY: Where?
DR LANGMAN: With the Sanitation Department.
GERTIE: When?
DR LANGMAN: By the end of the month.
SALLY *and* GERTIE [*together*]: Why?

[*A* TOWNSWOMAN *steps into view.*]

TOWNSWOMAN: I know why. Because of *him.*

[*She points to* DR PAPPENHEIM, *who is just emerging on the steps of the hotel.*]

⋆ This is a theatrical device first used by Arianne Mnouchkine in her production: *1789.*

Him and his festival and his singers and his readers and his musicians! Artists! They draw attention to themselves! The authorities don't like it. There's too much excitement, too much laughing and singing and late-night parties. Too much —

[*She is at a loss for words.*]

DR LANGMAN: — decadence!

KARL: What is he talking about?

DR LANGMAN: You don't know what I'm talking about?

KARL: Explain!

DR LANGMAN: You can't see how this, this, this bohemian second-rater has reawakened all the old ghosts from their slumbers?

KARL: Perhaps Dr Langman would like us to send our children to military academies.

DR LANGMAN: What's wrong with young boys engaging in sports? Why must it always be violins?

KARL: Because violins please me and physical exercise revolts me.

DR LANGMAN: Then *you* go to Poland. *You* join the Ost Juden. Sport revolts them too, the little Eastern European Jews busy in their busy little busy shops.

KARL: Far better the busy little shopkeepers than busy little steel-hearted army cadets.

SAMITZKY: Why is everyone talking about little Eastern European Jews? I'm a little Eastern European Jew.

DR PAPPENHEIM: Please, no quarrels because of me.

DR LANGMAN: Your festival awakens ghosts!

SAMITZKY: You mean me? I'm a ghost? Because I'm a little Eastern European Jew I'm a ghost?

[*In anger he goes to the bandstand and begins to beat out a rhythm on his drum.*

The other BANDSMEN *pick up his rhythm, which is the beat of a lively* Hasidic *dance.*

The square becomes alive with this dance, seething with a kind of defiant anger.

When it ends — blackout.]

PART THREE

THE TOWN SQUARE

Out of the darkness come sounds:
*   the barking of the Dobermanns; hammering; lorries arriving; harsh*
orders; motor-bikes . . . merging into —
*   — chamber music and the flashing on and off of lights in different*
parts of the stage, revealing couples telling each other:

VOICES: Mandelbaum's arrived! Mandelbaum's arrived! Mandelbaum's arrived!

> [*The music grows fierce.* THE MANDELBAUM TRIO *are*
> *rehearsing.*
>   *Lights build.*
>   *A crowd of* GUESTS *has gathered round a stern and haughty*
> *man —* MANDELBAUM.
>   *He is obviously of much greater renown and importance*
> *than those surrounding him. He should not be there. He's out*
> *of place.*
>   *Music stops.*
>   *Lights full on.*]

DR PAPPENHEIM: I thought you'd never make it. It's wonderful.
My festival is complete.

> [*A new occurrence is taking place.*
>   STRANGERS *are appearing in town. They are haggard and*
> *dishevelled as they wander through with their belongings.*
>   *The first to appear: a* MOTHER, FATHER *and* CHILDREN,
> *silently peering, frightened.*
>   MANDELBAUM *regards them with distrust. How is it that*
> *he shares his arrival with such as these?*]

MANDELBAUM: They caught up with us in Reizenbach. At first

the whole thing seemed like a joke but no sir! The Austrians turned out to be as efficient as the Germans. No beating about the bush! The locals were sent home and the Jews were put into quarantine! Yes sir! Plain and simple!

FRAU ZAUBERBLIT: What did you do?

MANDELBAUM: What did I do? What did I *do*? What I always do in such a case, send letters to my Academy.

DR PAPPENHEIM: Who acted at once of course.

[MANDELBAUM *laughs sardonically*.]

MANDELBAUM: Acted? Nothing! No action, no answers. Nothing. Can you believe that? The Academy ignored its president! Denied its founder! Isn't that food for thought, eh? It fed *my* thoughts I can assure you. I'm bloated with thought. Ha!

GERTIE: They'll be sorry one day.

SALLY: Won't they just! Sorry indeed.

DR LANGMAN: Forgive me asking, maestro, but how then did you get here to Badenheim?

MANDELBAUM: A young officer. In charge of events in Reizenbach. An honourable young Prussian. We asked to be transferred to Badenheim. We explained to him, there's a festival there, we've been invited, we simply had to get to Badenheim.

DR LANGMAN: Forgive me again, maestro. But what did the young officer say?

MANDELBAUM: Say? Say? He laughed and gave his permission. What else was there to say to such madness? Laughed, gave his permission, snap! Like that! No nonsense!

DR PAPPENHEIM: And now the maestro is here, and if the maestro agrees to appear, ah!

FRAU ZAUBERBLIT: It will be the experience of our lives.

SALLY: The guests are extremely pleasant here.

GERTIE: They couldn't be more pleasant.

DR PAPPENHEIM: And this year, due to the restrictions, the atmosphere is intimate.

MANDELBAUM: Me? Appear? I'm just a Jew, a number, a file. I'm not a rabbi, I'm not a cantor. What do you need me for?

DR PAPPENHEIM: You are our maestro, our one and only maestro and the only one we want.

[MANDELBAUM's *haughtiness has crumbled. Suddenly he is — one of them!*]

MANDELBAUM: Are we all Jews here?
DR PAPPENHEIM: The servants have run away —
HEADWAITER: — but I'm a Jew born and bred —
WAITRESS: — and I'm half Jewish.
SALLY: Everyone you see.
GERTIE: But not everyone in the town.
HEADWAITER: Here in Badenheim the maestro has many admirers.
MANDELBAUM: Badenheim is far more beautiful than Reizenbach, let me tell you. Had I known it was so beautiful I would have accepted your invitation years ago, Pappenheim. A man never knows where true beauty lies hidden or where his true admirers are.

[PRINCESS MILBAUM *arrives and stands to one side waiting for* MANDELBAUM *to see her and approach. They are obviously from the same high-flown milieu.*
    He sees her. Rises. The others make way to allow these two naturally 'superior' beings to meet in private. He kisses her hand.]

PRINCESS MILBAUM: So, Professor Mandelbaum too is amongst us.
MANDELBAUM: With you here, Princess, my disgrace becomes public.
PRINCESS MILBAUM: And what does the Royal Academy have to say?
MANDELBAUM: They ignore my letters.
PRINCESS MILBAUM: Sever your connections with them!
MANDELBAUM: Ha! That will I certainly do.
PRINCESS MILBAUM: Teach them a lesson. Some manners.
MANDELBAUM [*conspiratorially*]: And here?
PRINCESS MILBAUM [*arrogantly*]: Rotten to the core!

[*More* STRANGERS *pass through.*

MANDELBAUM's *ferocity returns. He strides into the hotel.*

The chamber music *of* THE MANDELBAUM TRIO *is heard again, furiously, till it reaches a certain musical passage which it keeps repeating.*

MANDELBAUM *is rehearsing them mercilessly.*

We hear his voice raging at the musicians.

The repetition of the music is nerve-racking. No one can think clearly, speak coherently, walk straight.]

SCHOOLGIRL: Someone should go upstairs and rescue them. Mandelbaum's torturing them. He's a sadist!

[*No one responds.*]

This company makes me sick. As though nothing was happening. I'm going.

[*She leaves them.*

SHUTZ *follows her like a dog.*

The music stops abruptly.]

TRUDE: You registered us?

MARTIN: We're registered.

TRUDE: So quick? You've only just left.

MARTIN: It was a simple process. The clerk asked, 'Jew?' 'Jew,' I replied. 'Wife, Jewess?' 'Wife, Jewess,' I replied.

TRUDE: And Helena?

MARTIN: I told him, my daughter is no longer a Jewess.

TRUDE: What did he say?

MARTIN: He asked a lot of questions about her.

[TRUDE *gazes out of the window, remembers odd Polish words. With each one she remembers, she smiles, as with a sense of achievement.*]

TRUDE: Suknia slubna? Piłka? Jarzyny? Góra? Czy może pan mi powiedzieć gdzie jest dworzec Kolejowy? (Wedding dress? Ball? Vegetables? Mountain? Can you tell me the way to the railway station, please?)

MARTIN: You are still living in the mountains.

TRUDE: If God wills it, a person returns to the land of her birth.

WAITRESS: Will they let me come with you?

CONDUCTOR: What a question! Who'll wait on us if not you?

WAITRESS: But I'm not fully Jewish.

CONDUCTOR: And me, am I fully Jewish?

WAITRESS: Both your parents were Jewish, weren't they?

CONDUCTOR: Yes, my dear, they were *born* Jewish but – can you believe it – they converted to Christianity.

WAITRESS: Converted?

CONDUCTOR: You can't believe it can you?

WAITRESS: Did you tell them that when you registered?

CONDUCTOR: I told them.

WAITRESS: What did they say?

CONDUCTOR: They wrote it down. Everything you tell them they write down.

FRAU ZAUBERBLIT'S ROOM

SAMITZKY *sits with* FRAU ZAUBERBLIT. *He is drunk. She is writing.*

SAMITZKY: Writing! Writing! Everybody's writing something down. What something down are you writing?

FRAU ZAUBERBLIT: I'm writing my will.

SAMITZKY: That's morbid.

FRAU ZAUBERBLIT: My daughter will arrive any day now.

SAMITZKY: She's come to be with you on your journey, what does she need your will for?

FRAU ZAUBERBLIT: I think I will leave some jewellery for the Yanuka for his musical education.

SAMITZKY: Lucky Yanuka!

FRAU ZAUBERBLIT: Some cash for the Twins.

SAMITZKY: Lucky Twins.

FRAU ZAUBERBLIT: Some clothes for Sally and Gertie.

SAMITZKY: Lucky Sally, lucky Gertie.

FRAU ZAUBERBLIT: I want Dr Pappenheim to say Kaddish for me and I do *not* want to be cremated.

[*She coughs violently into her handkerchief. Looks at it.* SAMITZKY *cradles, rocks her.*]

You are the only man I have ever loved to see drunk.

TELEGRAPH OFFICE

Full of people in a state of panic.

Collage of voices sending out telegrams.

The SANITATION INSPECTORS *appear and whisper something to each person, who then walks away.*

When the last person has gone, they shut up the office.

Only DR PAPPENHEIM *is left, crestfallen.*

THE MAJOR *approaches.*

DR PAPPENHEIM: I have not learned to do without letters and newspapers. I will *never* learn to do without telegrams.

THE MAJOR: I don't understand. Is there an epidemic?

DR PAPPENHEIM: A Jewish epidemic.

THE MAJOR: Is that supposed to be a joke?

DR PAPPENHEIM: Try to leave the town and see.

SANITATION DEPARTMENT

THE MAJOR: I demand to know when the telegraph office will reopen?

SANITATION INSPECTOR: Are you registered with us yet?

THE MAJOR: I'm an Austrian major of the last war and a registered citizen of Badenheim and I demand you reopen the telegraph office, the Post Office and the town gates; I demand that you take down the barbed-wire fences and those flags which are nothing whatsoever to do with Austria; I demand you restore order here.

1ST SANITATION INSPECTOR: Your name, please?

THE MAJOR: Do you realize no food supplies are getting through?

1ST SANITATION INSPECTOR: Your name, please?

THE MAJOR: My name is Major Kurt Hoffmansthal and I demand courtesy, respect and answers to my questions.

1ST SANITATION INSPECTOR: Jew?

THE MAJOR: Damn your Jews and damn your bureaucracy. What has any of it to do with closing down the Post Office and holding up supplies? We have lost contact with the outside world. Don't you understand that?

1ST SANITATION INSPECTOR: Sign here please, that way you can be registered.

[THE MAJOR *signs and leaves in a great distress.*]

FRAU ZAUBERBLIT'S ROOM

FRAU ZAUBERBLIT, *her* DAUGHTER, *and* SAMITZKY.

SAMITZKY: She doesn't look like you.

FRAU ZAUBERBLIT: She has never looked like me.

DAUGHTER: Please. I'm in a hurry.

SAMITZKY [*perplexed*]: They will let you out now you're in?

FRAU ZAUBERBLIT: When I sign this form they'll let her out.

SAMITZKY: More forms. Everyone's giving everyone forms to sign. What form can a daughter give her mother?

FRAU ZAUBERBLIT: A form renouncing maternal rights.

SAMITZKY: Renouncing maternal rights? How can you renounce maternal rights? They come with the blood!

FRAU ZAUBERBLIT: With forms you can renounce anything.

DAUGHTER: Please. I'm in a hurry.

FRAU ZAUBERBLIT: Is this what *you* want?

DAUGHTER: What I want and what my father wants.

[FRAU ZAUBERBLIT *signs.*]

SANITATION DEPARTMENT

PRINCESS MILBAUM *storms in*.

PRINCESS MILBAUM [*showing a form*]: What is the meaning of this?

1ST SANITATION INSPECTOR: Is it signed?

PRINCESS MILBAUM: How can I sign a form that's not accurate?

1ST SANITATION INSPECTOR: It's not signed yet. Please sign.

PRINCESS MILBAUM: Do you hear me, young man? I sent word of my titles. My first husband – a duke. My second husband – royal blood.

1ST SANITATION INSPECTOR: Your father's name was Milbaum. It's on the form. Sign please, that way you can be registered.

PRINCESS MILBAUM [*signing*]: I know who's to blame for this.

CONDUCTOR: When I went to register they showed me a book written by my father. About arithmetic. In Hebrew!

DR PAPPENHEIM: You didn't know?

CONDUCTOR: I didn't know. But in the Sanitation Department they knew. They know everything. It's very interesting what they've got there. And you know what? It's no trouble to them to show a man his past. They're happy to do it.

DR PAPPENHEIM: Parents baptized. I'd never have believed it.

CONDUCTOR: It doesn't make me proud. What my parents did it doesn't make me proud.

DR PAPPENHEIM: You could join the Order of Jews if you want. One of the best orders around.

CONDUCTOR: I don't believe in religion.

DR PAPPENHEIM: Who talks of religion? You could be a Jew without religion.

CONDUCTOR: With whose permission? The Sanitation Department's?

1ST MUSICIAN: We're visitors here, do *we* have to register?

DR PAPPENHEIM: Of course you must register. What kind of a question is that? Don't you know the Sanitation Department wants to boast of its important guests? Our names are going down in a Golden Notebook. Honoured we are.

1ST MUSICIAN: Perhaps it's because we're Ost Juden!

2ND MUSICIAN: In the souvenir shop they're selling maps of Poland.

1ST MUSICIAN: Why Poland?

2ND MUSICIAN: Historical necessity.

DR PAPPENHEIM: What does it matter, here, there? Perhaps our true place is really there.

1ST MUSICIAN: What will they do with us there?

2ND MUSICIAN: You'll be a musician like you've always been a musician.

1ST MUSICIAN: Do you remember anything from there?

2ND MUSICIAN: Nothing.

CONDUCTOR: My parents converted, damn it!

2ND MUSICIAN: So you can leave. Pack your things and return to Vienna.

CONDUCTOR: My dear friend, my name has a place of honour on their list. My father's book. On arithmetic. In Hebrew!

1ST MUSICIAN: If it is to be Poland we'll have to start studying.

CONDUCTOR: At our age? My dear —

1ST MUSICIAN: Polish. It'll have to be Polish.

2ND MUSICIAN: And Yiddish!

[DR LANGMAN *bursts in.*]

DR LANGMAN: This country is finished.

1ST MUSICIAN: Which is why we'll have to learn Polish.

2ND MUSICIAN: And Yiddish!

DR LANGMAN: I went to the department, saw the director, demanded a re-examination.

DR SHUTZ: Of what?

DR LANGMAN: Of my case. Of my specific case. I am an Austrian born and bred, and the laws of Austria apply to me as long as I live.

DR SHUTZ: But you also happen to be a Jew, if I'm not mistaken.

DR LANGMAN: Jew! Jew! What does it mean? Perhaps you would be so kind as to tell me what it means?

DR SHUTZ: As far as we're concerned you can renounce the connection any time you like.

DR LANGMAN: That's what I told them.

DR SHUTZ: And what did they say?

DR LANGMAN: They have their orders.

DR SHUTZ: So why are you getting angry with us?

DR LANGMAN: Because of what Pappenheim keeps saying. Don't you hear him? All the time? Calling us the order of Jewish nobility?

DR SHUTZ: I heard him. I didn't know he had such a sardonic sense of humour.

DR LANGMAN: You can't say such things with honour!

SCHOOLGIRL: Take me away from here. Can't you see I can't stand it any longer?

DR PAPPENHEIM: The child is unwell. Bring her some brandy.

DR LANGMAN [*to himself*]: My God but the Jews are an ugly people. No use to anyone.

> [*Sound of gunshot.*
> *Sound of singing.*]

THE CONCERT HALL

THE YANUKA *is singing.*
An audience gathers.
A dead MAJOR *is carried through.*
STRANGERS *appear. Bewildered. Frightened.*
Blackout.

PART FOUR

HOTEL FRONT DOOR

Late evening.

A commotion. One of the STRANGERS, *well dressed, middle aged, has the* HOTEL OWNER *by the scruff of the neck, screaming at him.*

STRANGER: Ost Juden! Ost Juden! You're to blame!

HOTEL OWNER: Me? Why me?

STRANGER: I'll murder you all.

HOTEL OWNER: I'm to blame for nothing.

[*Others are trying to pull them apart.*]

STRANGER: You and your dirty little bohemian guests.

HOTEL OWNER: Take this madman off me.

STRANGER: You open your doors, you lower the tone, you anger authority!

HOTEL OWNER: Madman! I run a first-class house. Madman!

STRANGER: You!

HOTEL OWNER: Madman!

STRANGER: Your fault!

HOTEL OWNER: My fault – nothing!

[*The* STRANGER *is prised off, still screaming –*]

STRANGER: There was peace in the land, there was quiet in the land, there was dignity, there was order. And then came the festival, the artists and the whores!

[– *till he is pacified.*]

1ST MUSICIAN: Why scream? It's not the end of the world.

SALLY: Nothing is ever as bad as it looks.

GERTIE: It may *look* bad but it never is.

DR PAPPENHEIM: If you think there's been a mistake, the Board of Appeals will exempt you.

STRANGER: There's a Board of Appeals?

DR PAPPENHEIM: Every committee has a Board of Appeals. That's a well-known fact.

GERTIE: As everyone knows.

DR PAPPENHEIM: No committee can *ever* do as it pleases.

SALLY: Ever!

1ST MUSICIAN: There's a question of procedure.

DR PAPPENHEIM: And if the lower courts have made a mistake, there's always a higher court to remedy it.

GERTIE: So you see there's no need to get upset.

SALLY: Ever!

STRANGER: Where does the Board of Appeal sit?

DR PAPPENHEIM: They'll probably make an announcement soon.

STRANGER: I mean, am I a criminal to be thrown out of my own house? Tell me please, am I?

DR PAPPENHEIM: It's not a question of crime but of misunderstanding. We too, to a certain extent, in a certain sense, are the victims of misunderstanding.

HOTEL OWNER: Procedure and Appeal. Remember. Now. Rest a little. I have a spare room. Tomorrow we'll probably know more.

STRANGER: I'm sorry. Forgive me. Suddenly everything was taken away from me. They drove me here on the grounds that I'm a Jew. They must have meant Ost Juden. Not me. Me, I'm Austrian.

HOTEL OWNER [*taking him in*]: Come. You've been through a hard time. I'll find you pyjamas, a towel, you'll have a good night's sleep and in the morning, you'll see – the world will begin all over again.

STRANGER: My apologies, forgive me, you don't know –

[*They enter the hotel.*
   DR SHUTZ *and* SCHOOLGIRL *emerge.*
   She is in control. She is pregnant. She wants everyone to know.
   They walk off.]

DR PAPPENHEIM: Ladies, I think it's time for us to take a stroll too.

[GERTIE *and* SALLY *each take an arm.*]

SALLY: Now we know why she was moody.
GERTIE: I thought it was because the swimming-pool closed.
SALLY: She belonged to the water.
GERTIE: It was her element.
SALLY: Such a pity they cut off the water supply.
GERTIE: Just when we'd learned to swim.
SALLY: And closed the tennis-courts.
GERTIE: Just when we'd learned to play tennis.

THE PASTRY SHOP

GERTIE, SALLY *and* DR PAPPENHEIM *stop outside the pastry shop, which has closed down and over which creepers have grown.*

GERTIE: And now the pastries are finished too.

SALLY: Another shop closed down.

GERTIE: What will we eat on the train journey?

DR PAPPENHEIM: Oh, they'll be selling chocolates at the station for sure.

[*The* CHEF *from the pastry shop appears in his suit.*]

DR PAPPENHEIM: Getting ready are we?

CHEF: *I'm* ready, at least.

DR PAPPENHEIM: No hurry, there's still time.

CHEF: I wanted to ask you, Herr Doktor, how will the transfer take place?

DR PAPPENHEIM: By train. Won't that be nice, ladies? Don't you just enjoy long journeys?

GERTIE: It's been so long since we've taken one.

DR PAPPENHEIM: Then you have a treat in store for you.

CHEF: May I be permitted to ask a personal question, Herr Doktor?

DR PAPPENHEIM: Anything, anything!

CHEF: I've been working here for thirty years. Will my pension be recognized there too?

DR PAPPENHEIM: Everything will be transferred. Have no fears. No one will be deprived.

SALLY: And what will we do there?

GERTIE: What would you suggest, Dr Pappenheim?

SALLY: I imagine that in the evenings we might be able to attend a course of lectures.

GERTIE: All large cities have lecture courses in the evenings.

DR PAPPENHEIM: Of course. You will be able to attend lectures but I – I think I would like to go back to research.

> [*Silence.*
> *They are held between what they hope for and what they vaguely and inexplicably fear. Then –*]

SALLY: I feel sad.

GERTIE: Me too.

SALLY: Doktor! Mr Bloomfeld! A drink in the bar! How is that for a good idea?

CHEF: They still have drinks in the hotel bar?

DR PAPPENHEIM: I'm ready for anything!

HOTEL BAR

Levity.

The SIX-MAN BAND *have become a jazz band.*

MITZI *dances with a new stranger,* SALO, *the salesman.*

The WAITRESS *dances with the* CONDUCTOR. *She's showing a lot of leg.*

SALLY *and* GERTIE *dance with each other and a clumsy* DR PAPPENHEIM.

Most are there – THE YANUKA, THE TWINS, KARL *and* LOTTE, DR LANGMAN.

The dance ends. Applause.

DR PAPPENHEIM [*breathless*]: Oh! It will be a brilliant season.

SALLY: And if we *have* to emigrate –

DR PAPPENHEIM: – we'll emigrate! There are wonderful places in Poland. In a few days' time everything will be different. We are on the threshold of a radical change.

[*The* WAITRESS *takes the stage. She drinks continuously.*]

WAITRESS: Who am I?

[*She imitates* MANDELBAUM *playing a violin. We hear it. Applause.*]

Who am I?

[*She imitates* THE YANUKA *singing. We hear it. Applause.*]

Who am I?

[*She imitates* THE TWINS *reciting. We hear it.*]

The Years go by . . . and yet, as in a train
we're going, years stay like landscape which we pass

64

and look at through our rattling window glass
which frost bedims and sunshine clears again.

[*Applause.*]

Thank you, thank you, thank you! Quiet now, please, quiet.

[*She tells a joke.*
Laughter. Applause.]

[*raising her glass*] Down with Austrian cabbage!

[*Laughter. Applause.*]

Ladies and gentlemen, I give you a toast. [*turns to* DR PAPPEN-HEIM] To Doktor Pappenheim's Jewish Order!

DR LANGMAN: That's not funny!

WAITRESS: To which I swear an oath of loyalty!

DR LANGMAN: Don't say such things!

[*He's booed down, storms off.*
SALO *and* MITZI. *She's flirting with him desperately.*
They're high and panting.]

MITZI: You're a lucky fellow to have landed up here on your business travels.

SALO: But Poland? Return to Poland? I ran away from Poland.

MITZI: We all did once. Now we're going back.

SALO: So long as the firm's prepared to foot the bill for such a long journey I don't mind. It'll be a rest. A rest at the firm's expense is worth its weight in gold.

[MITZI *cries. Maudlin tears.*]

SALO: What's to cry about?

MITZI: I had a postcard from an old lover.

SALO: And that makes you cry?

MITZI: My husband works and works and works. His stupid book which no one will read.

SALO: Your husband's a brilliant man. With a mind like that what else can he do?

MITZI: You haven't been here long. Wait till you hear the Mandelbaum Trio rehearsing. They'll drive you crazy.

SALO: Don't you like music?

MITZI: No! I don't like music. And I don't like travel. The idea of a long journey frightens me very much.

DR PAPPENHEIM: What's to be afraid of? There are many Jews living in Poland. A man has to return to his origins.

[MITZI *weeps and sinks into* SALO's *arms.*
He pulls her up and away with him.
She follows, feigning a coy reluctance.]

SALO: In Poland it'll all be different. You'll see.

[WAITRESS *takes the stage again. She is now very drunk.*]

WAITRESS: Samitzky! A drum roll, please.

[SAMITZKY *obliges.*
The WAITRESS *provocatively raises her skirt, unhitches a suspender, and peels down a black stocking. She slaps her ample thigh.*]

Austrian flesh! The Sanitation Department didn't register that.

[*Laughter. Applause. Another drum roll. Another stocking.*
Approaches DR PAPPENHEIM. *Offers her thigh.*]

WAITRESS: Isn't my meat tasty?

DR PAPPENHEIM: It's certainly tasty.

WAITRESS: So why don't you take this knife and help yourself to a slice?

DR PAPPENHEIM: Do I look like a butcher?

WAITRESS: You don't need to be a butcher to taste a slice of me.

SALLY: Leave the poor Doktor alone. You know he's incapable of cutting a fly let alone your flesh.

WAITRESS: In that case, I'll cut it myself.

[*She saws her thigh.*
Blood.
Screams.]

MARTIN *rips a tablecloth to bind her.*]

You won't leave me here. I'm coming too.

DR PAPPENHEIM: Silly woman! What did you imagine? Wherever we go you will go too.

[MARTIN *and* CONDUCTOR *take her away.*]

WAITRESS [*desperate; insistent*]: I'm coming too. You won't leave me here. I must come too.

[*The atmosphere in the bar has changed.*
People move off.
Gloom.]

DR PAPPENHEIM: Oh, this is no good. No good at all. What have we been thinking of? This is madness. We should be rehearsing. The services have been cut off, supplies of food in the hotel are down to nothing, it can only mean one thing. We'll soon be on our way! Rehearse, children, rehearse! Artistic standards in Poland are high!

[*Music.*
A work for trio *and* brass band. *The musicians are working hard, and together.*
The next scenes happen wordlessly as the music plays.]

FRAU ZAUBERBLIT'S ROOM

Two SANATORIUM MEN, *not unlike the* SANITATION INSPECTORS, *are standing waiting for* FRAU ZAUBERBLIT *to finish packing. One takes her case, another offers his arm.*

THE CHEMIST'S SHOP

TRUDE *opens her arms to greet her daughter,* HELENA.

She stands by her side triumphantly facing MARTIN, *as though saying, 'I told you she'd return.'*

MARTIN *falls on his knees and kisses his daughter's hands.*

HOTEL LOBBY

LOTTE *and* KARL *stare at the illuminated aquarium. Fascinated. Anxious.*

THE TOWN SQUARE

FRAU ZAUBERBLIT *is leaving with the* TWO SANATORIUM MEN.
She sees THE YANUKA *staring after her. Kisses him goodbye.*
Pauses to listen to the music. At that moment it is drums.
SAMITZKY *unknowingly is saying goodbye.*
She smiles, happy.
Leaves, coughing.

THE HOTEL CELLAR

The HOTEL OWNER *is opening a door to his hidden cellar, revealing it to the* HEADWAITER. *Inside it glows like an Aladdin's cave. It is full of food and wine.*

The HEADWAITER *is amazed.*

He picks up one tin after another. One box after another. Uttering the names in awed whispers.

HEADWAITER: Liqueurs. Swiss chocolates. Pecans. Peach preserves. Caviare. [*beat*] French champagne!

[*On 'champagne' the music changes abruptly to a tango.*]

THE CAFÉ TABLES AND TOWN SQUARE

Lights up on a now seedy town square.
  Neglect. Dilapidation.
  Couples dance the tango.
  The last of the food is being served.

DR PAPPENHEIM: A farewell feast to remember for ever!

  [DR LANGMAN *and* PRINCESS MILBAUM *sit aside, scowling on the proceedings.*

   MITZI *and* SALO *tango round them, tantalizingly, till, exhausted, they flop beside them while the tango continues.*]

SALO [*breathlessly to* DR LANGMAN]: There's no help for it. Everyone has to go.
PRINCESS MILBAUM [*to* DR LANGMAN]: Riff-raff!
SALO: There's nothing to be afraid of. In Poland there are lots of Jews. They help each other.
PRINCESS MILBAUM: Leave us alone.
SALO: I know because I spent my childhood in Poland. A year or two among them and you'll forget everything. You'll get up in the morning and go to synagogue. Is that bad? You'll pray. Is that bad? And if you're lucky you'll find a shop in the centre of town and you'll earn a living. Is that bad? Even the pedlars make a living. My father was a ped-lar and my mother had a stall in the market place. We were a lot of children at home. I was the seventh. You listening?
DR LANGMAN: No!
SALO: Don't put on airs. My advice to you — leave your arrogance behind. In Poland people treat each other with respect.

DR PAPPENHEIM: He's right! What do you say? Dr Langman? Duchess? *Pace pactus?* East and West will be as one?

PRINCESS MILBAUM: I will have none of it!

DR LANGMAN: Cheap romanticism!

DR PAPPENHEIM: Come now. We have drunk the last of the wine, eaten the last of the tinned preserves and —

THE CHEMIST'S SHOP

TRUDE, MARTIN, HELENA.

TRUDE [*to* HELENA]: – and soon we'll go to Poland and all will be well.

MARTIN: Your mother kept saying: 'Helena's on her way! Helena's on her way!'

TRUDE: Your father's excited.

MARTIN: And I never believed her.

TRUDE: Look at him how excited he is.

MARTIN: Was it bad. *Did* he beat you?

TRUDE: A goy is a goy. You mustn't blame him. What does he know better? I'm not sorry.

MARTIN: We were a little worried.

TRUDE: I was never worried.

The food queue.

HEADWAITER *and* WAITRESS *behind a huge pot of soup on a trestle table.*

WAITRESS *moves with difficulty. Her thigh is bandaged. A cane leans against the table.*

Everyone is there.

MITZI [*to* SALO]: What do you say to a strawberry tart and a cup of coffee?

SALO: I'd give the world for them.

1ST MUSICIAN: Look at him.

[*Eyes turn to* SAMITZKY, *who is sullen and withdrawn.*]

Have *you* been able to get a word out of him?

2ND MUSICIAN: They told her: 'Our sanatorium is emigrating too.' So she sells them: 'But I'm registered here, you know?' 'Never mind,' they said, 'why not go with all your old friends from the sanatorium?'

1ST MUSICIAN: He hasn't spoken since. Just smashes things up and quarrels.

DR PAPPENHEIM: They say the air in Poland is purer. The purer air will do her good.

[MARTIN *runs up. Frantic.*]

MARTIN: They've looted my shop. Someone's taken all the drugs. And I know who it is. Don't think I don't know who it is.

[*He turns to* KARL *and* LOTTE.
They are strange.
KARL *stares all the time at* DR LANGMAN.]

DR LANGMAN: Stop staring at me! He stares! All the time he stares like a madman. Are you a madman or something? Stop staring at me!

KARL: Sport! He preaches sport.

DR LANGMAN: Finish with this sports thing! I haven't spoken about sport for weeks.

KARL: He'd like us all to be in military academies hunting and shooting and being healthy.

[PRINCESS MILBAUM *pulls* DR LANGMAN *away*.]

PRINCESS MILBAUM: Ignore him. We'll eat later.

DR LANGMAN: He's mad. I warn you all. This man is dangerous.

PRINCESS MILBAUM: It's a mistake to be here. I should never have allowed my twins to perform at this festival.

[KARL *imitates a 'healthy soldier'*.]

PRINCESS MILBAUM: There are civilized Jews and uncivilized Jews, Dr Pappenheim, and you have gathered around your festival the uncivilized ones.

DR PAPPENHEIM: But who, gracious lady? Mandelbaum and his trio? The band? The Yanuka? Your twins, the readers?

PRINCESS MILBAUM: You know perfectly well who I mean.

[KARL *taunts* DR LANGMAN *with his 'healthy soldier' act*.]

DR LANGMAN [*leaving*]: Go stare at your fish, you crazy man you. That's where you belong – in an aquarium!

[DR LANGMAN *and* PRINCESS MILBAUM *leave*.]

KARL: I want no one to use the word 'sport'.

LOTTE: Please, Karl.

KARL: 'Sport' is a word that's taboo.

LOTTE: Karl, stop this, please.

KARL: Do you all understand? 'Sport' – taboo!

LOTTE: Let's go for a walk. We'll eat later.

KARL [*he's very high*]: And what about the fish? Do we abandon them to their fate?

LOTTE [*pacifying him*]: God forbid.

KARL: We're not Junkers and we're not Prussians. We feel sorry for the little fish in the aquarium. As long as we live we'll feel sorry for the little fish in the aquarium.

LOTTE: Of course we will.

KARL: It's food for *them* we must find. Us – we can always eat. But for them?

> [KARL *picks up dry bread from the table.*
> *Leaves with* LOTTE.]

DR PAPPENHEIM [*to a forlorn* MARTIN]: Do you know what I heard? That the musicians have looted the cutlery and silver from the hotel. To take with them!

> [*At which he laughs. Uncontrollably.*
> *The laughter stops when a new crowd of* STRANGERS *appear.*
> *Among them is an* OLD RABBI *in a wheelchair.*]

1ST MUSICIAN: Is that our old rabbi?

2ND MUSICIAN: I thought he had a stroke and died years ago.

> [*A silence. They look at the* OLD RABBI.
> *The* OLD RABBI *looks at them.*]

OLD RABBI: Jews?

HOTEL OWNER: Jews!

OLD RABBI: And who's your rabbi?

HOTEL OWNER: You! You are our rabbi.

> [*The* OLD RABBI *is hard of hearing.*]

[*repeating*] You! You are our rabbi.

OLD RABBI: Are you making fun of me?

HOTEL OWNER [*shouting*]: Have you forgotten? Years ago.

1ST MUSICIAN [*shouting*]: We thought you were dead.

HOTEL OWNER: Can we offer you some soup?

OLD RABBI: Kosher?

[*Embarrassed silence.*
  He declines.]

And what are you all doing here?

SAMITZKY: We're getting ready to return to Poland.

OLD RABBI: What?

SAMITZKY: To return to Poland.

OLD RABBI: Are you all from Poland?

SAMITZKY: What does it matter? It's where we're all going.

DR PAPPENHEIM: For my part I've had a letter from the Sanitation Department demanding that all my artists be registered with them. It can only mean one thing. A comprehensive concert tour awaits us!

GERTIE'S AND SALLY'S FRONT-ROOM

It is GERTIE's *fortieth birthday party.*
  The music comes from their old horn gramophone.
  GUESTS *are coming in one by one or in couples.*
  DR PAPPENHEIM *first. He kisses* GERTIE's *cheeks.*

DR PAPPENHEIM: It's been a long time since I was last here.
GERTIE: It's been a long time since any of you were here.
SALLY: Counts, industrialists –
GERTIE: – salesmen, tired intellectuals –
SALLY: – a long time.
DR PAPPENHEIM: But I'm the bearer of good news today. The emigration procedures have already been posted on the notice-boards.
GERTIE: Well how about that!

  [DR SHUTZ *and the* SCHOOLGIRL.
    She has a quiet authority. After greeting SALLY *and* GERTIE
  she backs away.
    This party is full of silences.]

GERTIE: Have you heard? The emigration procedures have been posted on the notice-boards.

  [DR LANGMAN *brings a bottle of liqueur. Kisses* GERTIE's
  hand.]

DR LANGMAN: I found this. Don't ask where.
GERTIE: Oh! *Something* to drink.

  [*Each is given a small glass.*]

DR LANGMAN: How nice it is here.

[*Silence.*]

Karl refuses to budge from the aquarium. What does he expect from fish?

SCHOOLGIRL: He changes the water and feeds them bread crumbs.

[*Silence.*]

DR PAPPENHEIM: I tried to persuade Mandelbaum to come. Hopeless. Rehearse, rehearse, rehearse.

[THE TWINS *and* THE YANUKA *arrive. Shy and awkward. They just sit.*
SALO *and* MITZI *arrive next.*]

SALO [*to* GERTIE]: So, you're forty!

GERTIE: And only yesterday I was thirty.

SALLY: Only yesterday . . . Counts, industrialists –

GERTIE: – salesmen, tired intellectuals . . .

[*Silence.*]

SALO: Karl's determined to take the fish with him.

[*Silence.*]

SALLY [*to* THE TWINS *and* THE YANUKA]: What can we do to gladden the hearts of the artists?

[MITZI *laughs.*]

SALLY: Why are you laughing?

MITZI: No reason. People make me laugh. That's all.

[*Silence.*]

DR PAPPENHEIM: I must say, the emigration procedures seem very efficient. Very efficient indeed.

DR SHUTZ [*to* SCHOOLGIRL]: In that case there's much we can look forward to.

[*She ignores him.*]

DR PAPPENHEIM: You'll be able to teach in the mathematics department. Poland is a very cultured country you know.

DR SHUTZ: Are they connected to the University of Vienna?

DR PAPPENHEIM: They must be. All centres of culture are connected to Vienna or Berlin.

[*Silence*].

GERTIE: I feel so ashamed that we've nothing to offer you.

DR PAPPENHEIM: Never mind. You'll give us a party in Warsaw. A lavish party.

GERTIE: That's a promise.

DR PAPPENHEIM: Ah, what a wealth of folklore there is in Poland. Authentic folklore. In Poland we'll be able to diversify our festival.

SALO: I remember now. I once saw a wonderful Yiddish play in Warsaw. I think it was called something like *Bontze the Silent*. My father took me.

[*Silence.*
DR PAPPENHEIM *stands.*]

DR PAPPENHEIM: Goodbye, house. Au revoir, house. You're staying here and we're setting off on our travels.

[*Two shots ring out.*]

SALLY: I think the headwaiter has shot his dogs.

GERTIE: They refused to eat.

SALLY: Kept running away into the bushes.

GERTIE: Seemed very confused.

DR PAPPENHEIM: And au revoir, maidens, until tomorrow morning at seven o'clock sharp on the hotel steps, where the dawn and a new life will await us.

[*Slow, slow blackout.*]

PART FIVE

THE HOTEL STEPS

A clear, cold, frosty morning.
    THE MANDELBAUM TRIO *arrive first, dressed in white suits.*

MANDELBAUM: Where's the carriage?

   [DR PAPPENHEIM *appears, anxious about his artists.*]

DR PAPPENHEIM: The emigration arrangements are evidently not yet complete.

MANDELBAUM: In that case we'll have to waste our time here doing nothing. And the pastry shop? What's happened to the pastry shop?

DR PAPPENHEIM: Everything's been closed down in readiness for the emigration.

MANDELBAUM: In that case we'll have to wait for coffee until we get to Warsaw.

DR PAPPENHEIM: Has the maestro already appeared in Warsaw?

MANDELBAUM: A couple of times. An enthusiastic and sensitive audience, more so than the Austrians I should say.

DR PAPPENHEIM: I'm happy to hear it.

   [DR SHUTZ *and* SCHOOLGIRL *arrive next.*
       He is now weak and feeble and stooped. A wicker basket rests with pathetic domesticity on his arm. She is upright and proud.]

DR PAPPENHEIM: Allow me to introduce Dr Shutz.
MANDELBAUM: Honoured.

   [DR SHUTZ *fumbles.*]

DR SHUTZ: And this is my wife.

[SCHOOLGIRL *turns away in anger.*
   MARTIN, TRUDE *and* HELENA *followed by* KARL *and*
LOTTE.
   KARL *cradles a huge glass jar with fish in it.*
   *They take their places in silence. His, the silence of madness;
hers, of patience.*]

MANDELBAUM: So, we're late as usual, Dr Pappenheim!

[MITZI, *very made up; her husband,* PROFESSOR FUSSHOLDT,
weighed down by boxes of proofs and papers.]

DR PAPPENHEIM: May I introduce Frau and Professor Fussholdt.
  Dr Mandelbaum.
MANDELBAUM: So, Fussholdt is with us too?
PROFESSOR FUSSHOLDT: Honoured.
MANDELBAUM: What a shame I didn't know.

[*The* HOTEL OWNER *next. Sad.*
   Followed by the SIX-MAN BAND *carrying heavy bags of
loot and their instruments.*
   The CONDUCTOR *stands aside from them with the*
WAITRESS.]

1ST MUSICIAN [*to* CONDUCTOR]: Stop glaring at us. If we come
back we'll return them.

[HEADWAITER *arrives. Depressed.*]

MITZI: I'm sorry about the dogs. What were their names?
HEADWAITER: Lutzi and Grizelda.
MITZI: I could never tell them apart.
HEADWAITER: Lutzi was quiet. A dog with a lot of complexes.
MITZI: Such a pity!

[SALO *next in his salesman's uniform with his battered
old case. He stands with the* SIX-MAN BAND.
   SALLY, GERTIE *and* THE YANUKA. *He's very changed.
More a man, in a suit that fits him. He speaks with a heavy
accent.*]

THE YANUKA: Hey, Salo. My new clothes. What do you think? Sally and Gertie say: 'You like a fairy prince!'

SALO: And right they are.

THE YANUKA: So — the 'prince' commands you — that box of sweets — in your pocket.

SALO: Not sweets, my dear. A pair of women's stockings. I'm the agent for a well-known firm.

OLD RABBI'S VOICE [*from inside*]: Are you leaving me here?

[DR PAPPENHEIM *and several* MUSICIANS *go to help bring him and his wheelchair down the steps.*]

DR PAPPENHEIM: We're all still here, but it was cold outside.

KARL [*to* HEADWAITER, *showing him the bottle*]: What do you think?

HEADWAITER: If it's not too long a journey you might be able to save your fish.

KARL: I've got an extra bottle of water.

HEADWAITER: That's good, then. Thoughtful.

[DR LANGMAN, PRINCESS MILBAUM *and* THE TWINS *appear at the hotel door but refuse to join the others at the foot of the steps.*

PASTRY-SHOP CHEF *appears.*]

HOTEL OWNER: Where's your employer?

CHEF: Refuses to come.

[HOTEL OWNER *walks over to the dilapidated pastry shop.*]

HOTEL OWNER: Peter? Peter! You're contravening a municipal ordinance.

PASTRY-SHOP OWNER: I'm not coming. Not with Pappenheim, anyway.

DR PAPPENHEIM: Why me? What harm have I ever done him?

HOTEL OWNER: You're an intelligent man. How can you be so irresponsible?

PASTRY-SHOP OWNER: I'm staying.

HOTEL OWNER: Take my advice. Join us. For your own good. We have a rabbi with us.

PASTRY-SHOP OWNER: I'm not religious.

[*One of* THE MANDELBAUM TRIO, *to keep himself warm, takes out his fiddle to play a fierce* cadenza.

The PASTRY-SHOP OWNER *comes out and takes his place.*

STRANGERS *join them.*

SANITATION INSPECTORS, *like policemen, unarmed, encircle them.*

A whistle is blown.

They move off. Everyone is relieved. Happy.

SAMITZKY *is the last to come out, his anger still clinging to him.*]

ROAD TO THE STATION

The motley crew 'walk'.
  Badenheim passes them. The countryside passes them.
  THE MANDELBAUM TRIO *at the head.*
  SALLY, GERTIE, THE YANUKA *between* THE TWINS.
  DR LANGMAN *and* PRINCESS MILBAUM.
  SIX-MAN BAND.
  CONDUCTOR *and* WAITRESS *with a heavy cane stick.*
  HOTEL OWNER *pushing the* OLD RABBI.
  PROFESSOR FUSSHOLDT, MITZI, *and* SALO.
  The HEADWAITER, KARL *and* LOTTE.
  MARTIN, TRUDE *and* HELENA.
  DR SHUTZ *and* SCHOOLGIRL.
  PASTRY-SHOP OWNER *and his* CHEF.
  SAMITZKY.
  STRANGERS.
  DR PAPPENHEIM *moves here and there, checking.*
  The SANITATION INSPECTORS *linger behind, guarding, silent.*

CONDUCTOR [*to* WAITRESS]: What I've never told you about
  is my inheritance and my savings. My Christian parents left
  me a little money, you know. Not a fortune, but enough! *And* I
  saved.
WAITRESS: So you're a rich man? My parents left me nothing.
  An Austrian father who was a pig. And if he hadn't been a
  pig he still wouldn't have left me anything.

  [*Walk in silence.*]

IST MUSICIAN: I tell you, I need the change. Perhaps we'll work
  fewer hours.
SALO: You can be sure of it.

1ST MUSICIAN: In fact, I wouldn't mind a couple of years' leave. The sound of brass is driving me out of my mind.

SALO: But be careful. The years on the threshold of retirement are critical. I've already collected twenty years of seniority without missing a day. I've got a month's annual leave coming to me. I promised my wife a holiday in Majorca.

1ST MUSICIAN: Majorca? I've never heard of it.

SALO: A warm, wonderful island. I owe it to her. She brought the children up. Wonderful children.

1ST MUSICIAN: Do you think we'll be able to save something in Poland?

SALO: You can be sure of it. Prices there are much lower, and if we continue getting our salaries in Austrian currency we'll be able to save a lot.

> [*Walk in silence.*
> *The* WAITRESS *weeps.*]

CONDUCTOR: What's this? Tears? For what? We'll reach the station soon. Soon we'll be in Poland! New sights, new people! A man must broaden his horizon.

> [*Walk in silence.*
> MITZI *approaches* DR LANGMAN.]

MITZI: I had this dream last night. I was a little girl of six. My father took me to Vienna, to the Prater. It was a wonderful autumn day, and we walked and walked and I realized he was only trying to tire me out so that I wouldn't resist having my tonsils out. And then I was in the hospital and I saw all the nurses and doctors running towards me and they performed the operation. I dreamt all that last night. It was such a vivid dream, I can't tell you. I saw everything.

> [*They walk in silence.*
> *Suddenly the* OLD RABBI, *who has been sleeping, wakes up.*]

OLD RABBI: What do they expect? All these years they haven't paid any attention to the Torah. Me they locked away in an old-age home. They didn't want to have anything to do with me. Now they want to go to Poland. There is no atonement without asking forgiveness first.

MITZI [*excitedly*]: Look! The station! The station! We've arrived!

THE STATION

People scatter to do various things.

SALLY *and* GERTIE *buy sweets for* THE YANUKA, *cigarettes for themselves, vodka for* SAMITZKY.

DR LANGMAN *buys a financial paper. Reads. Laughs.*

Suddenly a strange, glorious light breaks over them. It is a light which tells of the earth's beauty and abundance.

Everyone looks up, their spirits risen.

DR PAPPENHEIM [*almost in tears of joy*]: What did I tell you! What did I tell you!

[*The sound of an engine shunting into the platform.*
  Not carriages. Freight wagons.
  Everyone is stunned.
  Do we see the freight wagons?
  Are they projected on huge screens?
  Do we guess what is there from their faces peering out at us?
  Does someone say something to inform us?
  The last image is of crestfallen humanity.
  Silence.]

DR PAPPENHEIM: Well! If the coaches are so dirty it must mean that we have not far to go.

[*No sounds.*
  No orders.
  No weeping.
  No sentimentality.
  Just a cold dying of the light.]

BEORHTEL'S HILL

a play for Basildon
in two acts

with incidental music specially composed

Blaendigeddi
4 December 1988

Beorhtel's Hill was commissioned by the Colway Theatre Trust and first performed at the Towngate Theatre, Basildon, on 5 June 1989. The directors were Jon Oram and Steve Woodward. Design was by Chris Lee (costumes) and David Rennie (set and properties). The music was composed and directed by Ian Stewart and choreographed by Ginnie Woolaston.

The cast was drawn from the people of Basildon and its surrounding areas.

ACT ONE

Vast empty area, oval shaped.

Audience surrounds it, standing, sitting, but does not *promenade.*

House lights down, followed by stage lights to complete darkness.

Slowly, a light builds and finds a circle of fifteen figures shrouded in grey, like monks, hooded, faces unseen.

They are CHORUS *and scene-changers, the sound-makers and providers of light, the controllers of the traffic, of characters and crowds on stage, the pointers of their destiny.*

The circle faces inwards.

CHORUS: All things tire of themselves: the demagogue of his tongue, the revolutionary of his fervour, the singer of his song, the sower of his seed.

[*They bend forward as though to hide what they do.*

Slowly, the light builds and builds and builds, until everywhere is bathed in a dazzling, ethereal luminescence like a portent of some millennial event.

The CHORUS *step back and away.*

In the centre of the space can be seen a single, magnificent red rose in a beautiful ornate 'art nouveau' vase, and alongside it a fresh plaited loaf of bread.

The light fades, slowly, slowly, to complete darkness again.

Light picks out BRENDA, *a married woman who keeps a diary. She sits at an old desk, obviously chosen by her with love. Her position is permanent. Her diary entries are punctuation marks along the way.*

Light picks out NARRATOR, *aged around fifty-five, grey and slightly bucolic, standing in the centre where the rose and loaf were.*

His is a nature by turns benevolent and fierce, reassuring and acerbic, bemused and angry. He is a restless and unpredictable personality who charms and challenges, flirts with and castigates his audience.

In his hand is the rose. He places it in his button-hole as we hear BRENDA *read from her diary.*]

BRENDA: 17th August 1964. We have been offered a new house in a new town called Basildon. New house, new town, new life! We will accept but I am terrified. On the other hand, the past is dead like a bowl of decayed fruit – the juices dried up, the aroma faded, the sweet taste gone. And I am tired . . .

[NARRATOR *takes out a hip flask to drink from – an action he will repeat intermittently throughout.*
As he drinks –]

CHORUS: All things tire of themselves. The heart of its sadness. The rose of its scent. The city of its dreams.

NARRATOR: Who are *they*? I know who I am. I'm the community drunk. People love a drunk. There's something honest about him, they think. He seems to have a sense of desperation so extreme that nothing will be held back. No inhibitions. That's what they say. Well – I've me doubts. A drunk is boring, selfish, self-centred, lachrymose, a ham actor, and there is nothing in the books to guarantee that honesty, inebriated or otherwise, equals intelligence. A drunk can be an honest idiot and frequently is, so let's not be sentimental about drunks.

[*He drinks.*]

CHORUS: All things tire of themselves.
CHORUS 1: Youth of its certitude.
CHORUS 2: Manhood of its bravery.
CHORUS 3: The lover of his passion.
CHORUS 4: The cynic of his sneer.
CHORUS: The rose of its scent. The city of its dreams.
CHORUS 5: The sower of his seeds.
NARRATOR: Not true! The sower never tires of sowing his seeds.

The most deep-seated instinct in people is to make things grow. Food, flowers, cities, the child in the womb, a work of art – from a seed! Explode! Pwuch! [*Imitates an explosion.*] A miracle! Who *are* you anyway?

BRENDA: 5th January 1965. Today we moved our worldly belongings into our new house and arranged them in the clean, bright, white painted rooms.

[*Rain! The sound of rain!*]

It has rained steadily since we arrived, churning up the mud of unmade roads. The mud here is like glue. I feel slightly uneasy and depressed, but that's probably tiredness. On the other hand, rain makes things grow, at least there is the blossom to look forward to. New house, new town, new life, new risks, new blossom. I hope it *is* just tiredness.

[*Rain, rain, rain.*
    Light picks out another figure, RILEY. *Old Cockney dressed in an overcoat, muffler, peaked cap, an umbrella in one hand, a plastic shopping-bag in the other. Sticking out of his bag is a bunch of red roses.*
    He approaches NARRATOR, *beckoning him to come in close and share a secret.*]

RILEY: 'Ere, 'ere! Come 'ere a minute. To save yer sweating.

[*A long cautious pause. What can he want?*]

The worst part of the dream is – that when I wake up, I find that Maggie Thatcher is still alive.

[*Without bothering to wait for a response, he shuffles away to the other end of the space, where he stops, as though in reverie.*
    Sounds of high winds. A gale is blowing up, slowly, to become a violent storm.
    The CHORUS *flash lightning, rattle thunder.*
    The storm howls. The three figures, each in their different worlds and time, stand/sit facing away from each other, listening, thinking, remembering.]

The storm dies. Bright sunlight takes over one half of the space (not the same as the first ethereal light). It will gradually take over the whole space, chasing away the dark storm clouds.

Before this happens, a rainbow appears. A hologram of lights traverses the theatre's interior.

Five KIDS *between the ages of eight and eleven run on near to where* RILEY *stands. They're dressed in clothes of around 1914/18.*

Because one of them, 5TH KID, *stands with his back to* RILEY, *we know he is* RILEY *as a child.*

They are staring in wonderment and silence at the rainbow.

Sighs, exclamations, awe. Nothing raucous. Then —]

1ST KID: I can see red and orange and yellow . . .

2ND KID: I can see green and blue and violet . . .

3RD KID: And what's the other?

1ST KID: What other?

3RD KID: I can count seven colours.

[*Pause.*]

4TH KID: I think it's called indigo.

[*More sighs and exclamations.*]

Where we come from, down Stepney way, there was once a rainbow stretched from Spitalfields Church to Shoreditch Church.

1ST KID: Where d'yer think this one stretches from?

2ND KID [*working it out*]: It stretches from . . . Langdon Hill to . . . Barstable Hall.

[*Long pause.*]

5TH KID [*significantly*]: I know where Barstable Hall is.

[*Without anyone saying anything, just an exchange of daring, audacious looks, they have reached an agreement.*]

Come on then. Let's find it.

[*With a whoop of 'YEAHHHHHH!', they rush towards the other end of the space.*]

Halfway across, from different sides, two groups of three other KIDS *appear and ask —*]

KID 1: What's up?
KID 2: Where you going?
5TH KID: To find the end of the rainbow. Coming?

[*With another whoop of 'YEAHHHHHH!', some dozen* KIDS *run off.*
Silence. Then —
Rain again, rain, rain, rain!]

BRENDA: 14th April 1965. I have settled the children into school. Bluehouse County — evocative of gentlemanly sports. It is a low, sprawling collection of boxes set in the middle of several flat, windy fields. There seems to be another estate of houses being built behind it, ugly and grey like blocks of cement. I wandered back along the Link, woodland on one side and a tangle of undergrowth and trees on the other. What a pleasure to find a part of Basildon that isn't neat and clinical.

[*From the corner where the* KIDS *disappeared, come a couple of very brisk, very gaudily but expensively dressed housewives of today, umbrellas up, pushing supermarket trolleys overloaded with groceries.*
RILEY *turns and shuffles towards them.*]

RILEY: 'Ere, 'ere. Come 'ere a minute. To save yer sweating.

[*They slow down sufficiently to hear him out, but never quite stop.*]

The worst part of the dream is — that when I wake up, I find that Maggie Thatcher is still alive.
1ST HOUSEWIFE [*picking up speed*]: Silly ole bugger.
2ND HOUSEWIFE: Silly old sod.
1ST HOUSEWIFE: This town's full of silly ole buggers.
DAUGHTER: And silly old sods.

[2ND HOUSEWIFE *takes a swipe at her daughter, who dodges out of the way.*]

1ST HOUSEWIFE: From the old days.

2ND HOUSEWIFE [*calling back*]: You wanna watch who you accost like that.

1ST HOUSEWIFE: I like Mrs Thatcher.

2ND HOUSEWIFE: Don't know when they've got it good.

1ST *and* 2ND HOUSEWIVES [*together*]: Silly ole buggers! Silly ole sods!

[*They're off.*]

NARRATOR: They came as strangers to this town, from prefabs that lasted twenty years beyond their allotted time, with their broods, their steely eyes and high hopes, strangers in a rural midst. And once they were grateful for the warmth and friendliness of silly ole buggers from the old days. But now? Ah . . . now . . .

[*Movement! Energy!*

The space becomes criss-crossed with GANGS *and* INHABITANTS. *All, except members of* GANGS, *are holding umbrellas, rushing from somewhere to somewhere: home to work, work to home, from shopping, to shopping, pushing prams, pushing trolleys, carrying briefcases, tool bags, pulling children, muttering as though to themselves, sometimes hurling their words at* NARRATOR.

One young woman, INHABITANT 2, *stands by a bus-stop (brought on by one of the hooded* CHORUS).

All is very carefully orchestrated and choreographed for pace, movement and sound.

Only one group remains still, beneath their umbrellas, watching, bewildered and lost, as INHABITANTS *and* GANGS *rush by in the rain.*

They are an ASIAN FAMILY. *New arrivals. Parents and three children. At their side, cases. In the hand of the girl, a bunch of red roses.*

Movement! Energy!]

INHABITANT 1: Depressing! Bloody depressing town. Nothing ever happens . . .

INHABITANT 2: Boring, boring, boring, boring, boring, boring, boring . . .

INHABITANT 3: Looks good and tidy, but underneath, cor . . .

INHABITANT 4: Wonderful town! Great little town! Keep your London, stuff your Paris, burn New York! Basildon for ever is what I say.

INHABITANT 5 [*exuberant, singing, dancing*]: 'I'm singing in the rain, just singing in the rain, what a glorious feeling, I'm happy again . . .'

INHABITANT 6: If I won the pools, I'd leave — quick as a wink . . .

[*A* GANG *from one area chase another* GANG *across the space, menacing and shouting* —]

1ST GANG: Stacies! Stacies! Stacies' lot! Stacies' lot! Stacies! Stacies! Stacies' lot! Stacies' lot! . . .

INHABITANT 7: Everyone comes from the East End, that's the trouble. They all look alike, dress alike, talk alike, think alike, joke alike, eat alike . . .

INHABITANT 8 [*and her eager brood of four*]: Fish fingers, baked beans and chips, that's what you lot get tonight.

BROOD 1: Meat pies! Jellied eels!

BROOD 2: Fish and chips! Egg and chips!

INHABITANT 2: Watery vegetables! Over-cooked meat!

BROOD 3: Sausage and chips!

BROOD 4: Hamburger and chips!

EVERYBODY: Chips! Chips! Chips! Chips! Chips! Chips! Chips! Chips!

[*Rain still. Rain, rain, rain!*
   The GANG *who were chased chase back; it's their turn to shout and menace* —]

2ND GANG: Subway! Subway! Subway's lot! Subway's lot! Subway! Subway! Subway's lot! Subway's lot!

[*A* 3RD GANG *follow on, chasing yet a* 4TH GANG. *The air is filled with violence.*]

3RD GANG: Pitsea! Pitsea! Pitsea's lot! Pitsea's lot! Pitsea! Pitsea! Pitsea's lot! Pitsea's lot!

[*And still a* 5TH GANG *chasing a* 6TH GANG.]

5TH GANG: Basildon! Basildon! Basildon's lot! Basildon's lot! Basildon! Basildon! Basildon's lot! Basildon's lot!

INHABITANT 2 [*diminishing whatever glamour emerges from this ugly moment*]: Boring, boring, boring, boring, boring, boring, boring . . .

INHABITANT 9: You get used to the violence, you get used to it. That's the bloody trouble, you get used to any bloody thing!

INHABITANT 4: They took my mum and dad from the slums and gave them a palace. We grew up in paradise. Keep your London, stuff your Paris, burn New York. Basildon for ever is what I say.

INHABITANT 5 [*still singing*]: 'I'm singing in the rain, just singing in the rain . . .!'

[*Silence – but for the rain.*
Empty – but for the ASIAN FAMILY *standing mute, bewildered, abandoned.*
RILEY *wanders up to them.*]

RILEY: 'Ere, 'ere. Come 'ere a minute. To save yer sweating. The worst part of the dream is that when I wake up, I find that Maggie Thatcher is still alive.

[*He shuffles to a corner but not out of sight.*
ASIAN FAMILY *move away.*
Empty space.
The rain. The rain.]

NARRATOR: Strángers in their midst. Mark that, dearly beloved. I too came as a stranger to this place. Fought for it, schemed for it, dreamed for it, invested my best years in it. But I've a confession to make – I'm lonely here. There are no – poets here. Oh yes, one or two. There's always one or two, but mostly only makers of money. If I want to feel alive, emotion-

ally charged, inter-bloody-lectually stimulated, I have to
escape to the bleedin' metropolis. Makers of money. Lonely.

CHORUS: All things tire of themselves. The storm of its turbulence. Words of their meaning. Evil of its tyranny. The rose
of its scent. The city of its dreams.

NARRATOR: Who *are* they?

[*The rain has been dying out.*
Stillness.]

BRENDA: 21st August 1965. Once back inside the house, loneliness lurks in the empty rooms. There are a constant stream of
callers — offering to deliver milk, to clean carpets or to save
my soul, but no one I can really talk to . . .

[*The light fades, fades.*
The space is in darkness.
Suddenly — here, there — a glow, another, and another, and
another, all on the outer band of the oval space. An assortment
of old hurricane and tillie lamps has been lit. It's the early
1920s.
Four East End families, the PLOTLANDERS, *have come to*
their plotland bungalows for the weekend. They are:
PLOTLAND FAMILY 1: NELL *and* BERT, *their children*
FLO, ELSIE *and* JACK, *and* NELL's *mother,* GRAN.
PLOTLAND FAMILY 2: MAVIS, *her children* STAN *and*
DORIS, *and* DORIS's *betrothed,* MICK.
PLOTLAND FAMILY 3: MAUREEN *and* ALF, *their daughter*
MABEL.
PLOTLAND FAMILY 4: IVY *and* ERNIE, *their son* SAM
and ERNIE's *old* AUNT GRACE.
(*Note: The 'children' should be played by young men and*
women, which is what they'll become.)
A bungalow is delineated by its floor space, covered in
furniture which the CHORUS *pull on trucks into its space.*
Each bungalow occupies a corner of the oval area, but
leaving a lot of space between and in the centre.
In each household are flowers in vases. Roses — plus.]

Everyone is engaged in a different activity. An evocation of the times!

Some are preparing food – peeling vegetables, rolling dough, cleaning fruit, stirring soup. Other activities are: ironing with heavy old irons, darning socks on a wooden mushroom, sewing net curtains, simple carpentry, polishing brass and cutlery, snobbing shoes and any activity which the cast can discover.

Cooking and the heating of the iron are done on paraffin stoves. All the implements are of the time.

Can someone be churning butter?

Dare anyone get into the tin bath, which is being filled from a drum of rain water, and have his back scrubbed?

The CHILDREN *are involved in indoor games or pastimes: snakes and ladders, flicking cigarette cards, rolling marbles, reading comics, cleaning a bike, constructing a ball-bearing scooter, and any activity of the period which the youngsters in the cast can discover.*

NARRATOR, *restless, walks amongst them, looking in on their lives. Individual members of the families will come and talk to* NARRATOR *as though he were the interviewer, but they'll continue working at something. Living never ceases. Always something to be done.*]

NARRATOR: They came by train from Fenchurch Street Station for weekends and summer holidays to get away from the noise and the grime of their East End streets, lured by offers of cheap plots of land.

BERT: Twenty feet by a hundred and sixty.

NARRATOR: Price?

MAVIS: Anything from £3 to £6.

ALF: We had our fares paid and we was given champagne by the landowners.

ERNIE: Plotlanders! They called us the plotlanders!

NARRATOR: They came to Dunton, Laindon, Little Burstead, Vange – I love the names of places – Pitsea, Nevendon, Fobbing, Lee Chapel. Sounds! Full of stories! Langdon Hills, Basildon, or Beorhtel's Hill, as it was known in Saxon times.

BERT: Used to be farming land. For centuries.

ALF: Poor quality, though.

BERT: Good for cereals. Heavy London clay. Yellowish.

ERNIE: Then they started importing cheap corn from America, didn't they?

BERT: Never mind the poor soddin' farmers!

NARRATOR: And between 1870 and 1880 the harvests were so poor that the poor soddin' farmers sold out to land speculators.

MAVIS: Harry Foulger and Thomas Helmore of Laindon.

IVY: James Humm and Robert Verty at Vange and Pitsea.

NARRATOR: Came the Boer War, the developers combined with the London, Tilbury and Southend Railway Company to auction plots. Played the old game of holding back land to keep up prices.

ALF: But our offers were still low.

NARRATOR: The main plots developed around Laindon and Pitsea railway stations. Inevitably! But some of the plotlanders became so addicted to fresh air and the dawn chorus that they braved muddy footpaths, substandard dwellings and bad sanitation to leave London and live here for good, look.

ELSIE: Not us. My family didn't come to live till 1942, halfway through the war.

NELL: But we bought the property in 1924.

NARRATOR: The stories begin. And they better be good!

ELSIE: My mother was an East Ender.

NELL: Born in Bow.

ELSIE: But my father, he was a Wickford man.

BERT: Came to London to join the Metropolitan Police force for security.

ELSIE: And one morning he said to my mother –

BERT: I'm going out to buy a field because if I can't get away from people one day a week, I'll go insane.

ELSIE: So my mum said jokingly –

NELL: Well, whatever you do, don't spend more than £240 because that's all we own.

ELSIE: He came back and he said to her –

BERT: I took you at your word, I've bought a four-acre field with a white bungalow and I only spent £250.

[*The other families applaud her story.*]

NARRATOR: They've all got stories. And they tell them to each other endlessly. I mean not earth-shattering stories, not dazzling ones about larger-than-life personalities and extraordinary deeds. Just little ones, about tiny deeds and small braveries by unextraordinary people.

NELL: I'm not sure I like your tone.

NARRATOR: I'm not sure what I think of your lives!

Wars come, wars go, revolutions in art that changed ways of seeing, revolutions in thought that changed notions of liberty, revolutions in science that took cameras to Saturn, and here's your old man spending his family's last penny on four acres of field to get away from people and grow cucumbers!

GRAN: I don't think I know what he's talking about.

NARRATOR: Soon someone will say, 'We're only simple, working-class folk.'

GRAN: We're only simple, working-class folk!

NARRATOR: 'Don't bamboozle us with your high and mighty ideas.'

MAUREEN: Don't bamboozle us with your high and mighty ideas.

[*Focus shifts to* BRENDA.]

BRENDA: 2nd December 1965. I walked the quiet streets again today. There seems to be no place where life can be watched, no railway sidings, no wharves, no rivers to gaze at. No park with ducks to be fed, no teahouse to congregate around, nothing within reach, just open green and windy fields or clean streets with boring bare lawns. A toy town made of building bricks where the people are put into the correct places and life is neat and well ordered.

[*Focus back to* PLOTLANDERS.]

SAM: *My* father was a shipwright.

NARRATOR: The stories continue.

ERNIE: Worked on the London docks.

NARRATOR: Always best to ignore the community drunk.

SAM: Around the year 1915 he heard about the sales from his mates. Land sales at Laindon.

ERNIE: Bought one half an acre for £18 15s, your grandfather bought another.

IVY: Eight plots each.

ERNIE: Twenty-foot frontage by one hundred and fifty feet deep.

IVY: In New Century Road.

FLO: £18 15s for half an acre was a lot in those days.

AUNT GRACE: In those days, see, you could pay off for any land you bought at 2/6 a week. Ten shillings a month. But if you got behind in your payments, you lost your freehold.

NARRATOR: Freehold! Remember that, dearly beloved. Freehold! Very important principle. There's a great rumpus gathering on the horizon over that principle. Mark it. Freehold! Strangers in their midst! Mark them!

ELSIE: Our four-acre field was overgrown with blackberry and hawthorn bushes except for a small area round our white bungalow, and whatever the weather, my father came down on his leave day and us kids would come down with our mum every third or sixth weekend.

GRAN: Came down on a Friday and stayed right through to Sunday.

ELSIE: And we noticed, my brother and sister and I, that the train was full of people doing the same thing. They'd come down with their little bundles of wood –

JACK: – mostly from fish boxes –

ELSIE: – tied up, slung over their shoulders or in their little Rexine shopping-bags, wood to build their bungalows.

NARRATOR: Bungalows built of fish boxes! Wonderful! From the slum dwellings of the East End, they built themselves slum dwellings in the Essex countryside.

MAVIS: They were not slum dwellings!

NARRATOR: Slum dwellings! Made out of fish boxes!

MAVIS: Some of them, maybe but –

ELSIE: Friday, they'd travel down with their fish boxes but on Sunday they'd all go back carrying produce from their gardens – beans, cabbages, cauliflowers –

BERT: – carrots, peas, parsnips –

ALF: – onions, lettuce, tomatoes –

NARRATOR: – and cucumbers!

IVY: And flowers! Bunches and bunches of flowers! All our own! Which we'd grown! Everybody loved growing things.

MAVIS: Call that a slum?

NARRATOR: An untidy, hotchpotch of development! Mushrooming like some Wild West town. Without a sheriff!

MAUREEN: We were pioneers! Frontiers men and women!

NARRATOR: 'I knew the place when Indians were still hiding in the bushes.'

MAUREEN: I knew the place when Indians were still hiding in the bushes.

ERNIE: There were twelve shipwrights in our road.

IVY: Only it wasn't a road, was it? Just pegs in the ground. No roads, no sewage, no gas, no water, no electricity.

NARRATOR: Frontiers men and women, see!

ERNIE: Our lighting, our heating, our cooking – all paraffin.

AUNT GRACE: On the old-fashioned Beatrice stoves. We cooked on the old-fashioned Beatrice stoves in wooden huts, never thought anything about the dangers.

MABEL: You'd sit round the Beatrice stove to keep yourself warm. One of my first childhood memories.

ERNIE: Paraffin! Four pence a gallon!

ALF: Where d'yer get your water from, missus?

NELL: Rain-water tank on the corner of the hut.

BERT: Where d'yer bath, missus?

MAVIS: In a tin bath in the kitchen.

NARRATOR: Charming? Charming!

ELSIE: We'd come down for these weekends and first thing we always did was to raise the flag and show everyone we were there!

NARRATOR: Well, it was their castle, wasn't it? They were like royalty, weren't they?

JACK: Next thing we did was walk right round our boundary.

GRAN: Your father did that. Right the way round, checking the fences and the posts.

NARRATOR: Property! Mark that. An Englishman's home is his castle. Property! Freehold! Strangers in their midst!

[*Focus shifts to* BRENDA.]

BRENDA: 14th April 1966. In the early hours of this morning, my pains began. We have no car or telephone and Basildon has no hospital, so a frantic figure ran through the darkness into the centre of town to summons help. At half past nine in St Andrew's Hospital, Billericay, our son was born. The one member of the family who really belongs to Basildon. The price for our ticket to the new life has been paid . . .

[*Focus back to* PLOTLANDERS.]

STAN: My dad died when he was forty-eight.

MAVIS: A young man.

STAN: Used to be general foreman bricklayer at Runwell Hospital and I used to work under him. I suppose I must've been about fifteen then, and I was sitting having me dinner with him at half past twelve, and by one o'clock he'd gone!

MAVIS: Thrombosis!

STAN: He'd just erected a mortuary slab in the hospital and he was the first to lay on it!

MAVIS: We managed, though.

STAN: We managed.

MAVIS: I was a jolly sort.

STAN: Right!

MAVIS: I used to love people's company.

STAN: Right! My dad used to go down to Southend dogs, he used to be one for the greyhounds, my dad, but he never used to like my mum going out. He used to be selfish like that.

MAVIS: Well, that's how it used to be that time of day, didn't it?

NARRATOR [*mocking*]: 'Well, that's how it used to be that time of day, didn't it?'

MAVIS: And I loved the Salvation Army.

STAN: And Dad used to laugh. 'You'll come home with one of them bonnets one night,' he used to say. He wouldn't stop her but he didn't like her going.

MAVIS: Well, that's the way people were that time of day. It was the Victorian times. He was the breadwinner of the family and that's how it used to be, didn't it?

NARRATOR: 'That's how it used to be, didn't it?' People will take anything for a quiet life. Employees will take it from employers, citizens will take it from politicians, wives will take it from their husbands.

MAVIS: Tell them, though, Stan. Tell them. Your mum did get to sing once with the Salvation Army.

STAN: It was outside the Five Bells Pub and she saw this man struck by lightning –

NARRATOR: – which cured him of his rheumatism.

STAN: – which cured him of his rheumatism!

NARRATOR: You can see my problem, can't you?

STAN: She swore it!

[*Focus shifts to* BRENDA.]

BRENDA: 9th October 1966. Everyone is asleep. I have been looking at the sky. The stars are very bright. They have looked down on towns and villages and people like me for ever. The sky is part of my past and my future. It has continuity. But have I?

[*Focus back to* PLOTLANDERS.]

MABEL: *My* mum used to make butter. In a churn. We had cows and we used to sell the new milk three ha'pence a pint and the surplus milk that was left over she got some big flat pans and next day, she'd skimmer cream off for the butter and sell what remained a penny a quart.

DORIS: Where did you keep your food?

MABEL: Not in a fridge, that's for sure. In a two-foot square box with perforated zinc sides and a door.

MAUREEN: And it hung at the rear of the bungalow exposed to the elements.

AUNT GRACE: Like our outdoor lavatory. *We* were exposed to the elements too. A timber shed with an ever-open window and Venetian door and a bucket on a concrete slab for which your dad made a hinged seat.

IVY: And the garden was big enough for the contents.

AUNT GRACE: And the garden was big enough for the contents.

ELSIE: After we'd come to live here for good, we got a pig.

BERT: Lived at the bottom of our garden.

GRAN: Instead of fairies!

JACK: Dad always fatted a pig every year to be killed in the autumn by Uncle Frank, who was a butcher.

BERT: He took half the fresh pork and *I* took the other half, and I had a big oak tub which stood that high where I salted and pickled its hands for six weeks in brine, my own brine, look, and it had to be turned every day, and then at the end of the six weeks, I'd send them to Luckin-Smiths at Chelmsford to be oak-saw dried.

ELSIE: And Mother made brawn and sausage from it.

GRAN: And the chidlins! Don't forget the chidlins!

ELSIE: The innards of the pig! And Saturday night we used to have them served for tea and if there was any left over, Dad had them fried up Sunday morning with his bacon.

STAN: When I was ten years old, I did two jobs.

NELL: Intestines! With bread and butter. Lovely!

STAN: A paper round and cleaning for a chemist's.

NELL: And it gave me enough lard to last me till the spring too.

ELSIE: Nothing was wasted in our house.

STAN: I used to be up at five o'clock in the morning, I used to be at Wickford Station at ten to six, I used to get all the papers off the first train from London to Southend, I used to go all round Swan Lane and all round the Gardens and then I used to have to be back at ten to eight to start the chemist job at eight, where I used to have to clean all the measures out, and the scales which was all brass that time of day. And I had to sweep all three shops for them. And when that was done, I used to go home round quarter to nine just to have a quick breakfast, 'cos I had to be at school at nine o'clock. And there was no being late that time of day or you got caned.

[*Focus shifts to* BRENDA.]

BRENDA: 21st December 1966. I sit here writing this diary of my passing days and I wonder — what's the purpose? Wouldn't it be better to write about the past? Recapture the days of my youth? The days of dreams and roses? But I wouldn't believe myself. I don't trust memory. Better to record the days as they come. Instant pain, instant relief . . .

[A SPECTACULAR HAPPENING.

A plotland bungalow is to be erected. The parts have been prefabricated elsewhere.

The grey-hooded CHORUS *bring on the pieces.*

BERT, ALF *and* ERNIE *build it.*

Music features strongly as the background to these final passages of reminiscence.]

SAM: We lived in a new terrace house in Barking. 71 Keith Road. Six shillings a week inclusive. And in our back garden, my dad erected and bolted together the frame of our Laindon house.

IVY: He was a very versatile man, your dad. Could turn his hand to anything — iron, woodwork, joinery, bricklaying. And he could draw his own plans.

AUNT GRACE: And he finished every job he began.

[*Music.*]

MABEL: My dad worked on the railways and when it was foggy weather, he had to get his men out to man the line and he had to see they were well supplied with food and drink because those days were the days of the pea-soupers and when it came down, it came down!

MAUREEN: And I hated him being out in the pea-soupers, hated it! I was frightened and just hated it.

[*Music.*]

ELSIE: There on the farm, they had the most wonderful tree. These days, you'd tell your kids don't go near it but for us, it was a wonderland.

JACK: It had these great thick branches which had been hollowed out and we used to play families in it.

ELSIE: We had the dining-room, we had the sitting-room, we had the kitchen, the scullery, the bedroom and we'd play and play and it was fairyland, just fairyland.

[*Music.*
The bungalow continues to be assembled.]

MABEL: They were a wonderful couple, my mum and dad. They loved each other deeply and desperately, they really did, and they gave us a wonderful, settled and safe childhood. It was summer all the time for us.

[*When the bungalow will be completed, there will be a double celebration.* DORIS *and* MICK *are preparing to marry, dressing up in black suit and white gown.*]

SAM: I remember that summers were warm, that we picked lots of bluebells in the Crown Woods, Langdon Hills, and whenever I smell blackberries, I remember all the blackberries we picked for jams and pies which my mum made.

MABEL: I remember we went gleaning, picking up heads of corn that was cut too short so they couldn't pick it up with the forks. Mother made up bags, which we tied round us and filled with the heads of corn to give to the chickens.

STAN: I remember we went wooding, picking up wood the wind had blown off trees. For the fires.

ELSIE: I remember my parents knew magic. We had a magic lantern and a horned gramophone and my mum played the piano and we sang a lot.

[*Piano.* Song. Everyone sings.*
After a first verse, they continue singing, but more quietly.
Against the background of quiet singing, focus shifts from singers to BRENDA.]

BRENDA: 14th February 1967. Today my world shattered into guilty fragments at my feet. My mother died and I wasn't there with her. If I had still been living round the corner when she collapsed, maybe I could have saved her, but I had moved to Basildon and left both my parents behind. The funeral was so sad and pathetically short. I wept silently. But tonight back in Basildon, I walked alone in the woods beyond the Link and howled like an animal into the quiet night air.

[*Focus shifts to* NARRATOR.]

NARRATOR: So, they came from London, strangers into the rural midst of villagers who had lived there for centuries.

NELL: Centuries!

NARRATOR: And were you made welcome by those villagers?

NELL: Some eyed us strangely, but yes, we were made very welcome. Everyone got to know everyone else: neighbours, shopkeepers, delivery men.

IVY: When we all fell ill once, the grocer missed us. Brought us a selection from his shop.

MAUREEN: Can't see supermarket managers doing that.

NARRATOR: Strangers made welcome. How many of us have been strangers at some time or other in our lives? And were we warmly received? And did we receive warmly?

The stranger in our midst! Freehold! Property! What, dearly beloved, is being woven here?

AUNT GRACE: I can remember that when there used to be a wedding, the best man used to stand at Laindon Station platform, he used to wait for the London train to pull in, then he used to tip the driver to sound his whistle on his way to London. The newly-weds used to board the train, it used to

---

* In the Basildon production an actor was able to play an accordion.

go off and the whistle used to ring out cock-a-doodle-do! Cock-a-doodle-do! All the way to Dunton and beyond.

[*Music.* BRIDE AND GROOM *pose for a photo — one of the sepia ones.*
Train whistle: 'Cock-a-doodle-do! Cock-a-doodle-do!'
Beer and celebratory cries as the bungalow (completed) becomes the train which is pulled away by the hooded people in grey, the MARRIED COUPLE *on it.*
PLOTLANDERS *freeze.*]

BRENDA: 10th May 1967. I perform all the normal functions of living as if I were still alive, but inside I have died a death. How I wish I had someone to talk to. I am beginning to hate this new, self-contained life in this new, self-contained town. Basildon, Basildon, bloody Basildon!

[*The dozen* KIDS *chasing the end of the rainbow appear, still searching, but now dressed as in the 1930s.*
Halfway across, they again encounter two more groups of three who come at them from different sides to ask:]

KID 3: What's up?
KID 4: Where yer going?
5TH KID: To find the end of the rainbow. Coming?

[*With an even louder whoop of* 'YEAHHHHHH!', *the enlarged battalion of youngsters continue their quest.*
Into the space now.
AN AMAZING SIGHT. THE BALLET OF STREET GAMES.
These games must be expertly carried out by children who have been specially selected and who have trained to be spectacular.
Spinning tops: Those coiled in string and flung to the ground; those flung to the ground by a whip; those spun and thrown high from string between two sticks. The tops are brilliantly coloured so that when they spin, the floor is ablaze.

> *Skipping: Breathtakingly fast and rhythmic skipping such as is not seen today. Individuals and groups.*
>
> *Ball games: Bouncing it under legs with one arm behind back, and many such difficult feats from the past which I've forgotten.*
>
> *The whole to be carefully choreographed.*
>
> *During the previous time* JACK *has been putting on an army uniform, a portent of the cataclysm to come. As the children play their games, he wanders among them, waving goodbye, picking up a small one for a final hug.*
>
> *Towards the end of the Ballet of Games, come the growing sounds of war.*
>
> *Siren. Planes. Bombs.*
>
> *The children stop their games. Look up. Gather their toys and run off screaming.*
>
> *The remaining* PLOTLANDERS *form a tableau of fear.*
>
> *Anti-aircraft guns. Fire engines. Explosions. A cacophony of terrifying sound.*
>
> *Against the background of on-going war-sounds, the men relate war experiences in tones of distress.*]

RILEY: I can remember, in 1937, couple of years before war broke out, I went to work at Shell Haven, loading boats. And what were we loading? Pitch! The Germans were building autobahns and we were sending all the pitch over to them. Used to be put in five-gallon barrels which were stored till the German boats come in and then for about four or five days, we'd load the boats and off they'd go to build Adolf's autobahns. And I could never understand why they couldn't see what he was doing. They knew he was preparing for war, but they never done anything about it, look!

NARRATOR: Well, he talks like that now. Hindsight, it's called. Very clever people are with hindsight. But ask him, would he have gone on strike to stop the rearming of Germany? Ask him, would he have agreed to sanctions to stop the rise of the Nazis über alles? Ask him, did he even bother to find out what the Nazi Party was all about! Ask him! Ask him! I love the barrack-room lawyer mentality of the working class, don't you? Heartfelt, deeply felt ignorance! Nothing like it!

[*The sounds of war continue.* NARRATOR *ducking all the time. Searchlights sweep the sky. Anti-aircraft blasts. Somewhere there is a flickering red of flaming ruins.*]

SAM [*in great distress*]: My company helped to free Belsen and I got photographs to prove the atrocities what took place there. I got photographs! It was horrifying. We saw the incinerators filled with bones, we saw the gold they pulled out of dead Jews' mouths, we saw a heap of spectacles eight foot high. And I helped to bury the dead. You had to use bulldozers to dig the graves. There was one grave, well, it was about three quarters of a mile long and at the end of it, we put up a plaque saying 36,000 bodies lie here. 36,000!

NARRATOR: We don't believe you, do we?

SAM: Well, you better believe me 'cos I saw it.

NARRATOR: All fabricated lies!

SAM: I got photographs to prove it.

NARRATOR: A Jewish plot to justify taking land away from the Palestinians!

SAM: Oh well, I don't know about any of that.

NARRATOR [*in fury*]: 'Oh well, we don't know anything about that!'

STAN: But *I* know what the Nazis was like 'cos I was guarding a prisoner of war camp in Trieste. The German soldiers looked after themselves, see. Very efficient. Kept to the same discipline like as if they was still in the army. And we fed *them* proper 'cos they worked. Not the Nazis, though. We had 'bout forty or fifty of them and they were kept separate 'cos they refused to work. They spoke English, see, and they used to call us all the Bs under the sun. Well, they still wasn't defeated in their eyes, see. You'll never change our way of life, they said, you laugh now but we laugh last. I used to feel like putting a bullet through them. Terrible people. But the women was the worse. We had a lot of women SS, like the men, only worse.

You couldn't believe how they were. Brutal! Tear anybody to pieces with their hands. I mean – well – I mean – it's dreadful, war, and to me there's no cause for it. I mean I got no grudge against any foreigner.

[*Sounds of war continue all the time.*]

NARRATOR: But ask him, did he protest when the British government turned back refugees fleeing from the Nazi extermination camps? Ask him!

STAN: I mean, why can't everyone be friends in this world?

NARRATOR: Ask him, did he open his arms to the foreigner then? The stranger in his midst? Ask him!

[JACK *is in uniform, writing a letter home.*]

JACK: We may be winning, but you've still got to be careful, though. Never know where the snipers are. But I tell you this, Mum –

[*Sister* FLO *takes over reading the letter.*]

FLO: – when we get back, we're going to build our very own and golden cities.

[*A rattle of machine-gun fire sounds especially loud.*
JACK *falls dead.*
The CHORUS *of grey-shrouded people raise him high. Carry him round for all to see. They carry him off.*]

STAN: Why can't we all live in peace? There must be an explanation there somewhere.

NARRATOR [*as they're carrying* JACK *off*]: Oh, the innocence of it! Oh, the bewildered, uncomprehending naïvety of it! Well, yes! There *is* an explanation to it somewhere. Because life is a conflict of interests between the vain and the vain, the greedy and the greedy, the fanatic and the fanatic, and it's all sanctioned by the unthinking, the ill-informed, the pious, the lazy, the illiterate, the easily-incited-led-by-the-nose-flattered-and-fooled majority. Not us, of course. I'm not talking about you and me. We're not like that, are we? We read books, we talk to one another, we travel, we entertain dissent, don't we? We applaud non-conformist, unconventional, unfashionable ideas, don't we? It's the others! Out there! Always the others out there, isn't it?

[*The sounds of war seem to rise to a crescendo as though matching the* NARRATOR's *anger. And then — slowly — dies away.*

In their scramble to evade the bombing, the families have knocked over things. Created chaos. Now, wearily, they gather the pieces together.

The MARRIED COUPLE *are changing from their wedding clothes to everyday wear. As this takes place —*
music — and the CHORUS.]

CHORUS:

All things tire of themselves.
The demagogue of his tongue.
The revolutionary of his fervour.

AUNT GRACE: The singer of his song?
CHORUS 1: The singer of his song.
GRAN: The heart of its sadness?
CHORUS 2: The heart of its sadness.
CHORUS: Be glad. Be comforted. All things tire of themselves.
NARRATOR: Who *are* these people?
SAM: The longing for revenge?
MAUREEN: The tiny satisfactions of spite?
CHORUS:

All things, all things.
Not only hope but despair also.
The smile may fade
But the crying cannot go on.

NARRATOR: Will we ever know who they are?
NELL: The rose of its scent?
IVY: The city of its dreams?

CHORUS:

> And silence too.
> All things tire of themselves.

DORIS: And passion?
CHORUS: And passion.
DORIS:

> How can that be?
> How can such energy and joy come to an end?

CHORUS: It does. It does.
MICK:

> How can that ever be?
> My images are sharp and glowing.
> My language is on edge.
> My heart is high.
> And all my nerves are ringing! Ringing!

CHORUS:

> It can be!
> Passion does tire of itself
> As all things do
> Be glad. Be comforted.

CHORUS 3: If confidence falters.
CHORUS 4: And holy grails fade.
CHORUS 5: Unhappiness wearies also.
CHORUS 3: The mocking wear their shrillness thin.
CHORUS 4: Contempt withers.
CHORUS 5: The sneer dissolves.
CHORUS:

> All things! All things!
> All things tire of themselves.

CHORUS 6: Childhood of its childishness.
CHORUS 7: Youth of its certitude.
CHORUS 8: Manhood of its bravery.

CHORUS 9: Evil of its tyranny.
CHORUS 10: The long storm of its turbulence.
CHORUS 11: The rose of its scent.
CHORUS 12: The city of its dreams!
NARRATOR: Does anyone know who the hell they are?
CHORUS:

> And if madness follows
> Will that too not tire of itself
> As all things do?
> Though no joy lasts
> No pain lingers
> Though the sower flags
> The flower blooms
> What tires of itself – revives!
> Be glad. Be comforted.

[*The low roar of the* KIDS *is heard offstage, in first gear.*]

RILEY: 'Ere, 'ere. Come 'ere a minute. To save yer sweating. The worst part of the dream is –

[*He doesn't complete his sentence but moves sadly away.*
Focus shifts to BRENDA.]

BRENDA: 3rd August 1967. My baby was playing happily one minute and the next he began to choke. Picked him up and thumped his back, but he kept fighting for breath and started to turn blue.

[*The low roar of the* KIDS *is heard offstage, becoming louder.*
Second gear.]

Put my fingers down his throat. Felt something hard and sharp. Pulled. He screamed and coughed blood but at least he was breathing. Covered him with a coat and ran in the rain to the doctor's surgery. No one there. Shops shut, telephone round the corner out of order. Returned in misery to the house. Badly needed someone to talk to. Knocked on house next door. No reply. Felt so alone. Must make friends and learn to fit in here if I am to survive.

[*The roar of the* KIDS *grows as the enlarged battalion chasing the end of the rainbow appear, still searching but now dressed in the clothes of 1945.*

Halfway across, they again encounter two more groups of three who come at them from different sides to ask:]

KID 5: What's up?

KID 6: Where yer going?

5TH KID: To find the end of the rainbow. Coming?

[*With an even louder whoop of 'YEAHHHHHH!', they continue their quest, but —*

— this time, they don't leave the space. They run in slow-motion on the spot and are caught in strobe lighting, so that we can see the eagerness, the hope, the excitement of 'the quest' on their young faces.

THE KIDS *run and run and run, ever hopeful.* NARRATOR *moves among them.*]

NARRATOR [*to* KIDS]: Go on! Run on my lovelies! Run! Go for it! Remember what the hooded ones said: 'Though the sower flags, the flower blossoms. What tires of itself — revives.'

[*to audience*] I know what you're thinking. Look at those kids, you're thinking. The innocence and the hope that something's there at the end of a rainbow, and all he can be is sour about it.

And listen to those lovely silly old buggers, you're thinking, with their romantic memories, their endeavours, reaching to clutch a share of the beauty there is in this sad old world — and all he can be is sour about it. That's what you're thinking, aren't you?

Well, nothing's simple. I'm sour and sweet by turns. I'm impressed and bored. Gloomy and hopeful. I can be tempted to hope like a virgin, then disappointed like a neglected spinster. That's how I am.

[*to* KIDS] Go on! Run! Don't give up! Take deep breaths and run! Run!

[*to audience*] I mean, how many people do you know who

make things happen? Most people are just not vivid, interesting. So, these plotland people, well . . . well . . .

[*The glow on the faces of the* KIDS, *the shine in their eyes, seem to make him doubt his thoughts.*]

On the other hand, I'll never forget a line in a poem by the Russian poet Yevtushenko. No one's completely uninteresting, he says, because:

> *When a man dies, there dies with him his first snow and his first kiss . . .*

[NARRATOR *takes the rose from his button-hole and hands it to a running* KID. *The lights fade on them running, running, running — ever hopeful.*

The last glow of light holds the image of the old man handing the young one his rose.

The CHORUS *form a bowed circle of hooded grey around them.*]

NARRATOR: I wish, I wish, I wish I knew who you were.

ACT TWO

From darkness, a burst into light, sound, movement.
  The stage crowded with celebrating Londoners.
  Noises of hooters and whistles.
  Parties! Beer drunk from bottles! Champagne popped!
  Singing! Dancing in the streets!
  The war is over.
  After some minutes, the crowds disperse, leaving . . .
  The CHORUS *of hooded forms, looming, ever present.*
  And the NARRATOR, *drunk.*
  The PLOTLANDERS *are dressed in the costume of the 1950s.*
Older.
  The interiors of the bungalows have appropriate changes and additions.
Fresh flowers.

NARRATOR: 1946! We'd won the war! The spirit of the times
  was 'Never again!'

  [*The* PLOTLANDERS *take up the chant –*]

PLOTLANDERS: Never again! Never again! Never again! Never
  again . . .!

  [*Which continues as background to –*]

NARRATOR: How excited we become with the glory and drums
  of war. Then our fathers and sons die and after the first
  euphoric spree, we remember them and victory turns stale
  and we stand in church or by gravesides and we swear with
  hand on heart, eyes up-turned to God – never again!

  [*Chanting stops.*]

But time passes! A new generation! Youth becomes excited all over again because youth has no imagination and you can sell youth anything from third-rate music to third-rate wars.

[*Protest from* PLOTLANDERS.]

That's right. Dismiss me, shout me down. I'm just the community drunk.

Listen to them! The same voices — the same voices — first they loved him, then they swept him aside, the man who'd led them to victory, the old Tory with his cigar, poor old Winnie Churchill.

ALF [*imitating Churchill's famous speech*]: You can fool some of the people all of the time. You can fool all of the people some of the time.

EVERYONE: But you can't fool all of the people all of the time.

NARRATOR: No! But can you fool enough of the people for enough of the time? And anyway, it wasn't Winston Churchill who first said that!

[*Protest from the* PLOTLANDERS.]

NARRATOR: Yes, yes! That's right. Shout me down.

BRENDA: 25th December 1967. Christmas. My past has been left behind, closed like a chapter in a book. This new chapter has no substance yet, I feel as though I am floating with no anchor to hold me, no harbour to which I can return. I am one stranger among many in a strange land.

[RILEY *shuffles to the* NARRATOR.]

RILEY: 'Ere, 'ere. Come 'ere a minute. To save yer sweating. The worst part of the dream is —

[*Sound of the* KIDS' *roar off stage interrupts him. Their sound is in first gear.*]

Hear them? Hear that sound? *That's* the sound of a dream. Street kids. Ever-hopeful street kids. Street-wise they say.

NARRATOR: Street-bloody-stupid, more like. If you stay on your street corner, what can you know of life except what's on your street corner?

[*The* KIDS' *roar goes into second gear.*
The PLOTLANDERS *take up chant again –*]

PLOTLANDERS: Never again! Never again! Never again! Never again!

NARRATOR [*over the chanting*]: Never again! Away with the Tories, who'd let us in for the war in the first bloody place. Bring on Clem Attlee and the Welfare State! The Socialists would build the new Jerusalem.

CHORUS 1: A health service!

CHORUS 2: Equality for women!

CHORUS 3: Distribution of wealth!

CHORUS 4: Jobs for all!

CHORUS 5: Education for all!

CHORUS 6: New thinking!

CHORUS 7: New towns!

CHORUS: 1946! The New Towns Act!

[NARRATOR *is ever perplexed by them. Each one he approaches to peer at or speak to backs away.*

Meanwhile – sound of roaring KIDS *enters third gear as they rush on, now dressed in style of the 1950s.*

Once again, the even larger group are met halfway by two more groups of three.]

KID 7: What's up?

KID 8: Where yer going?

5TH KID: To find the end of the rainbow. Coming?

[*With a renewed roar of* 'YEAHHHHHH!', *thirty kids rush off to continue their quest.*

Three gavel knocks on a table. A meeting of four members of the Housing Committee of the Billericay Urban Council (BUC).]

CHAIRMAN 1: Gentlemen! Gentlemen! Ladies! This meeting of the Housing Committee of the Billericay Urban District Council is brought to order. First on the agenda – the New Towns Act. Here's how I see it. For some time, the state of the Laindon–Pitsea area of the county has been causing concern. A large, scattered community has grown up, plotlanders they're called, and a situation has been reached in which most of the population in our district are living in substandard dwellings which urgently require water, sewerage, gas, electricity and roads. Installation of these services is our responsibility and – to put it bluntly –

BUC 1: We're broke!

BUC 2: Can't afford it!

BUC 3: A new town would generate rates –

BUC 4: – which would pay for the services.

CHAIRMAN 1: Right! Now, what do we do?

> [*Three gavel knocks on a table.*
> *A meeting of four representatives from the East and West Ham Borough Councils (EWBC).*]

CHAIRMAN 2: Gentlemen! Gentlemen! Ladies! This joint Housing Committee of the Boroughs of East and West Ham is brought to order. First on the agenda – the New Towns Act. Here's how I see it. As you all know, due to six years of war, two factors have contributed to the dire housing problems we both face: the destruction of property by severe bombing and the building of little or no housing due to labour and materials being diverted to the war effort.

EWBC 1: The East End is congested!

EWBC 2: We've reached bursting point, I'm warning you!

EWBC 3: One of those new towns would go a long way –

EWBC 4: – to ease congestion!

CHAIRMAN 2: Right! Now, what do we do?

> [*Both committees join and face the* MINISTER OF TOWN AND COUNTRY PLANNING. *He's dictating a letter to a secretary,* MISS MATHIESON.]

MINISTER: To the Town Clerk, Billericay Urban District Council. What's his name?

MISS MATHIESON: Mr Alma Hatt, Minister.

MINISTER: I see you've had your hair permed.

MISS MATHIESON: It's the new style.

MINISTER: Looks very nice.

MISS MATHIESON: Thank you, Minister.

MINISTER: Dear Mr Hatt. As the person most responsible for arguing the claims for your district to be designated a new town area, I am happy to inform you that my ministry is granting provisional approval for the setting up of a new town with a 50,000 population to be called Basildon.

> [*Applause and hurrahs from* COUNCILLORS.
> *A roar of* 'NO – OOOOOO' *from the* PLOTLANDERS.]

BERT: What about our homes?

MAVIS: Our sacrifices?

ERNIE: Our livelihoods?

ALF: Our rights! Our rights! What about our rights?

NARRATOR: Here we go again. Conflicts!

BERT: You're denying us the fruits of old age.

IVY: You're taking away our friendly corner shops.

MAUREEN: Strangers will come!

MAVIS: They'll destroy our neighbourhood.

NELL: Disturb its spirit.

MABEL: And what will happen to our countryside?

NARRATOR: Conflict, conflict, conflict!

MINISTER: I have no desire to inflict injury or harm on anybody in the course of carrying out these proposals. But I must remind you – government has a duty and wider responsibility to help others. East and West Ham has one in four houses flattened by bombs, and some 20,000 people are on the housing list waiting for homes.

BERT: And what will happen to our freeholds?

NARRATOR: Freehold! Property! Strangers in our midst! Life is a conflict of interests, dearly beloved. Not only between the vain and the vain, the greedy and the greedy, the fanatic and the fanatic – but between the state and the individual. On my left – the individuals!

> [*Brass and drums.*

Enter from all corners GROUPS OF PROTESTERS *behind banners declaring:*

DUNTON RESIDENTS PROTECTION
   ASSOCIATION
LAINDON RESIDENTS PROTECTION
   ASSOCIATION
BASILDON RESIDENTS PROTECTION
   ASSOCIATION
VANGE RESIDENTS PROTECTION
   ASSOCIATION
PITSEA RESIDENTS PROTECTION
   ASSOCIATION

Men and women with sandwich boards declaring:

MPs DO YOUR DUTY
NO JUSTICE, NO FREEHOLD
WE FOUGHT FOR ENGLAND, NOW WE
   FIGHT FOR FREEHOLDS

The bungalow with a man, MR BIRCH, *astride its roof, rifle in hand, is pushed on again by the hooded circle of grey.*]

MR BIRCH: Our resolution passed this day 14th September 1948: 'Compensation for property and land is grossly inadequate and bears hard on their owner-occupiers. The loss of freehold would be a heart-rending blow to those of us who have striven for years to acquire a small portion of their mother soil. We have built our own homes to free ourselves from the burden of rent and fear of ejection. By our thrift and self-sacrifice, we have placed ourselves beyond the need of the state's assistance. Are we now to be penalized by the state for our spirit of enterprise and public responsibility?'

[*Roar of support from the* PROTESTERS.]

NARRATOR: And on my right – the state. Minister of Town and Country Planning.

[*Roar of boos from the* PROTESTERS.]

MINISTER: Your enterprise was privately motivated, not publicly responsible. We must live with one another. No man is an island unto himself. It is in the public interest that the community and not individuals should hold freeholds. I want you to go away and think this out calmly and dispassionately.

[*Protest. Protest.*]

You have an opportunity of rendering service to tens of thousands of people like yourselves. I have spoken to hundreds from West Ham and East Ham and they are just living for the day when they can come here. Strangers in your midst. I want you to make them welcome.

[*Protest. Protest.*]

I warn you! People will come whether you like it or not because this is an area ripe for development. The real choice which lies before you is whether in the long run this town is going to be built in a proper planned manner and inhabited by people who make a real home of it, or through chaotic development, by people who will come in sporadic fashion to make quick profits from jerry-built houses.

MR BIRCH: But you're not even offering a fair price for my property!

[*The two committees of Billericay and East and West Ham have joined as one to become the Basildon Corporation.*

Each of the eleven members holds a large card with a letter on it.

As the CHORUS *speak, the cards are revealed one by one to spell out two words.*]

CHORUS: In the beginning was the dream.

CHORUS 12: And the dream created the Corporation and the Corporation was without form and voice, and darkness was upon its face.

CHORUS 11: And the spirit of the dream moved upon the face of the Corporation and said let there be life and there was life.

CHORUS 10: And the dream looked upon the Corporation's life and saw it was good.

CHORUS: And the Corporation became God.

[*The cards have spelt out* BASILDON CORPORATION.
The CORPORATION *take over the circle of the hooded grey ones and surround* MR BIRCH *on his bungalow roof.*]

CORPORATION: We offer you £500 for your house and land.

MR BIRCH: It's valued at £2,000.

[*He fires a shot in the air.*
The circle retreats in fear.]

NARRATOR: Conflict! Conflict! The Corporation began to terrorize inhabitants to accept their offers.

[*The circle regroups.*]

CORPORATION: We'll offer you £750 for your house and land.

MR BIRCH: It's valued at £2,000.

[*He fires a shot in the air.*
The circle retreats in fear.]

NARRATOR: The elderly became very frightened.

[*The circle regroups.*]

CORPORATION: We'll offer you £1,000 for your house and land.

MR BIRCH: It's valued at £2,000.

[*He fires a shot in the air.*
The circle retreats in fear.]

NARRATOR: His case became a *cause célèbre* in the nationwide press.

[*The circle regroups.*]

CORPORATION: We'll offer you £1,400 for your house and land.

MR BIRCH: It's valued at £2,000.

[*He fires a shot in the air.*
   The circle retreats in fear.]

NARRATOR: Families like him were holding up the building of recreation facilities for the new town. They were offered to Billericay and Brentwood instead. Divide and conquer!

[*The circle regroups.*]

CORPORATION: Our last offer, £1,750!

[MR BIRCH *stands triumphantly aloft his bungalow as the hooded* CHORUS *of grey push him off amid hurrahs and applause from the* PROTESTERS, *who set up a chant,* –.]

PROTESTERS:

> BEORHTEL'S HILL SAX-ON
> WE DON'T WANT NO BASILDON
> BEORHTEL'S HILL SAX-ON
> WE DON'T WANT NO BASILDON

[*Against which* –)

NARRATOR: So, we applaud! The hero! The individual who stood up for his rights, defended his castle, got the right price for his property. The state didn't understand and had to be taught – think about it – with a gun! And we approve! We applaud? Think about that, dearly beloved.

PROTESTERS:

> BEORHTEL'S HILL SAX-ON
> WE DON'T WANT NO BASILDON
> BEORHTEL'S HILL SAX-ON
> WE DON'T WANT NO BASILDON.

[*And on and on* – *as background to* NARRATOR's *next speech.*]

NARRATOR: Conflict! Conflict! Conflict!
   'We have done this,' he said, 'in order to build our own home and free ourselves from the burden of rent and the fear of ejection.' Very moving! But thousands were homeless! So,

planned town or chaotic development? Beorhtel's Hill or
Basildon? And where do *we* stand, dearly beloved? With the
silly ole buggers and their romantic memories, their sacrifice?
With the homeless of East London? Chaotic development
could mean character, variety. Planned development *could* mean
dull monotony. Think about it – dearly beloved –

[*Chanting stops.*]

– for here comes the biggest conflict of them all – the dream
versus the reality.

[*The space darkens.*
Thunder – lightning –
– music of the spheres!
A light burgeons from above as though the heavens were
opening to reveal God.
Unfortunately, God had engagements elsewhere but we
have secured the services of angels, male and female, wings and
all!
The ANGELS *sing.**
As they sing, the transformation takes place. The grey-
hooded ones pull, one by one, the PLOTLANDERS' *bungalows*
off-stage, amid gestures of protest.
In their place they wheel on, one by one, four huge models
of the four most recognizable buildings of Basildon.
The new town takes shape before our eyes as it is being
sung about.]

ANGELS:

And this was the dream.
Within twenty years
From the devastation of war
From the deprivation of slums
From the poverty, the poverty
A phoenix!

* In the Basildon production a choir of about twenty 'angels' were used.

From the misery, the misery
A phoenix!
And this was the dream.

And this was the dream.
Offices of glass
From the shadows into sunlight
From the night's fears into morning
From the dark myths and the squalor
A phoenix!
From the pavements into parklands
A phoenix!
And this was the dream.

And this was the dream.
Diversity!
Sing praises to diversity!
Sing high, sing low
Sing black and white
Sing brick, cement and stone.
Sing typist neighbour to the nurse
Sing doctor neighbour to the dustman
Sing library, church, theatre, school
Sing clinic, pub and swimming-pool
A phoenix! A phoenix!

And this was the dream
Which every citizen could boast
And all the world would marvel at
Sing Art
Sing Industry
Sing sweet contentment
And this was the dream.

[*The singing and music end.*

   Sounds. Building-site sounds. Orchestrated sounds of pneu-matic drill, petrol-driven rammer, the shovelling of gravel, the chug of tractor engine.

   The town is being built.

These sounds fade into the background.

Stage empty except for the four huge models, the NAR-RATOR, RILEY, BRENDA and the CHORUS of grey figures.]

BRENDA: 24th May 1968. The town has no continuity. It has taken into its midst everything that couldn't be moved or destroyed. The sheer power of its newness and creation has overwhelmed any character that it might have built on. There are isolated pockets of resistance, but rather like the Indians in America — if they resisted too much, they were either killed or herded into small areas and forgotten; if they co-operated, they lost their identity. I have severed my own umbilical cord and must find my own nourishment in a town that seems to have none to offer.

[*Rain again. Rain, rain, rain.*

The ASIAN FAMILY reappear beneath umbrellas and watch the INHABITANTS who, as before, rush across the space, umbrellas up, pushing prams, supermarket trolleys.]

NARRATOR: So, the town was begun! Messily, but begun.

INHABITANT 1: Houses were built before roads and shops and social services. Bloody daft!

INHABITANT 2: There was a lot of mud and a lot of trudging.

NARRATOR: The first house was completed in 1951, the thousandth house in 1955.

INHABITANT 3: We had our own bathroom for the first time in our lives.

INHABITANT 4: We had a garden!

INHABITANT 5: Fresh air!

INHABITANT 6: Open spaces!

INHABITANT 5: They built paradise for us!

NARRATOR: Some of the protesters achieved their demands — a fair price! A freehold for a freehold!

INHABITANT 7: But they kept changing the master plan, didn't they! Public inquiry after public bloody inquiry!

NARRATOR: In 1964 it was agreed that Basildon could expand to take not 50,000 but 140,000 by the end of the century!

INHABITANT 8: But by 1983 there were 160,000 inhabitants, look! Seventeen more years till the end of the century.

NARRATOR: Ten thousand properties were knocked down –

INHABITANT 9: – protected buildings along with the rest!

NARRATOR: And – and here's the really interesting bit – as government and the times changed, so did principles change. Designated land bought for a pittance from the plotlanders was later auctioned off by the Basildon Corporation to private speculators at a huge profit. Ha! Freehold! Property! The stranger in our midst! The dream versus the reality! Conflict, dearly beloved! Conflict! Conflict!

INHABITANT 10: If the world had piles, it would be here!

INHABITANT 3: This is my town and I love it. It's got all *I'll* ever need in this life.

INHABITANT 2 [*at her bus-stop*]: It's a town waiting, this place. Bloody standing still and waiting.

INHABITANT 4: It's given me schools for my kids.

INHABITANT 11: There's a buzz but no explosion. One endless bloody fuse.

INHABITANT 12: And has anybody lit it yet? Has anybody even got a light?

INHABITANT 5: It's given me work, shops, clinics –

[*The* 6TH GANG *of youths chase the* 5TH GANG *across the space.*]

6TH GANG: Chalvedon! Chalvedon! Chalvedon's lot! Chalvedon's lot! Chalvedon! Chalvedon! Chalvedon's lot! Chalvedon's lot!

INHABITANT 13: It's a place to be born, a place to die, but it's no place to live!

INHABITANT 3: I tell you this, mate. Basildon has a future in Europe like no other.

INHABITANT 4: Shopping centre, sports palace, industry, the arts – you name it, we've got it.

INHABITANT 2: It's all money, isn't it! Work harder! Build bigger! Buy more! Money, money, money, money, boring, boring, boring, boring, boring!

[*The* 4TH GANG *chase the* 3RD GANG. *This time more stylized — like a ballet movement, moving slowly to the rhythm of their own chant —*]

4TH GANG: AL-CA-TRAZ! AL-CA-TRAZ! We're the gang from AL-CA-TRAZ!

INHABITANT 2: Boring, boring, boring, boring . . .

INHABITANT 8: You get used to the violence, you get used to it. That's the trouble, you get used to any bloody thing.

INHABITANT 5 [*exuberant, singing, dancing*]: 'I'm singing in the rain, just singing in the rain . . .'

[*Silence.*
Empty stage, except for the ASIAN FAMILY.]

BRENDA: 19th August 1968. The bulldozers have moved into the woods on the Link. They are flattening the trees and destroying the wild life. A housing estate is taking their place. I shouldn't mind, really, after all I have a house, so why do I begrudge others the same opportunity? I shouldn't mind, but I do. How difficult it is to welcome the stranger into your midst, but welcome them we must or die.

[NARRATOR *walks round and round the* ASIAN FAMILY.]

NARRATOR: Conflict! Property! Freehold! The dream versus reality! The stranger in our midst.

MR PATEL: At first Amin threw out only the British Asians from Uganda.

MRS PATEL: We heard about it on the radio and TV.

MR PATEL: Ninety days to sell our property and make our arrangements. Ninety days! We were promised safety and fair dealing but —

MRS PATEL: — but not all promises were kept, were they!

MR PATEL: Then in 1972 Idi Amin —

MRS PATEL: Idiot Amin we used to call him.

MR PATEL: Quiet, woman. Idi Amin visited Gadaffi, who promised to open a bank in Uganda if he threw out the Israelis.

MRS PATEL: The Israelis! Who were building vital roads and factories for Uganda!

MR PATEL: Will you please let me tell the story?

MRS PATEL: Are men stupid, tell me, are men stupid or not?

MR PATEL: Enough, Farida. Then he visited Bokassa in Central Africa, who gave him the idea to throw out the Germans and all the Ugandan Indians as well. Africa should be only for blacks, he said.

MRS PATEL: Stupid? Answer me! And we keep giving them such responsibility, *such* responsibility.

MR PATEL: And with Amin came the soldiers out of the barracks, crying, 'The Indians are milking the cows.'

MRS PATEL: Soldiers! The stupidest of the men are made soldiers. The ones who can't do anything constructive in life, they put them in uniform to destroy life!

MR PATEL: I was kept in prison for two days and I could hear the screaming from the torture.

MRS PATEL: Drunk and illiterate!

MR PATEL: They ripped off finger-nails and put salt there.

MRS PATEL: And the violations? The violations? Tell them about the violations!

MR PATEL: On the way to the airport, I saw bodies of men, women and children floating in the water.

MRS PATEL: He had brain damage. The man had brain damage from being a boxer in the army. His own soldiers joked about it. And they made him president of the most beautiful country in the world!

NARRATOR: When the full scale of the problem had been gauged by the Conservative government, they made their position very clear.

[*The voice of the Prime Minister, Edward Heath, is heard as if on the radio.**]

PRIME MINISTER'S VOICE: Those who have been forcibly ex-

---

* Edward Heath *did* record this speech, which he rewrote himself.

pelled from Uganda are British citizens. Your government is determined to honour its obligations towards them. We shall not fail in our responsibilities towards our fellow citizens.

Accordingly, I have asked each local authority to take in at least five families. In this way the burden on each one authority will be kept to a minimum.

Arriving families will be met by the immigration authorities, who will deal with the necessary formalities as quickly and as sympathetically as possible. Special reception teams will also be on hand at Heathrow, Gatwick and Stanstead airports. These will be comprised of volunteers from organizations such as the WRVS, the Red Cross and the St John's Ambulance Brigade. Altogether, forty-eight — note that — forty-eight organizations have offered to help.

[*Voice fades.*

The CHORUS *in grey surround the* ASIAN FAMILY *and walk in a circle round them, chanting.*

NARRATOR, *still bewildered as to who they are, walks around them in the opposite direction, hoping for a clue as to their identity.*]

CHORUS:

All things tire of themselves
The demagogue of his tongue
The revolutionary of his fervour
The singer of his song
The sower of his seed
The rose of its scent
The city of its dreams.

NARRATOR [*thinking he understands them at last*]: The city of its dreams! The rose of its scent and the city of its dreams! [*to the* ASIAN FAMILY] They're telling you too! I don't know who they are or where they come from, but they're also telling you. You think you've come to a city of dreams, don't you? Basildon! A town of working-class strangers taking over from plotlanders who were themselves working-class strangers.

Basildon! A town built for the disinherited, the slum-dwellers, the bombed out! Basildon! A phoenix from the ashes! A town of pity and dreams! And what happened?

[*Two men appear. They are* COUNCILLORS *of the time.*]

NARRATOR: We won't name names. We'll call you Dave.

DAVE: And we'll call you Tom.

NARRATOR: And they were both from the same political party. Labour councillors of Basildon!

DAVE: You never understood my arguments.

TOM: I understood them right enough.

DAVE: I *wanted* us to house those Ugandan Asians. I wanted the people of Basildon to welcome the strangers into their midst, but gently. Gradually.

TOM: There was no time. It was a crisis. These people were exiles. They'd lost everything.

DAVE: If you want to get emotional, let me remind you of the mother of two in a caravan with bronchitis and an ulcer. What would she have said to see an Asian family just arrived moving into a new home she'd been told she'd have to wait for?

TOM: There was no comparison. We were talking about people some of whom had committed suicide, some of whom had breakdowns from which they never recovered.

DAVE: I understood the problem. I knew about poverty and suffering and the iron fist of a ruling class. I grew up in the East End, didn't I? All I was suggesting was that we stagger them on the housing list. Not allocate five houses off the top but put them fifth, ninth, thirteenth, like that.

TOM: The issue was a moral one, not a pragmatic one.

DAVE: And I'm telling you it was a racial one. Pushing Asians on top of the housing list and claiming priority for them was creating racialism. We still had people looking for jobs, children looking for schools, patients looking for doctors!

TOM: That's demagogy! Absolutely unforgivable. To exploit genuine anxieties about jobs and social services in the face of human tragedy. The people of Basildon were capable of understanding the urgency of the situation. We insulted their intelligence and their humanity.

DAVE: Did we, Tom? Did we?

NARRATOR: Did they? The Labour motion to house the five Asian families was put to the council, where they had a majority of just 5 over the 19 Tories and Residents in the Opposition. 26 for, 16 against.

DAVE: And I abstained.

TOM: You betrayed.

DAVE: Not my beliefs. I didn't betray them.

NARRATOR: Passions were high. Councillors raged and accused and counter-accused. The Labour group was split. One Labour councillor resigned and put himself up for re-election as an Independent in order to test the avowed intelligence and humanity of the people of Basildon. Did they want strangers in their midst or not?

DAVE: No! I'm afraid they didn't! He was re-elected. The voice of the people of Basildon! They did *not* want strangers in their midst!

TOM: But did we always listen to 'the voice of the people'?

NARRATOR: So encouraged by the people of Basildon, the Tories put another motion to the council.

DAVE: That in the light of the result of a recent election in Barstable West Ward showing clearly strong public feeling in the matter, that this council rescinds the decision contained in Resolution 3 of Minute No. 1972/1488.

NARRATOR: The Billericay Residents added an amendment.

DAVE: That this council agrees to the acceptance on the housing list of five Ugandan Asian families expelled by the Ugandan government but after one year's residence in the United Kingdom.

TOM: But we had to integrate those people at once! The problem was not going to be solved by keeping them waiting for a year or more. And where? In camps? Refugee camps in Britain? Our council had *always* housed people out of turn for reasons of dire distress. Five homes! Five! A small contribution towards solving an international problem. We were given the chance to be magnanimous in the international arena and what did we do? Socialists! What did we do?

NARRATOR: Conflict! Conflict! Conflict!

The new motion was put to the vote. 22 for, 22 against. 5 Labour rebels voted with most of the Opposition and the Labour Chairman put his casting vote in favour of the resolution. The Socialist Group was defeated and Basildon said no to the stranger in their midst. Is it any wonder that heads had to roll? That rebels were expelled? And who was right, dearly beloved? Who represented the voice of the people? The comrades or the rebels? And if the rebels represented the voice of the people, should one always listen to that voice of the people? Conflict, dearly beloved, conflict, conflict, conflict.

[KIDS *in first gear.*]

RILEY: I remember that. Ashamed, I was. I remember that the Tory council down the road in Southend took in seven families.

NARRATOR: But the Basildon Corporation moved quietly in the background. The bloody old Corporation! Everybody's favourite villain! Under a certain Mr Charles Boniface, I remember.

[KIDS *in second gear.*]

Gave two fingers to the council and allocated five of their own homes to the Asians. Got it right for Basildon. Saved them; atoned for them.

[DAVE *and* TOM *leave.*

Thirty KIDS *rush on. They're dressed in the style of 1989. Again, they're met by two groups of three more* KIDS.]

KID 9: What's up?

KID 10: Where yer going?

5TH KID: We're going to find the end of the rainbow. Coming?

[*With a roar of 'YEAHHHHHH!', they rush forward. But,*

*as at the end of Act One, they do not move off stage. Instead
they run on the spot in slow motion.*]

BRENDA: How difficult it is to welcome the stranger into your
midst, but welcome them we must or die!

RILEY [*to* CHORUS]: 'Ere, 'ere. Come 'ere a minute. To save yer
sweating. The best part of the dream is that when I wake up I
can see flowers in my garden. Masses of them. I grow flowers,
y'see. Always have done.

[*And now the most extraordinary image of the evening. From
every part of the theatre, the people of Basildon appear with
flowers from their gardens. Not a few bunches in vases.
 Not a few dozen. But hundreds. Vases full of cut flowers.
Pot plants. All shapes. All colours. The floor is covered,
every inch. The models are strewn.*]

FULL CAST [*singing*]:

And this was the dream
Which every citizen could boast
And all the world would marvel at
Sing Art
Sing Industry
Sing sweet contentment
And this was the dream.

[*The lights go slowly down on the running youths, who leave
the* 5TH KID *to be surrounded by the* CHORUS *of grey. They
bow to him in a circle as he runs and runs and runs to find the
end of his rainbow.
 The* NARRATOR *pushes through them and, as before, hands
the runner a rose.
 Then he turns to the hooded circle of bowed grey forms.*]

NARRATOR: Who *are* they? If only I knew who they were.

[*The last glow of light is upon the runner with a rose held
triumphantly high in his hand. The bud opens up into bloom.*]

THREE WOMEN TALKING

a play in two acts

Blaendigeddi
July 1992

For MoJo

CHARACTERS

MINERVA, a business woman, aged 50
MISCHA, an academic, aged 42
CLAIRE a political researcher, aged 39

The three male characters are all played by one actor

MONTCRIEFF, a writer, aged 55, who left his wife, MINERVA
LEO, a financial analyst, aged 44, who was left by his wife,
   MISCHA
VINCENT, a shadow cabinet minister, aged 40, Scottish, who left
   his mistress, CLAIRE

Three Women Talking had its world première at the Northlight Theatre, Chicago, 15 January 1992. The cast was as follows:

MISCHA	Carmen Roman
MINERVA	Mary Ann Thebus
CLAIRE	Margo Buchanan

All three husbands:
LEO	
MONTCRIEFF	David Downs
VINCENT	

Director	Russell Vandenbroucke
Set Design	Michael Merritt
Costume Design	Nan Cibula-Jenkins
Lighting	Linda Essig

ACKNOWLEDGEMENTS

I am grateful to the director, Russell Vandenbroucke, for his intelligent and sensitive suggestions for changes which we discussed during four days in Blaendigeddi, 20–24 July 1991.

Further changes were made during rehearsals in Chicago, December/January 1991/2.

I added a new last scene 13 February 1992.

SETTINGS AND RELATIONSHIPS

Four areas.

Central, the largest, is the apartment of MISCHA, eclectic but exquisite taste.

In it she and her two friends, CLAIRE and MINERVA, have gathered for a meal.

Three other areas surround the central one. They will be occupied by the one actor playing each of the women's men, whose names are MONTCRIEFF, VINCENT and LEO.

LEO's space: a hint of garden, garden shed, garden bench, lawn-mower.

MISCHA left him six months ago, but he refuses to accept her absence, imagines she's always there in the house, talks to her.

VINCENT's space: section of a TV studio.

He is being interviewed. A married man, he has just ended an affair with CLAIRE.

Looming at an upper level is MONTCRIEFF's space: a hint of a study.

He's MINERVA's ex-husband. He left her five years ago, talks to someone off stage who's not there — his idealized mistress.

The women have gathered to share a three-course meal, each part of which one of them has elaborately prepared.

They will talk about their dish and the wine they have chosen to accompany it, but the scenes will be so arranged that the actors will have no need to be seen eating and the plates will be empty. Their descriptions will suffice.

Necessity requires that the opening of the play reveals its joints: the actor playing all three men must be seen changing from one character to another.

Clarity requires a kind of prologue,* a stylized opening in which the women reveal who they are and their relationships to the men — without it an audience's attention is distracted trying to work out who is who.

When the play opens all three women are in place in MISCHA's apartment in line with the spaces of their men.

* Though not, definitely not, addressed to the audience.

ACT ONE

[*Light on* MISCHA.]

MISCHA: I'm Mischa Lowenthal, lecturer in Hebrew studies. I left my husband, Leo, a stockbroker, six months ago – birth!

SCENE I

Garden.
    LEO, *professionally strong and able but emotionally adrift.*

LEO [*calling*]: MISCHAAAAAAAA.

> [*He has hauled out a lawn-mower from the shed and is confronting it like a strange beast he's never before encountered.*
>
> *He seems to remember you need to pull out a choke. Does so. He next remembers the pull start. He jerks it once, twice, three times, to no avail. He sits, easily defeated, exhausted, bewildered.*
>
> *A thought, like a slowly gathering storm, is assembling in his mind.*]

The universe is a ball
bounced by a child
living on a planet
placed in a universe bounced
by a child
living on a planet
placed in a universe bounced
by a child

living on a planet
placed in a universe bounced
by a child
living on a planet . . .

[*He finds the image a gloomy one. He looks up.*]

You gave me that, Lord. Don't blame me.

[*His thoughts, his memories overwhelm him. He cries out again –*]

MISCHAAAAAAAA!

[*Takes control of himself. Speaks to his wife rather than the Lord.*]

Sorry. You don't like shouting. I know. Forgive me. I'll get over it, only it takes time.

I remember, you used to ask me: 'What one, unexpected thing would you like to do in your life? You're a financial analyst for a big stock-broking firm but what,' you asked, 'is the one secret thing you've really always wanted to do? Something *really* surprising.'

And I never knew what to reply. Used to drive you mad, I know, but what could I do, Mischa? I just didn't have a secret ambition. Forgive me.

[*softer*] Mischaaaaaaaa!

[*Lights up on* MINERVA.]

MINERVA: Minerva Thompson, a business woman, ex-wife of
Montcrieff Hardy, a writer, he left me five years ago – chaos.

SCENE 2

MONTCRIEFF'*s study.*

MONTCRIEFF: And she blackmailed me with it, my wife, Minerva. 'I had the pain you had the pleasure.' But I didn't want
the pleasure, I wanted the pain. I *wanted* to have babies. Yes,
my love – birth! More than anything in the world I wanted
to give birth, my own children, not be dependent on the
blackmailing female of the tribe.

[*calling*] Are you listening in there? If we're to become
new partners in life you must know about me. I don't only
want to give birth to a literary masterpiece I also want to give
birth to a life.

What's that you say? Too late? Men can't give birth after
fifty? You're right! And didn't she know it. 'Men can't give
birth after fifty,' she mocked. Taunted me with my limitations. 'I had the pain you had the pleasure.' An emotional
terrorist, my wife. Leading light of the women's mafia. The
Godmother!

[*Lights up on* CLAIRE.]

CLAIRE: Claire Hope . . . political researcher . . . Vincent Ferguson . . . a mistress . . . pain.

SCENE 3

TV studio.
VINCENT *preparing to be interviewed.*

VINCENT: Yes, I know the questions become very personal at
the end. I'm one of the millions who gawp at your pro-
gramme. You're quite merciless on occasions. But I think I
can cope, I've nothing to hide. Though I'm not ashamed to
admit, I'd sooner face my opposite in the House of Commons
than face that evil eye there. How's my tie? I can never get
my tie right. First the wide end's too long, then the thin end's
too long. I tie and untie a dozen times before they come
equal. Or nearly equal. The wide end always has to be a wee
bit longer, I'm aware of that. I'm jabbering, aren't I? I'm
aware of that too. Nerves. I'll be all right, though. Once your
camera's turning and you're asking me difficult questions, I'll
be away. This idiot you see before you will turn into an
oracle, a sage and wit of the kind we in Scotland produce
endlessly, much to the envy and chagrin of the English who
are cool, calculating and boring – I promise. Does the light
have to shine so brightly?

SCENE 4

MISCHA's *apartment.*
    MINERVA *is decanting a bottle of red wine.*
    MISCHA *is laying the table.*
    CLAIRE *is rubbing wine glasses to shine with a cloth. She seems* obsessive.

MINERVA: Men! They're all the same! Interchangeable!

    [*Pause.*]

Look at the colour of this wine.

    [*Pause.*]

And they're incapable of making decisions.

    [*Pause.*]

Now there, sisters, is a colour speaks of passion. Just look.

    [*She holds it up to the light for them to see, slightly tipping the glass.*]

And no drop. Clings with confidence to the glass.

They hover. Have you noticed? Men hover, like birds before a window-pane, fluttering their poor wings at reflections instead of the real world. No comprehension of what they're looking at.

There's this marvellous cartoon of a vast woman with a fully dressed city gent over her shoulder. He hangs there, ecstatically, his briefcase still in his hand. And she's saying to him: 'Now, burp!'

    [*She holds up the decanter to continue pouring.*]

Regard! Centuries of good earth and the summer of '55 soaked up there. Enough to make you believe in God. You'll know all about heaven after a glass of that.

[*She places decanter in the middle of table.*]

Flutter and hover! You have to make all the decisions *for* them so that when you finally kick them out they can say, '*You* did it! *You* closed the door,' which, as you, I and all the world knows, is the way my bold ex-husband, Montcrieff, explained it happened.

MISCHA: Montcrieff? I thought you hated Hardy being called Montcrieff.

MINERVA: That was when I loved him.

MISCHA: Strange names parents give their children.

CLAIRE: Well, Mischa isn't exactly everyday nomenclature.

MISCHA: It *was* where *my* parents were born.

MINERVA: Have you got any *middle* names?

MISCHA: Stephania. The Jews name their children after dead relatives, never live ones. Stephania after my grandfather, Solomon; Mischa after my grandmother, Miriam.

[*They carry on their different tasks in silence.*
   MINERVA *is trying to peel off the label from the wine bottle.*
   After some seconds —*]

MISCHA [*to* CLAIRE]: Claire? Do *you* have other names to go between Claire and Hope?

CLAIRE: Dawn.

MISCHA: Nice.

MINERVA: Claire! Dawn! Hope!

CLAIRE: You've got it. My parents wanted all my dawns to be 'claire' and my days to be full of hope. They revealed it on my twenty-first birthday presented with a necklace of twenty-one pearls, bought one a year.

MISCHA: The schemes of our parents!

[*Continue in silence*]

[*to* MINERVA] Minerva?

MINERVA: I was hoping you wouldn't ask.

MISCHA: We have done.

MINERVA: Minerva Avril Loretta Thompson.

[*Silence. The others cannot see what is wrong with the name.*]

MALT! I was a war baby. M-A-L-T. My parents swore by malt. *Please* let's change the subject. My parents are not my favourite people.

SCENE 5

MONTCRIEFF's *study*.

MONTCRIEFF: *No* one was really her favourite person. Except me. I was the centre of her life. That was her downfall. But I was wild, full of appetites and divine discontent, the kind of man women find a challenge. Like cowboys tame wild horses, certain women are driven to tame wild men.

[*calling*] Are you listening? Are you there, my dream girl, my lucky find, my once–in–a–lifetime lover?

I could never understand why Shakespeare created a Katharina to be tamed by a Petruchio. Got it wrong again, didn't he? Got Richard Three wrong; got de ole black man wrong; got the Jew wrong. And women! Except in love. He knew about love and passion. Ah! Old Will! Where there's a will there's a play!

But tame me she could not, my ex! 'Frivolous! Infantile! Failed!' she scoffed. I am not, I hasten to assure you, entirely failed – I do make a living as a writer. And not entirely frivolous either. Not English enough to be entirely frivolous. Have you observed the neurotic drive of the English to be ever flippant? Tiresome, don't you think? Or are you irretrievably English? Perhaps you're not English at all but helplessly foreign! Or English with foreign extractions? I don't really know what you look like. Blonde? Brunette? Grey? [*Beat.*] Black? White? Asiatic?

[*Pause.*]

Would you like me to cook for you? It's true I can't have babies but I'm a very good cook, and when you got broody I'd get broody and I'd look after you wonderfully.

[*Pause.*]

She will answer me one day, won't she?

[*Mind wanders.*]

MISCHA's *apartment. Everything is prepared for the meal.*

MINERVA: Now. We're agreed. No cocktails. Just drink with the meals. And we each talk about the dish we've prepared and the wine we've selected *before* we eat.

MISCHA: Agreed!

MINERVA: Claire?

[CLAIRE *is distrait. The others are aware of her state. The meal is not the reason why they have assembled.*]

Claire Dawn Hope?

CLAIRE: Agreed.

MINERVA: And then – men! We are gathered, dearly beloved, to talk about men, especially your Leo, her Vincent and my 'Mont-bloody-crieff', and to help Claire face desertion!

MISCHA: We are here 'dearly beloved' to eat a good meal and help Claire if Claire wants help. Claire might even change her mind and want to watch Vincent being interviewed on telly.

MINERVA: Don't be daft! It was bad enough she had to deny being his mistress.

CLAIRE: Please! Let us agree not to talk about Vincent.

MISCHA: Did they have any suspicions?

MINERVA: They probed a bit, hoping for dirt. Even if she hadn't been his mistress the researchers would have thought she was. Never work with pretty women!

MISCHA: I think he's insane. No one's ever come away from that interview unscathed.

MINERVA: First they lull you into false security so's you imagine you've got the interviewer eating out of your hands and then

– crash! bang! Down come careers, families, a life's work . . .
But our saint here remained loyal to her bastard despite all.

MISCHA: Vincent's not a bastard, he's an old friend who's
impetuous, needs constant cautioning and I should have talked
him out of it. [to CLAIRE] *You* should have talked him out of
it, Claire.

CLAIRE: Can we please change the subject?

MISCHA: Yes, but not to talk about what women are supposed
to talk about when they get together.

MINERVA: You will before the evening's out, I promise you,
there will be no pussyfooting around this dinner table.

MISCHA: Can I remind you that it is *my* dinner table?

CLAIRE: That's how her business flourishes.

MISCHA: She was always Miss Bossy Pants.

MINERVA: Don't talk about me as though I'm not here. I'm
here! And let me say in my defence with no concession to
modesty – for I can see it is to become an evening of 'no holds
barred' and I may be in for a rough time – that, though I am
often judgemental, and who isn't – I am also loved, admired,
depended upon and the softest touch in town.

So. Let's start with Mischa's hors-d'œuvre. What is it, what
wine is it to go with, and why?

MISCHA: I wanted to visit the land where the cedars come from
before I began translating the Song of Songs –

MINERVA: – which is Solomon's –

MISCHA: – which is *not* Solomon's. Ernest Renan, who as you
probably know –

MINERVA: No! I probably *don't* know!

MISCHA: – was the eminent membre de l'Académie française
and –

MINERVA: I can't bear it when people assume I share their
erudite, cultural framework.

MISCHA: – and wrote a celebrated *Life* of Jesus, also –

MINERVA: My father was a ticket-collector, I *have* no cultural
framework, and I'm –

CLAIRE: I hope she doesn't plan to say she's proud of it.

MINERVA: Oh you're still alive then?

[MISCHA *smothers the moment before it grows.*]

MISCHA: Ernest Renan also put forward the theory that the Song of Songs is not really a long poem by Solomon but a kind of play *about* Solomon. About Solomon and a Shulamite shepherdess who was *abducted* by Solomon when he saw her tending the vineyards one day. Far from loving Solomon, she's really very unimpressed with him and longs for her true love, who is a shepherd.

CLAIRE: In my teens I had a boyfriend used to quote verses from the Song of Songs. Used to stroke my belly round and round and recite:

> *Thou art beautiful, O my love, as Tirzah,*
> *comely as Jerusalem —*

MISCHA: — says Solomon to his Shulamite, and then he adds 'terrible as an army with banners'. Now why does he add that? Why does he tell her she is as terrible as an army with banners? Renan thinks the answer lies further down in verses 11 and 12 of Chapter 6.

> *I went down into the garden of nuts to see the*
> *fruits of the valley and to see whether the vine*
> *flourished, and the pomegranates budded.*
>
> *Or ever I was aware, my soul made me like the*
> *chariots of Ammin-a-dib.*

Oh fatal step! A visit to the vines and there she was — lifted into the chariot of a king's train.

MINERVA: Poor Shulamite! Plunged into the arms of lecherous old Solomon!

CLAIRE: How do you know her shepherd wasn't a lecher, or wouldn't become one?

MINERVA: We'll come to you, Claire, when the time is right. So, Mischa, the Song of Songs, Solomon and —?

[MISCHA *plonks wine on the table.*]

MISCHA: And red wine from Lebanon. Kosraia '64!

MINERVA: Why Lebanon?

MISCHA: Solomon made himself a chariot of the wood of Lebanon. His palace was in Lebanon. The shepherd tells his Shulamite love: 'and the smell of thy garments is like the smell of Lebanon'. So, I had to see Lebanon. The tiny village of Kosraia, in the south, a lush, hilly area called Alboukah.

MINERVA: And the hors-d'œuvres?

MISCHA: I'd been walking all morning, before the sun became too hot, and had to stop in a restaurant for a coffee and a mid-morning snack. A little restaurateur – he spoke Arabic, French and English – we began talking. And when I told him that I was making a new translation of the Song of Songs in the shape of a play, to my surprise he asked, 'From which language – Hebrew or Latin?' I told him, 'Hebrew.' 'You're Jewish?' he asked. 'I'm British,' I said, 'but a Hebrew scholar.' 'You're Jewish,' he said, 'don't be afraid. We all have our madmen. I'm not one of them. Here,' he said, and he took out a plate from his rusty, peeling old fridge, 'here, a taste you will never taste anywhere else in the world. I had it from my parents who had it from their parents who had it from their parents all the way back to Suleman – Kibbey Nayeh.' Fresh raw lamb, minced; crushed wheat; raw onion, cut small, crisp; one beaten egg; Arabic sweet pepper; salt; and a local herb impossible to buy here called Kamoun. I begged it from a Lebanese restaurant in Piccadilly.

[MISCHA *pours out the wine. They raise their glasses to each other, drink, then turn their attention to 'the dish'.*]

Taste!

SCENE 7

LEO *by the garden shed. He's contemplating the lawn-mower again —
something he has always hated but must now confront. Again he pulls
the cord, again it refuses to come alive. He has no idea what to do. He
has never mowed a lawn before. Machines confuse him.*

LEO: Gardeners! Why do employees fall ill?

[*Cups hands to his face and again cries out to the air in
desperation —*]

MISCHAAAAAAAA!

[*Long silence. He calms down.*]

She stopped loving me, what could I do? Stopped! Ceased!
Dried up! Childhood friends, thirteen years married, two
children and I became unlovable! Unloved any longer. Like
this lawn-mower. Though this lawn-mower I never loved.

It's not a crime — to stop loving me. To stop loving me I
could not say with my hand on my heart was heinous. It's
everyone's right to love, not to love, to love less, to stop
loving.

But of course it was not so simple, because she liked me,
perhaps even more than liked me. And why not? I was a good
man — faithful, loyal, dependable! I'd given her the best years
of my life, her beloved children, days of roses and wine and
verse beneath the bough. Why shouldn't she like me a little,
even a lot?

But love? That searing madness? That insatiable longing?
That absurd thrill of one finger on a cheek? That ache to be
there all the time? That sharp nerve-end sharing of every
domestic detail of the day: she watching him peel her an

170

apple, him watching her drying her skin, she watching him shaving, swimming together, walking together, listening to music, watching a movie, just holding on to one another for the dear last years of life? None of that. All that dead and gone. Affection in place of passion ... Sad ... Sad and over ... Batteries run out ... Sing lullabies for the day's end ... Sing lamentations ... For the night has come ...

SCENE 8

MISCHA's *apartment. They have finished the hors-d'œuvre.*

MINERVA: Oh my God! That was a taste to excite and a wine to weep for.

MISCHA: Come, it was an exquisite wine but no wine is to weep for.

CLAIRE: Do you think only human beings are to weep for?

MISCHA: Mostly, yes.

CLAIRE: I once visited a stone garden in Kyoto that made me weep.

We were there two years ago you'll remember – a parliamentary delegation trying to persuade the Japanese to lift their trade barriers. He and I took off, as we often did on such journeys, broke away – he needed to explore the ceramics industry, he said. Kyoto.

We entered a temple. The temple of Ryoanji. He told me to close my eyes, took me by the hand, led me, then said, 'Open them.' It was a shock. Rocks, moss, furrows of small stones. Laid out by two brothers six hundred years ago. My eyes saw it, my stomach felt it. What? I never know the word to use when I talk about it – rightness? harmony? courage? All those things. But more. It was to do with the unexpected. Those brothers had the courage to imagine that a juxtaposition of the unexpected was right, harmonious, perfect. It was the courage of the unexpected made me weep.

[*Of course she wants to weep for her life going wrong. Restrains herself.*]

MINERVA: I don't believe in perfection. Human *beings* aren't perfect and what they *produce* shouldn't be.

MISCHA: *Shouldn't* be? You're *dictating* imperfection?

MINERVA: *Can't* be, then.

All things are literally better, lovelier, and more beloved for the imperfections which have been divinely appointed, that the law of human life may be effort, and the law of human judgement, mercy.

[*Pause.*]

Ruskin.

[*Pause.*]

On the Nature of the Gothic.

[*Pause. She feels she has to explain how she came by the quotation.*]

[*sheepishly*] Evening Institute course on British Cathedrals . . . cultural frameworks and all that!

[*Awkward silence.*]

CLAIRE: I know a very funny story about an American football player called Puzaltski.

MISCHA: *You* know an American story? But there's no one more English county than you.

MINERVA: You don't *have* to hide behind laughter, Claire.

MISCHA: The English! We have this great need to defuse our emotions with giggles.

MINERVA: On the other hand – I need laughter. If I was given the choice between laughter and money I'd have no hesitation in choosing. I need laughter like I need oxygen.

[*Awkward silence.*]

CLAIRE:

I charge you, O ye daughters of Jerusalem, by the roes, and by the hinds of the field, that ye stir not up, nor awake my love, till he please.

MISCHA [*reminding them*]: Said the shepherd to the women of Solomon's harem.

CLAIRE: And he rubbed and he stroked and he rubbed and he stroked, in small circles, quoting without pause.

[*Silence.*]

I thought one was supposed not to decant good wine any longer.

MINERVA: Well, like Moses you supposes erroneously. It's impolite to leave wine in the bottle so that guests can see how expensively they're being hosted.

CLAIRE: Disagree. It's more polite to please your guests with information about what they're drinking. There's pleasure in labels.

MINERVA: *Visual* pleasures! I prefer tastes – like people – to come through with*out* labels.

SCENE 9

TV studio. VINCENT *is being interviewed.*

VINCENT: There is no doubt in my mind that the three major issues to confront the twenty-first century will be world poverty, environment, and a conflict between believers and non-believers. Or, to be more optimistic, between countries driven by religious fanaticism and countries with a tradition of religious tolerance. But those are the chapter headings not the subheadings, and it's the subheadings which are crucial.

[*He pauses as though listening to an interviewer's question.*]

What do I mean by that? What I mean by that is – take the problem of the conflict between religious fanaticism and religious tolerance. Voltaire thought it was solved 250 years ago when the age of reason dawned over Europe, but reason and tolerance didn't, like spring, burst out all over. Now, why? We have to be able to identify the spiritual bacteria that inflame bigotry. Or do we just pacify religious states with a kind of soothing, there-there-we-love-you diplomacy? Is education the answer to fanaticism? Or must we make damn sure we've got a good military defence against holy wars?

Here's a formulation which I think should be printed as huge posters and stuck on walls all over the world:

My respect for your liberty to live and pray and believe as you wish does not mean I have to respect what *you believe,* how *you live or the* content *of your prayers.*

[*Pause.*
Listening.]

Yes. I *am* a believer, believe it or not!

MISCHA's *apartment.*
    MINERVA *lays out her three fondue sauces. 'Lights' the paraffin. Pours wine for them.*

MINERVA: The bastard left me but he knew how to cook, and petty will I not be. The fondue, sisters, is the first meal he ever prepared for me and though I hate and despise his frivolous and infantile spirit yet will I honour his culinary memory.

    You have before you one red, one green, one yellow sauce, these being the traditional colours of the fondue meal. My red is sour cream, reddened with a tomato paste, heated with a touch of cayenne pepper, chilli and some drops of Tabasco. My green is mousse of avocado with *crème fraîche* and drops of lemon. My yellow is as much to do with textures as tastes — mayonnaise which I made myself, mandarin slices — from the tin, I'm afraid, and crushed walnuts. Sweet, crunchy, velvety, and softly fatty. On the small plates you will find raw mushrooms, raw onion, and slices of green pepper to spear with your beef which is — I promise you — best fillet no expense spared.

    The wine comes to me from other sources and marks the end of my marriage. Between this fondue and this red wine stretches, sisters dear, a quarter of a century of married bliss and blood. Could a graph be drawn it would show a steady decline from the heights of unimaginably original passion to the lows of unbelievably original venom. By the end we were lacerating one another into emotional cubes which, like the meats we are about to deep-fry, we deep-fried in our very own and seething blue angers.

The details are banal, and just as banal was the fact that I loved him throughout. Until he left me. Then I hated him. To go through all that pain and misery and not reap the pleasures of hate? Not this sister, my sisters. I could forgive the bastard not.

[*Pause. Waiting for a sign.*]

And do I hear you ask me *how* I discovered the wine?

MISCHA: Our eyes, our eyes, look at our eager eyes, for God's sake!

CLAIRE [*mocking*]: Wait we cannot!

[MINERVA *tells her story as though reading from a novel.*]

MINERVA: He stood me up for a concert one night. It was Bernstein conducting Mahler. Sold out. A man was looking for a ticket. An American professor of physics. I sold him mine. We sat alongside each other, saying nothing. Both of us afraid the other would mistake a word for a pass. Mahler flooded our emotions. At one moment I dared to glance at him. His eyes were closed. Ah! The sensitive soul, I thought. Until his head thumped loose on my left shoulder. Jet lag! Here was a boy needing to be tucked up in bed, not ravished by the chords of Jewish melancholy. I reassured him with the most sympathetic of my famed smiles. In the foyer he caught up with me.

'Could you direct me,' he asked with that special brand of mournful American courtesy, 'could you direct me to the nearest Underground?'

'Where are you making for?' I, with absolutely no intention of taking him there, responded.

'The Westbury Hotel,' he replied with the appeal of a lost and lonely visitor to strange lands.

'I'll take you there,' I said. Weakness overwhelmed my poor old woman's resolve.

On arrival he said: 'Whenever I come to London, which is at least four times a year for conferences and the theatre, the first thing I do is go to Berry Brothers at No. 3 St James's

Street, Piccadilly, to buy six bottles of good wine and one bottle of superb wine. In my room I have,' he continued in low, dark and confidential tones, 'already decanted by room service one hour before my expected return, a bottle of 1955 Château Margaux. Thirty years old, brown in colour and with an immense aroma of age and wisdom and utter, utter confidence. Will you,' he asked as though it was the last dance and he had finally plucked up courage, 'will you join me if I promise, hand on heart, to behave and advance you nothing but the story of my life?'

Fearing and hoping he would break his promise, I accepted. We drank this wine-from-another-planet and he told me that he was researching — wait for it — 'chaos'.

'Chaos,' he revealed to me, 'is the new discipline raging through and binding together all the disciplines of science which,' he informed me, 'during the last half century have been peeling away from one another into specialist corners.'

Did you know, sisters, that all is chaos in the physical world out there?

'Far from discovering a law and order to all things, as Newton predicted, nothing' — he was rivetingly dramatic about it — 'nothing happens in quite the same way twice. We are victims of,' and here he introduced me to one of the most tenderly formulated notions I've ever heard, so harken to it, sisters, 'we are victims of "the sensitive dependence on initial conditions".' I'll repeat it, for verily is it lovely: 'The sensitive dependence on initial conditions, a phenomenon known as: "the butterfly effect" which is,' he informed me, 'the notion that a butterfly stirring the air today in Peking can transform storm systems next month in New York. You hit a storm, you can feel it, but who will ever know which butterfly was where that caused it? Chaos!' he warned me, 'all is chaos.'

And when he asked me what *I* did I found myself weeping as I described how my husband had nagged me for years to found a business of vintage Christmas puddings and how I had resisted and he had been right and I became successful and now we lived in what he glorified as his 'divine discontent' but which you, I and all the world knows was blood, tears, and yes, chaos! I had told no one till then. The Château Margaux, assisted no doubt by Gustav Mahler, had released my confession and – here's the point – revealed the possibility of reconciliation. But, when I returned home, I discovered – he'd fled. Yes. Fled! Men don't leave, they flee – guilt in their hearts, terror and chaos up their arses.

Beware of the red sauce, sisters, it's hot!

SCENE II

MONTCRIEFF's *study. He's typing a sentence.*

MONTCRIEFF: 'The great attribute of chaos is that you can count on it! Chaos is dependable . . .'

    [*calling*] Is that *your* experience of life, my once-upon-a-time princess? That chaos is dependable?

[*Listens as though to her reply which gives him pleasure.*]

There's no chaos in *you*, is there? In you is the still centre all men crave. How fortunate I am to have found you. And I warn you I will keep you all to myself, tucked away in these hills, chaotic old humanity left far behind . . .

    My ex-darling was an archdeacon of chaos. Not her Christmas-pudding affairs, oh no! Those were kept in order. Her emotional affairs! Those! The chaos lay in her emotions. Her heart produced a turbulence the unpredictability of which had me and she and she and me buffeted around our lives like helpless flotsam in a gale.

    Oh, she told me about him, her physics professor. She couldn't resist letting me know every pass made after I left. One conversation with him about the new science of chaos and she knew all about it. The kind who attends a lecture on a complex subject and overnight is an instant expert! That was she. What I called 'a topper'! Any item of knowledge you presumed to offer a company, she could top it.

    'I see the Prime Minister has accepted an invitation to the Middle East.'

    'Ah, but have you heard his wife has refused to accompany him in protest against their treatment of women?'

    'They've reached the moon, then!'

'Yes. Took them twenty-seven hours and forty-three point two minutes.'

'I hear What's-his-name is going to star in Thingamebob's new movie.'

'Well that was the plan, dear, had their plane not crashed half an hour ago!'

I don't know where she got her information from. Her nipples seemed to act like antennae to the world's airwaves.

But I really didn't mind her knowing things. *That* wasn't our problem.

SCENE 12

MISCHA's *apartment. A pause in their main course.*

MINERVA: When I first saw him, I mean 'saw' him, you know what I mean — SAW! I thought — now — *that's* small. I thought that's probably the smallest I'd *ever* seen. Little! In fact it looked to me like it was growing inwards — in fear maybe, desperately trying to crawl back to wherever it came from. And I'd been waiting for this moment for a long time. Years! We'd been admirers for five years, contemplating each other from afar — until — this moment arrived. And I looked down and I thought: *this* is what you've been waiting for? All these years — *this*? I mean a stud he could never have been, except the kind that holds a collar in place, maybe. And when I told him —

MISCHA: You *told* him?

MINERVA: Of course I told him. No secrets if you want good love-making. And when I told him, he blanched, as though I'd told him in a roomful of friends.

MISCHA: Surprise, surprise!

MINERVA: But I mollified him. 'No malt during the war, huh?'

CLAIRE: They care about size, don't they? It really matters to them. No understanding of a woman's needs. Thick pricks and thick heads!

MISCHA [*shocked*]: Claire!

CLAIRE: We're here to talk about men, aren't we? 'Let's have an orgy of food, wine and derision,' Minerva said to me.

MISCHA: She didn't say it to me.

CLAIRE: You're so prudish about sex.

MISCHA: Not about sex but about —

CLAIRE: What? About what?

MISCHA: A certain respect. For the privacy of life.

CLAIRE: I don't think anything should be private.

MISCHA: That's an outrageous thing to say.

CLAIRE: Why? Literature is full of revealed private moments. That's what we turn to literature for – to pry into other lives.

MISCHA: That's not what *I* read literature for.

CLAIRE: And for what then *do* you read literature?

MISCHA: Illumination.

CLAIRE: The more intimate and private, the more illuminating!

MISCHA: About emotional pain, yes. Not physical deficiencies.

CLAIRE: Why?

MISCHA: Physical deficiencies make us vulnerable.

CLAIRE: And emotional ones don't?

MISCHA: Not in the same way.

CLAIRE: Explain!

MISCHA: Physical deficiencies invite derision, emotional ones invite pity.

CLAIRE: In the love and war of life, pity and derision are inevitable companions.

MINERVA: Well, you two are an exciting match. It's like tennis.

MISCHA: You *would* reduce life to a tennis tournament.

MINERVA: Don't get at *me*!

CLAIRE: Do you feel guilty for leaving Leo, Mischa?

MISCHA: No. I might have felt guilty if *he* had left *me*. I'd have feared I'd driven him away.

CLAIRE: Is she trying to tell us something?

MINERVA: I think I'll reheat the oil.

SCENE 13

MONTCRIEFF's *study*.

MONTCRIEFF: Our problem was me: I had broody longings for immortality. Babies and literature — she stood it for twenty-five years, then kicked me out. And who can blame her? Babies and literature. Lit-er-a-ture!

And what is it? Scavenging! A writer is a vulture that picks at the dead and the partly living. Well, not quite. But who can deny the element of scavenging in literature? Hovering over the livers and lovers, the mad and the dying, recording their passions, picking up their mistakes, weaving patterns out of their laughter and lunacy. All my best lines are other people's, Oscar, and I make my living from him and her and a soupçon of imagination the trick of which you can buy at any academic supermarket. Writer? Huh! I'm a picker-up, a pecker-off, a nibbler of this and that from here and there, an intellectual magpie, an emotional thief, a beachcomber of other people's lives. And when I've got it all down in a book I go into a market place and I take it out of my pocket like a vendor of dirty postcards, slightly ashamed. 'You buy? Cheap and lovely literature! Best art in town! Here, in my pocket! Ssh! Don't answer too loud. No one else must see and hear.'

You think I exaggerate, dearly beloved, my darling, my dove, my heart? Although there's nothing wrong with a little bit of exaggeration, I promise you I do not.

So what could she expect me to do with love, my ex, my producer-of-vintage-Christmas-puddings-out-of-which-she-has-made-a-small-fortune? What *is* love but another sack of discarded expectations to be sorted out, selected, listed and filed for lit-er-a-ture?

[*He picks up and reads from one of the letters he's been folding away in envelopes.*]

[*reading*] 'Dear Jason, my new novel is about chaos . . . in the past . . . you have published . . . but now I think . . . something new, something special . . . would you read . . .?'

[*Pauses to consider what he's written, sardonic and resigned.*]

Archivists, that's all we are, of other people's fond eccentricities, tragic errors, their lost illusions. Literature! Lit-er-a-ture! LIT. ER. A. TURE!
Are you still with me, my honey, my heart?

SCENE 14

MISCHA's *apartment.*

MINERVA: In the last years he began talking to himself. Lived in his head. His ideal women lived in his head, never the real world.

MISCHA: Do you think we can really be honest about men?

MINERVA: About them or with them?

MISCHA: With them, about them, either.

MINERVA: Well, I was honest *with* them. Credited the bastard with my business success; told him I loved him but that he was a bastard; confessed to a fantasy about making love to a stranger . . .

MISCHA: Claire? [*no response*] Claire, you don't seem really to be here? Are you sure you don't want to watch Vincent being interviewed?

[CLAIRE *abruptly deflects the question. What follows is a moment of coming together.*]

CLAIRE: Which of you wooed?

MINERVA: Wooed?

CLAIRE: Wooed! Wooed! I woo, he woos, she woos, they wooed . . .

MINERVA: And we'll all woo together . . . Yes! I've wooed, damn it! I've stood at the barricades of feminism and roared my fury at frivolous men and their infantile ways and yet —

CLAIRE: — and yet, admit! You have wooed like a slave.

MINERVA: Like a slave!

MISCHA: 'Come live with me,' you said to him, 'and I will be your factotum . . .'

MINERVA: Yes!

CLAIRE: 'Scream for me to scratch your back and I'll come running . . .'

MINERVA: Yes, yes!

MISCHA: 'I will be near you but not under your feet, I will comfort but not suffocate you, I will wait until you can bear no longer *not* to touch me!'

MINERVA: I promised! I pleaded!

CLAIRE: 'Of course I must work but – this will I do and that will I do . . .'

MISCHA: You plotted your seductions, planned your passions . . .

CLAIRE: Days of scheming, dreaming, gentle words and promises . . .

MINERVA: True! True! I even promised to change my fucking politics for them – all true! As soon as I found a man I wanted – into action! Instinctively! My whole being! Despite everything! I wanted to cook for him, iron his shirts, pour him drinks, cut interesting articles out of newspapers. I found a different hairstyle, tried new perfumes, new make-up. I bought new dresses to delight him, incredible nightdresses to entice him. I even went back to lacy, silk underwear and suspenders and rediscovered my pleasure in them. I was amazed and shocked how easily it all came back to me. I wanted – God damn it – I wanted to look after him!

[*Silence.*]

MISCHA: We all want to look after him.

CLAIRE: Speak for yourself. I want to be looked after. I want to be guarded against cruelty and stupidity, protected from dirty minds and ugly souls.

[CLAIRE *makes a sudden movement and knocks over a glass.*]

MISCHA: I'm worried about you.

CLAIRE: Well don't be!

SCENE 15

TV studio. VINCENT *is being interviewed.*

VINCENT: I'm glad you've asked me that question. But I'd better warn you my reply will be controversial. Few people know *how* to behave as equals. They either want to dominate or be subservient. It's a fraught problem, central to relationships between priests and their flock, politicians and their adherents, capital and labour, men and men, women and women, men and women!

Equality is a Queenly concept we all love to love because it flatters us. But she's not an easy lady to comprehend. Consider: if you place a simple mind alongside a wise mind and declare them equal in the sight of God you will at once intimidate the simple mind. It can't compete. If you place an *aggressively* simple mind alongside a wise mind that is totally *without* aggression, and declare *them* equal then you at once intimidate the wise mind. The one can't handle wisdom, the other can't handle belligerence.

Look at the problems between men and women – and I think we should because I believe the twenty-first century will be the century of the woman – though not without a kind of emotional bloodshed. Most women – and many are not going to like what I say, and I may be losing myself their votes but not too many I hope because I'd like to think I appeal to those who vote for honesty rather than demagogy – but most women seem not to *want* to behave as equals! They either want to dominate or serve. There may be historical or social reasons for this, but I'm not a sociologist, I can only describe my experience of those relationships.

We are here dealing with an uncomfortable concept. Most

men and women in their relationships do not eye one another as potential partners but as potential combatants. The question they present to themselves is not 'Do I love?' but 'Can I win?'

SCENE 16

MISCHA's *apartment. They have finished the second course.*

MINERVA: Was that good or was not that good?

MISCHA: It was very good.

CLAIRE: It was like nothing I've ever tasted before.

MINERVA: Let's not go over the top. Praise, I enjoy. Adulation is suspect.

CLAIRE: No! I mean it. I'm serious about food. I've had lots of fondues, and the sauces offered nearly always taste like each other. With these I had the feeling that each cube of meat came from a different cow. A cube of meat dipped in the avocado sauce seemed to come from Switzerland. The cube dipped in the yellow sauce was undoubtedly a cow from the Argentine. The cube dipped in the red hot sauce — don't expect any of this to be logical — although it was hot, was unmistakably a cow from England.

MINERVA: An English cow — curried?

CLAIRE: Just so.

MINERVA: I love that you've distinguished tastes in my food, sister dear, but sense you do not make.

CLAIRE: Don't *say* that! That's what *he* kept telling me: 'You do not make sense.' How I hate that sentence. [*mimicking*] 'Forgive me saying it but you do not make sense, my dear.' It was important to him to keep me just a few rungs lower.

MINERVA: I thought he was a generous spirited man your Vincent.

CLAIRE: He was, he was! Generous, able, dynamic company, an adequate lover too, but he was — oh, that special brand of put-downer. There I was — high on being the researcher and mistress of a shadow cabinet minister, but not a week went by

that he didn't talk about the brilliant, erudite talented women
of the past – George Eliot, Beatrice Webb, Virginia Woolf –
MISCHA: – Jane Austen, the Brontës, Mary Shelley –

[*A subtle change of tone emerges. A list that began as a whip
of the past turns into a panegyric roll of honour – another
moment of coming together.*]

MINERVA: Bodicea, Elizabeth I, Catherine the Great –
MISCHA: – George Sand, Rosa Luxemburg, Simone de
Beauvoir –
MINERVA: What about Héloïse, Beatrice, and Eve – who got us
out of boring old paradise?
CLAIRE: Right! A marvellous heritage of women. But Vincent
beat me with them, the greats of the past, as though he
himself was one of those very greats. And he constantly laid
upon me facts he knew I'd not be able to contradict. He
didn't do it maliciously, oppressively, there was no spite in the
man but – I don't know. It was as though he didn't know
how to behave as an equal. He *talked* about equality, talked like
one who *believed* himself your equal. But he seemed incapable
of *behaving* like one. Perhaps I *wasn't* his equal – he was after
all a very capable man: astute at political assessment, shrewd at
human assessment, quick-witted, good memory, widely read,
social graces and – something I admired in him more than
anything else – intellectual courage, he took risks in his career,
but – it was essential to his self-confidence that someone was
around twenty-four hours a day to reassure him that he was
superior, not by word but simply by *being*. I was that being.
With me he could be benign, generous, modest, helpful,
overflowing with advice. I made him seem wise to himself,
allowed him to bestow bounty, permitted his magnanimity to
blossom.

[*Her tone changes.*]

And I loved every minute of it.
MISCHA: That's awful, Claire. That's shocking and degrading.
CLAIRE: Ah, moral Mischa who imagines she's found her knight

in shining armour, her Prince Charming. Do you really think me shocking and degraded? Performing the service of making him appear wise and superior had the reverse effect of making *me* feel wise and superior. Permitting him to assume control simply meant *I* was in control. Do you think I *really* considered him wiser than me? As the servant who deferred, as his admirer who bowed, I was able to manipulate him for my own needs.

MINERVA: I think my Château Margaux '55 has got to her.

CLAIRE: And do you think I *loved* him? That I even like men as a species? I — have needs, they — provide. They fuck my appetites away and I can command high salaries.

MISCHA: Methinks the lady doth protest too much.

CLAIRE: For that I must dissemble a state of mind which allows them to imagine *they* are in control. But oh are they not! And *you* know they're not. Between ourselves let's be honest: men are for manipulating.

MINERVA: I'd drink to that if I had any more Château Margaux '55.

CLAIRE: Why else were we given tears?

MINERVA: I can open a bottle of lesser wine?

> [CLAIRE *drives on.*
> MISCHA *is watching her closely.*]

CLAIRE: And sighs and soft curves?

MINERVA: I think I *will* open a bottle of lesser wine. [*does so*]

CLAIRE: And what about eyes? What *can't* be put into eyes, tell me? Like bottles you can fill at will with different colours, so with our eyes — vessels to be filled with all those glorious shades of emotion. Gaiety one minute, vulnerability the next. A touch of melancholy here, a hint of longing there, the wicked brilliance of passion, the damp ducts of helplessness, the milky hue of modesty — whatsoever emotion is required for our ends we can call up into our eyes, and few men can resist.

   And let us not, sisters, let us not talk about our sexuality. That would be giving too much away, wouldn't it? You,

Mischa, ask can we be honest about men? You, Minerva, say there'll be no pussy-footing around this table? Right! Recall the moments, those splendid moments of total control, when you've stood naked and become triumphantly aware of the power in each moulded part –

MINERVA: Who on earth is she talking about?

CLAIRE: – when you've isolated each magnetic mound and known its sensuous weight in gold.

MINERVA: She's not talking about me.

CLAIRE: There you've stood, knowing the allure of breasts drew hands. There you've stood, knowing that mound at the base of your belly drew hands. And that belly – oh, I knew what drew my teenage lover to stroke and circle the palm of his hand round and round and round and round.

MINERVA: Nine out of ten women would not recognize themselves in any of that.

CLAIRE: Would not admit it! But – for most women there was at least one time in their lives when they stood before a mirror facing their flesh and aware that every voluptuous part was bewitching, delicious, magnetic! The curve of a neck, the long soft side of their arms, the down of a thigh, hips to be held, buttocks to be squeezed, fingers and toes and nipples to be sucked. Power! Pulsating, intoxicated, confident, through every nerve-end – power! The tool we must learn to handle for delight and the security of our lives – power! The power to bestow that one deep and excruciating pleasure that all men helplessly crave – it's ours! And with it we have them, malleable, for manipulating – men! Deny it if you dare, sisters dear! Contradict me if you dare, sisters dear! Talk to me of love if you dare, dear, dear sisters, dear!

MINERVA: I think it's time you presented us with your dessert, Claire.

ACT TWO

SCENE I

The garden. LEO *— his lawn-mower — three more attempts. Fails. Sits.*

LEO:

> The universe is a ball
> bounced by a child
> living on a planet
> placed in a universe bounced
> by a child
> living on a planet
> placed in a universe bounced
> by a child . . .

[*It is his private incantation, his secular rosary. But it is not really what is preoccupying him.*

Slowly, working it out, almost word by word . . .]

The real difference between men and women is that women have the power to *recognize* paradise when they see it, the emotional capacity to *hang* on to it, and the confidence not to care whether paradise wants them or not. Men are never certain it's *paradise* they see. That's why she stopped loving me – she'd seen paradise. A man who she knew, without the slightest, the merest, the merest, the slightest hesitation – she was in love with. And in she zoomed.

'You,' she said, 'do not support me emotionally, intellectually or in bed. You suffer from,' she said, 'constipation of the imagination.'

And she was right! I was dead! I only came alive in business conferences. What was wrong with me, was me!

What could I do? I had become – unlovable!

MISCHA's *apartment.*

CLAIRE *has calmed down. Contrite almost, as though she had shocked herself having gone too far.*

The others are waiting on her.

CLAIRE: Something light. A cheesecake. A lot of calories – I know – but – light. Fluffy.

[*Long pause.*]

MISCHA: And the dessert wine?

CLAIRE: Tokay. From Hungary.

MISCHA: Three or four star?

CLAIRE: Four.

[MISCHA *whistles in admiration.*
    Another long pause.]

MINERVA: No more? That's it?

MISCHA: When did you first eat it?

[*Even longer pause.*]

MINERVA: Well?

CLAIRE [*finally*]: In Auschwitz.

MINERVA: God help us!

MISCHA [*understanding*]: Another parliamentary excursion, no doubt.

CLAIRE: Yes.

MISCHA: Polish members of Parliament invite British members of Parliament to visit rebuilt Warsaw, beautiful Cracow, the ski slopes of Zakopane, and Auschwitz – obligatory.

CLAIRE: I didn't want to go. I hate confrontation with suffering, weeping tears I haven't earned.

[*Pause.*]

MINERVA: So?

CLAIRE: I held back.

MINERVA: And?

CLAIRE: Returned to the gate.

MINERVA: Where you were fed cheesecake? [*no response*] Jesus! It's like getting blood out of a stone.

CLAIRE: I saw a grey-haired old woman staring at me. She held a plastic carrier-bag in her hand which made me think she was a local. I nodded to her, and she spoke to me. It was quite a shock, actually. She had a heavy Polish accent tucked inside a heavy American one.

'You're not going to *visit* are you!' she said. She didn't ask, she stated. She seemed to know. 'I see many like you,' she said. 'They come to the gates but they can't go on. I don't blame them. *I* only come,' she said, 'because my family is here, and if my family wasn't here I wouldn't come either.'

And she told me this story, her entire family – parents, brothers, sisters, uncles, aunts, cousins and grandparents – all! Gassed! She survived because she was the clever one and the family saved up money to send her to study in Paris. And it seems her youngest sister, in the midst of all that deprivation, used to save crumbs to feed a baby bird she'd found.

'So I come every year to feed birds and visit my family.'

MISCHA: And *that* made you weep!

CLAIRE: Aren't you the clever one!

MISCHA: Not merely for her sister – the bird lover, but also for Environment Shadow Minister Vincent Ferguson, your own lover, and for the helplessness of that and most other things in life.

CLAIRE: The really clever one.

MISCHA: One event may prompt it but every tear is finally for everything.

CLAIRE: And to console me this grey-haired old woman fed me

her home-made cheesecake. 'Here,' she said. 'It's my own recipe. And I've given it a name.' I asked her what name? 'Five-thousand-years-of-suffering cheesecake,' she replied. Which made me laugh. We both laughed. Imagine – feeding birds, eating cheesecake and laughing at the gates of Auschwitz!

[*Silence.*]

MISCHA: *We have a little sister, and she hath no breasts: what shall we do for our sister in the day when she shall be spoken for?*

[*Silence.*]

MINERVA: Feel like telling the Puzaltski story?
CLAIRE: At this moment I think – no!

SCENE 3

MONTCRIEFF's *study.*

MONTCRIEFF: Travel! The one thing you and I are going to do is travel. When I think of all the exotic places I haven't seen I get into a panic. The Valois of France, the rain forests of Brazil, the back streets of Cairo, the deserts of Arabia, the temples of Thailand – panic! When I think of all the *books* I haven't read – panic! The tastes, the experiences, the challenges – panic!

[*Pause, as though listening.*]

Of course I get sea-sick! Sea-sick, car-sick, bus-sick, people-sick. You name it, I get sick of it.

[*Pause, as though listening.*]

What makes you think I'm a misanthropist? I'm just growing old, and growing old is the process whereby contempt for most humankind is confirmed.

[*Thinks sadly about this. Recovers.*]

But never mind, we'll take the car on the ferry, risk drowning, and I'll dance you through the Europe of my wild youth. Down and Out in Paris, the First Film Festival in Cannes, the Prague Spring, the Vienna Waltz, the Miracle in Milan . . . Isn't that what you're supposed to do with a young mistress? Take her back over your youth? Vivid times, my darling. BC.

[*Pause.*]

Before Cynicism.

[*Pause.*]

You're not really there, are you? I imagine you —

[*Pause, trying —*]

— invent you —

[*Pause, trying —*]

— *will* you into existence —

[*Pause. Finally, with a hint of sad envy —*]

Whoever you are *you* will always be the one who gives birth, won't you . . .?

MISCHA's *apartment.*
Each in her own way is a little tipsy.

MISCHA: I used to play this game with Leo, drive him mad. 'What,' I'd badger him, 'what one, unexpected thing would you like to do in your life? You're a financial analyst,' I'd taunt him, 'for a big stockbroking firm. But what — what is the one secret thing you've really, really always wanted to do?'

MINERVA: What'd he say?

MISCHA: Didn't! Couldn't!

MINERVA: Wouldn't, p'raps?

MISCHA: No! Couldn't! Constipation of the imagination! A genuinely sweet, genuinely kind man who genuinely comprehended nothing in the world except money. Machines, children, paintings, music, literature — all genuinely bewildered him. Had no meaning for him. What's the point of a child — it doesn't converse or produce? What's the point of a machine if it doesn't operate at a touch? What's the point of a painting — people and the world are there in front of you . . .? Even his own 'thing' bewildered him.

MINERVA: 'Thing'? 'Thing'? It's got a name. William! Willie for short.

CLAIRE: A marauder!

MISCHA: A shlong!

MINERVA: A totem-pole!

CLAIRE [*mock macho*]: 'Don't be frightened but here — are my credentials!'

MINERVA [*mock American macho, hand on imaginary zip*]: 'Are you sure you can handle this?'

[MISCHA *stands, legs astride, looking down.*]

MISCHA: Bewildered him! It was his stranger-in-paradise! He'd gyrate [*she does so*], watching it loll about. 'My sleepy lion,' he used to call it. It was the funniest thing he ever said. 'Look at my sleepy lion, ha ha!'

MINERVA: Whatever was Leo's attraction, for God's sake?

MISCHA [*giggling*]: His 'sleepy lion', I think.

MINERVA: She's off! I told you, dearly beloved, we'd gather to talk about men.

MISCHA: It was enormous! It used to hang between his legs and he'd stare down at it in genuine bewilderment, didn't seem to know what else it was for other than you-know-what

[*She's still there, staring down, herself a little unsteady.*]

Stare, waiting! Hoping something would happen by osmosis. He never quite made the connection between 'it' and the sexual act. I tried undressing slowly, slinkily, to help. No use! I'd finally have to manhandle it the way one slaps dough around the table

MINERVA: Ouch!

MISCHA: When it did finally lumber awake it was, I must confess, rather magnificent. But not for long. Without imagination it soon erupted and then collapsed like a dynamited old Victorian chimney-stack. Obsolete!

MINERVA: An obsolete cock! Yes – I'd say that describes most men.

CLAIRE: I think you're very unfair about Leo. He has limitations, who hasn't? He was gauche, his brain didn't live inside his body. But he was witty and generous and did you ever hear him on love?

MISCHA: He talked to *you* about love?

CLAIRE: I didn't love him. He could.

MISCHA: Perhaps he confided in you a secret, unexpected desire?

CLAIRE: Tell us yours, Mischa. What one, unexpected thing would *you* like to do in your life?

MISCHA: Can't say!

CLAIRE: Oh, go on. Tell us.

MISCHA: Too shy.

CLAIRE: What, between gals?

MISCHA: Especially between 'gals'.

CLAIRE: Well, that makes it immediately intriguing.

MINERVA: You weren't too shy to talk about obsolete cocks.

MISCHA: Tell us yours, Minerva. What one unexpected thing would *you* like to do in your life?

MINERVA: Oh, mine's easy. I'd like to climb the outside of Big Ben.

[*Her friends are incredulous.*]

MISCHA: Whatever for?

CLAIRE: I can't conceive of any more vacuous ambition in life.

MINERVA: That's because you don't suffer from virgo like I do.

CLAIRE: You mean vertigo.

MINERVA: That's what I said, vertigo.

CLAIRE: Do you think we're drunk?

TV studios. VINCENT *is being interviewed.*

VINCENT: If I were Prime Minister? I'm not sure that's the sort of question I should be answering. On the other hand I long ago decided – and our leader accepted this when I was invited to take up the post of Shadow Minister for Environment – that I was not going to tailor my personality to a political career. My political career would have to tailor itself to me.

A party leader is flesh and blood. A myriad of idiosyncrasies. Idiosyncratic habits, idiosyncratic tastes, idiosyncratic thoughts. Now, I'm against the cult of personality, but I can't be bland! I can't fade into an anonymous background.

So, if I were Prime Minister I'd want the people to be in no uncertainty as to the kind of person I am. They should know what I think, believe, fear and even doubt. Especially my doubts. I mean – there are a lot of very important issues to be considered: the eternal cycle of injustice, revolution, injustice, revolution . . . for example; the relationship of education to liberty; the role of envy in human conflict. It's not enough for a leader of a party to be good at putting pennies on a tax here and taking them off there – what's the quality of *thought* behind the decision, that's what *I'd* want to know.

So, if I were Prime Minister I'd set up a chain of key lectures. Say four a year. And my priority themes would be: the Individual Spirit – does capitalism release or shackle it? Second: Human Nature – good, evil or irrational. Third: the Decline of Language and Its Relationship to Inhumanity. Fourth: Violence to Achieve Ends – the vicious circle.

[*His last words fade away with the cross-fading lights.*]

SCENE 6

MISCHA's *apartment. The women are slightly tipsier.*

MINERVA: What do you look at first when you look at a man?

CLAIRE: His bum!

MINERVA: Only his bum?

MISCHA: Thighs for me.

MINERVA: Bums and thighs. Any advance on bums and thighs?

CLAIRE: His eyes, his eyes, I'm his for his eyes.

MISCHA: Shoulders, shoulders, I'm his for his shoulders.

MINERVA: Lips, lips. Let his tongue lick his lips.

CLAIRE [*singing it*]: And let us not forget the bulge.

[*All three find a simple harmony.*
Another moment of coming together.]

ALL: The bulge! The bulge! And let us not forget the bulge!

[*Laughter.*
Subsides.
Silence.]

MISCHA [*entering her own world*]: *I am the rose of Sharon, and the lily of the valleys.*

MINERVA: Mischa, Mischa, Mischa. Tell us your secret.

MISCHA: *As the lily among thorns so is my love among the daughters.*

MINERVA: Don't be shy with sisters who love you. What one unexpected thing would you like to do in your life? Climb a mountain? Cross the Sahara? Live a year with the Bedouins? Or in a nunnery? Would you like to get thee to a nunnery — which as we all know was Hamlet's inspired suggestion for the woman he loved?

204

MISCHA: *Stay me with flagons, comfort me with apples, for I am sick of love.*

CLAIRE: Oh wise, mysterious Mischa, who knows what we think before we have thought it, who will take her secrets to the grave.

> [*Something in this draws* MISCHA's *attention to* CLAIRE, *who turns away.*]
> MISCHA *lets it pass.*
> *Silence, then —*]

MISCHA: The truth about paradise is this: the serpent was Jewish!

Leo was obsessed with the thought that paradise lost was the cause of conflict between men and women. Men can't forgive women because Eve seduced Adam into biting the apple which lost them paradise. But he missed the point, my poor Leo. The conflict is not between men and women over the fall from grace, it's between men on one side and women and Jews on the other. 'Get thee with learning,' whispered the Jewish serpent. 'Bite! You'll see better!' *He* knew a useful tool when he saw it. So Eve, being a woman with an instinct for the good things in life, and having more courage than her male companion, bit, and got pregnant with learning and lost paradise! For all of us! [*Pause.*] Been hated ever since. [*Pause.*] Oppressed and hated. [*Pause.*] Jews and women! [*Pause.*] For knowing too much.

I read in the paper the other day that a woman got off for murdering her husband because he beat her, for long periods, cruelly, until she couldn't stand it any longer. And the occasion when he beat her most was when she used a word with more than one syllable. 'Don't you use educated words with me,' he cried at her. 'Don't you come the clever stuff with me. Bam! Wallop! Bash! Take that and that and that!' [*Pause.*] Women and Jews. [*Pause.*] For biting an apple. [*Pause.*] Funny old life.

> [*The speech came out of the air, and into the air disappears.*]

MINERVA: Claire Dawn Hope?

CLAIRE: Yes, Malt? What can I do for you, MALT?

MINERVA: Tell us, what one unexpected thing would *you* like to do in your life?

CLAIRE: I? Me? My secret unexpected hidden desire?

MINERVA: I know! Don't tell me! You want to be whipped!

CLAIRE: No! Though I'd quite like to be let loose with a whip on some men I know.

MISCHA: Come, Claire, you don't want to take your secret to the grave, do you?

CLAIRE: My secret wish has always been to sing a pop song. Just one. Specially written for me. Rehearse with a group for as long as it takes and then – cut a single! A song I can sing my heart out with, and everyone would dance to! Dance, dance, dance, dance, dance . . .

[MISCHA *is watching her very carefully as she dances.*]

SCENE 7

MONTCRIEFF's *study*.

MONTCRIEFF: Are you one of those young women who complain the world is dominated by men? Well you may be right, you may be right. We're a bullying lot. But here's some questions to ponder. Can men be said to have shaped the world when they're the sons of women?

And take the game of chess – a game I rarely play and when I do I can't think many moves ahead. Consider the Queen, her main task is to protect the King and attack anyone who threatens him. She can move where she likes – diagonally, horizontally, back and forth. And here's the question. Why do you think the Queen was chosen to be aggressive, defensive and free-wheeling, while the King creeps crippled across the board one step at a time?

[*Reaches for TV remote control, flicks screen alive. We hear* VINCENT's *voice.*]

VINCENT'S VOICE: I suppose this line of questioning means you're approaching dangerous terrain.

[MONTCRIEFF's *wicked chuckle as he settles down to enjoy his viewing.*]

SCENE 8

MISCHA's *apartment. She's serving coffee.*

MINERVA: The real problem with Montcrieff was that he couldn't face not being Dostoevsky.

MISCHA: Arabic coffee.

MINERVA: 'So what?' I'd yell at him. 'Absolutely no one else in the world is Dostoevsky either!'

MISCHA: With cumin seed.

MINERVA: He couldn't have our babies and he wasn't Dostoevsky so he left me.

MISCHA: That simple?

MINERVA: Nothing is that simple.

CLAIRE: And what drew Mischa to her Prince Charming, her knight on a white horse?

MISCHA: Harmony. His head was inside his body.

CLAIRE: Lucky you.

MISCHA: You don't like me any more, do you?

[*No response.*]

We were all such good friends.

[*No response.*]

I've never hurt you, betrayed you, spoken ill of you behind your back. You can't hold it against me that I suggested Vincent hire you, surely?

[*Long pause.*]

You think *I* talked him out of you, don't you?

CLAIRE: Didn't you?

MISCHA: Oh Claire. I have great faults but I'm not treacherous.

He's a family man with a political career. He made a choice.

[*No response.*]

I'd also love those days back. Good times. Shared pleasures, laughter, consolations, friendship . . .

CLAIRE: It's your 'wisdom' I can't bear, your fucking, melancholy Jewish wisdom. Not all those five thousand years of suffering have prevented you from dreaming on and on and on about your Prince Charmings, your knights on white horses, your Messiahs.

MISCHA [*bewildered*]: Why should that make you resent me so?

CLAIRE: Because all idealism offends me. There are no knights in shining armour out there. Prince Charmings live in the story books of silly girls. Messiahs never come. Leo was a good man with a sense of humour. Your families came from the same village in Russia. He was on his knees to you most of the time.

MISCHA: I didn't want that.

CLAIRE: He would have been your doormat.

MISCHA: I didn't want that.

CLAIRE: He dressed you, fed you, housed you, and answered your every whim.

MISCHA: I didn't want any of that!

CLAIRE: No! You wanted endless intellectual conversations, endless evenings out to the theatre, endless trips to historical sites, and an amazing circle of the endlessly interesting, the endlessly stimulating, the endlessly erudite.

MISCHA: What the hell is wrong with any of that?

MINERVA: What the hell is wrong with any of that is that no man is endlessly interesting for ever and ever and ever amen.

MISCHA: Is any woman?

CLAIRE: Is any*body*?

MISCHA: Bitterness is a cancer, Claire.

CLAIRE: There it is! Fucking melancholy Jewish wisdom again!

SCENE 9

LEO's *garden. Sitting on a bench. Disconsolate.*

LEO: Let us contemplate suicide.

First problem: how? Armoury? I do not possess. A knife in my heart? My hands would be unable to push. Sleeping pills? I would fall asleep before taking enough of them. Gas? She cooked by electricity. My car? Ah! My car! Close garage doors. Sit. Switch on. Breathe deeply. A comfortable way to go.

Second problem: why?

[*Long, long pause.*]

Third problem: a will. Is my will made out? Of course. All my affairs in order? All!

[*Pause.*]

Return to problem two: why? Everyone is interesting.

[*Pause.*]

Even when they're boring they're interesting.

[*Pause.*]

Only not for as long as those who are *not* boring.

[*Pause.*]

And *I* am definitely boring. I *am* boring! I am *boring*!

If I stop and try to make my mind think something interesting, I can't! Look! I sit here and squeeze and squeeze, like trying to get juice from a shrivelled-up old orange and –

[*Hold for a long pause as he tries to fill his mind with something to surprise himself.*]

– I can't! Nothing comes! Only if I think about – my job – my profession. *That* excites me – the flow, the placing, the reproductive mechanisms of money. I can't help it! Money excites me. Why should I be ashamed of that, Mischa? It helped you, your family, our friends.

[*Thinks about this.*]

Oh God! I'm so boring I bore myself. It's an illness. I need help, treatment, I need pity. Pity, not derision . . .

MISCHAAAAAAAA!

Hardy. Must phone Hardy. It's Hardy I need. He doesn't think much of me but he'll help. For old time's sake. I'll phone him now. [*rises*] I don't really want to die. I want to be loved. I do, I do. Loved . . . Looked after . . . I'll provide the money, somebody look after me. There must be a cure for an affliction like boringness.

[*Pause.*]

Is there such a word – 'boringness'?

[*Leaves, calling –*]

Hardy, Hardy, Hardy . . .

SCENE 10

MISCHA's *apartment*.

CLAIRE: The Puzaltski story.

[*All funny stories rely upon the teller. We write it out here but the actress is at liberty to restructure it to her own style of telling, like a solo violinist given free rein in a cadenza.*]

Puzaltski was the fourth reserve of a famous American football team. So famous that it always had star players and poor Puzaltski was never ever in fifteen years called on field to play a match.

Retirement is upon him. Comes the last Saturday in his career, he wakes up, sits down to his breakfast of steak and french fries and says to his wife [*in a heavy 'Brando Waterfront' accent*], 'Dat's it! Finished! I'm not going to de match!'

His wife is aghast.

'You're not going to the match? The last match! It's unprofessional not to play the last match!'

'Don't tell me!' cries a deeply unhappy and humiliated Puzaltski. 'But for fifteen years I've been fourth reserve and I ain't never ever been called to play a game. Fifteen years sitting on de sidelines. Do you have any idea what it's like only ever to sit on de sidelines and never be a player? What kindda life was dat?'

'Maybe today,' says his wife, 'today they'll call you!'

'Dey haven't called me in fifteen years, why should dey call me on my very last day wid de team?'

His wife is fearful.

'You skip the last match they'll cut off your retirement pension and then where will we be?'

'I'm not going and dey won't cut off my retirement pension and we'll be OK.' Puzaltski is adamant.

'*I'll* go!' cries his distraught wife. 'I'll *take* your place!'

'You?' laughs her husband. 'You're a woman!'

Mrs Puzaltski ignores him.

'I'll get to the locker-room early, I'll get into all that gear — who'll know?'

'It won't work.'

'It'll work! I'll just be a number sitting on the sidelines and I won't say a word. Did anybody ever talk to *you*?'

'Never!'

'So — it'll work!'

And away she goes. Locker-room. Changes. The coach puts his arm round her and pats her on the bum. Sits on the sidelines. First half of the match, as always, the team remains intact. Then, second half — chaos takes over! Down goes one player. The first reserve is called. Down goes a second player. The second reserve is called. A very nervous Mrs Puzaltski is sitting on the sidelines.

[CLAIRE *begins to titter.*]

[*carefully*] It is a game she does not know how to play!

[*As the story progresses all the women will gradually be drawn into infectious laughter even before the punch line.*]

Fifteen minutes before the end of the game the home team is losing, the fans are not very happy. Then, the unimaginable happens. A third player goes down and the cry goes up for the fourth reserve.

'PUZALTSKI!'

There's no way out. She has to go on to the field.

[CLAIRE *enacts it.*]

There she is, bending down, looking around, understanding nothing, praying she'll be called upon to do nothing, and the numbers come. Out of sequence. Meaningless. Fast. Nine! Seven! Three! Five! Two! Wham! She suddenly finds the ball coming her way. She catches! She runs! Of course she doesn't know what *should* be done, so she does the right thing in the wrong way. A crazy dash. While she runs with the ball, the players jump on each other. Touchdown! The fans go wild.

Who is this guy? They've never seen him before. The name is whispered. The whisper spreads and soon the name is on everyone's lips.

'Puzaltski! Puzaltski!'

Meanwhile Mrs Puzaltski is a very bewildered and frightened woman.

'This is not,' she says to herself, head bent down, 'a very wise thing to have done.'

The crazy numbers begin again. Different ones. Two! Nine! Seven! One! Ten! She understands nothing, but there again — wham! The ball's in her hands. She runs. Unorthodox. Another touchdown! The field's in confusion. The fans are delirious. They're chanting:

'PU-ZALT-SKI! PU-ZALT-SKI! PU-ZALT-SKI!'

Meanwhile the other side are getting very, very worried indeed, and they get into a huddle.

'I don't know what the fuck's happening,' says their captain, 'but one thing's for certain — we gotta nail that guy they call Puzaltski!'

So there they are again. Heads down, numbers flying, and every eye of the enemy team on Mrs Puzaltski, who by this time is beginning to enjoy herself. Five! Three! Seven! Two! Eight! Wham! The ball's in her hands again and in a flash eleven men are on top of her. She's out! Cold!

Next thing she knows she's in the locker-room, stripped, and the trainer is over her, pushing down at her breasts as though trying to get them to be somewhere else. She opens her eyes and it's obvious — she is amazed! The trainer bends over her full of admiration and reassurance and he says: 'Ya did good Puzaltski, ya did real swell. And don't worry about a ting. I'll have ya right in no time. As soon as I getcha balls back into place your prick will come out of hiding!'

[*They are convulsed.*]

SCENE 11

This scene will be played as a duet between two settings: MONT-
CRIEFF's *study followed by* MISCHA's *apartment.*

First: MONTCRIEFF's *study.*

*The phone rings — a ringing which will continue until the laughter
has died away and the scene settles.*

MONTCRIEFF *answers. It is* LEO, *who we hear as 'voice-over'.*

At the same time the TV set is on and we can see VINCENT *in the
last stages of his interview.*

*His voice will fade in and out but will always be there in the
background.*

Thus the three men perform a 'trio'.

LEO'S VOICE: Hardy? It's Leo, don't hang up.

MONTCRIEFF: Why should I hang up?

LEO'S VOICE: I know you don't like me but I've always rather
    respected you and I need to talk to someone. Someone who
    knew Mischa and me well.

MONTCRIEFF: Can I ring you back? Vincent's being interviewed.
    He should be writhing on the floor any minute now.

LEO'S VOICE: *I'll* ring back.

MONTCRIEFF: Why aren't you watching? Once-upon-a-time
    friends and all that.

LEO'S VOICE: I'm sorry to have disturbed you.

MONTCRIEFF: They've allowed him to be clever and urbane but
    now come the personal questions, and I can't wait to see what
    they've found.

LEO'S VOICE: It's important, Hardy. Life or death, I'd say.

MONTCRIEFF: Death? You? *You*, Leo?

[*But he's also listening to* VINCENT, *whose voice from the screen is louder.*]

VINCENT [*on screen*]: Well, it depends how far back you want to dig into my past, but I don't think there's anything I need be *too* worried about. Some apple-stealing from neighbours, a little cheating at school once, truant — that sort of misdemeanour. I mean I don't imagine you're going to ask me how my wife and I make love — [*Nervous laughter.*]

MONTCRIEFF: Leo, I don't really think we should be talking about this over the phone.

LEO'S VOICE: Hardy — would you ask her to come home?

MONTCRIEFF: Let her go, Leo. She's still in love with you-know-who. Accept it. Now put the phone down, switch on the TV and watch with bated breath.

LEO'S VOICE:

Did you know that our universe is a ball
bounced by a child
living on a planet
placed in a universe bounced
by a child
living on a planet . . .

MONTCRIEFF: LEO!

[*Fade in* MISCHA's *apartment.*]

MINERVA: Mischa! We still don't know which one, unexpected thing Mischa would like to do in her life. Claire wants to cut a disc, I want to climb a tower — what about you?

MISCHA: You want to know? Strip-tease!

MINERVA [*amazed*]: Strip-tease?

MISCHA: The one secret, unexpected thing I'd like to do in my life is a strip-tease.

MINERVA: The woman shocked by Claire's power-of-the-body theory wants to put her body to the test of power?

CLAIRE: She's lying.

MISCHA: I'm secure in my intellect, why should I be lying?

CLAIRE: She wants to be interesting.

MISCHA: In a really raunchy working-men's club where there is absolutely no brain at work, where the senses are uncontaminated by intellect, where the response is one hundred per cent pure contact between my body and what it makes a man feel, and where, incidentally, I could test Claire's power-of-the-body theory.

MINERVA: I understand my friends not.

CLAIRE [*disproportionately angry*]: She's mocking me.

[*Which makes* MISCHA *wonder at her even more.*]

MINERVA: Maybe I was wrong, maybe you *need* to watch Vincent being interviewed.

[MONTCRIEFF's *study.*]

LEO'S VOICE: Believe me! Women recognize paradise but men are never certain it's paradise they see.

MONTCRIEFF: Wrong! It's just that women are satisfied with *less* of paradise. Men want it all!

LEO'S VOICE: God! You're clever, Hardy. That's why you can be immune to feminine taunts.

MONTCRIEFF: Me? Immune to feminine taunts?

[VINCENT *on screen.*]

VINCENT: Yes, I had lots of girl-friends before I was married. In my degree course studying politics and economics were some of the most interesting female minds in our generation. For me there's nothing more sexy than an original mind.

[MISCHA's *apartment.*]

MINERVA: Claire? Vincent? The interview?

CLAIRE: No.

MINERVA: But they're coming to the decimating part and they're bound to dig up something you didn't know.

CLAIRE: I do not want to see his face, hear his voice, share his thoughts-for-the-day, or know anything about his life whatsoever.

MISCHA: Methinks the lady doth protest too much.

MINERVA: Methinks the lady she hath drunk too much.

CLAIRE: And methinks you're both getting on my tits [*to* MINERVA]. You're the one who's consumed with hatred of men.

MINERVA: Let's not exaggerate.

CLAIRE: I was just a married man's whore – period!

MISCHA: Oh come on, Claire, he didn't *pay* you.

CLAIRE: Not in cash but in kind, the good life, the good, good life – the rich, exhilarating, endlessly interesting good life.

MINERVA: There comes that ever-hopeful 'endlessly' again.

MISCHA: She always did have a weakness for self-dramatization.

CLAIRE: Oh did I now, Mischa the wise, Mischa the pure, Mischa the intellectual of us all? There's nothing you've done wrong in your life is there? Nothing really, really, really reprehensible. All sweetness and light!

[VINCENT *on screen.*]

VINCENT [*in fury*]: *That* is innuendo! That shouldn't even have been posed as a question. There was absolutely nothing beyond a professional relationship between Claire Dawn Hope and myself and I will take you and your muck-raking television company through every court in the land to prove it.

[*Pause. Listening.*]

What? That cannot be true – I don't believe – she could not possibly have –

[MISCHA *is looking intently at a miserable, distracted* CLAIRE.

The dialogue swings between the two settings.]

MISCHA [*to* CLAIRE]: You told them, didn't you?

MINERVA: You told them?

MONTCRIEFF [*incredulous*]: She told them.

LEO'S VOICE: Hardy, are you listening to me?

MONTCRIEFF [*to* LEO *on phone*]: Yes, of course she played that game with me.

MISCHA: Damn you, Claire!

MONTCRIEFF: And you know the one secret unexpected thing I'd like to have done in *my* life?

MINERVA [*dawning approval*]: She told them.

MONTCRIEFF: Given birth!

MISCHA: That television researcher who came to ask about Vincent's interests —

MONTCRIEFF: Yes, of course to a child, what else?

MISCHA: — you listed *all* of them, didn't you?

MONTCRIEFF: Penis–envy? Nonsense! They can have mine!

MISCHA: Didn't you?

MONTCRIEFF: More trouble than it's worth.

MISCHA: You listed *all* his interests . . .

MONTCRIEFF: Swap it for a womb any time!

MISCHA: . . . language, ceramics, stone gardens and Claire Dawn Hope.

MONTCRIEFF: My one envy of women is that they can give birth.

MISCHA: She promised silence but betrayed him.

MINERVA: Do I condone or do I not condone? That is the question.

MONTCRIEFF: Pain? Pain? What pain?

MISCHA: How can you condone? She's destroyed a life.

MONTCRIEFF: Women always want to exclude you.

MISCHA: She promised the affair would remain just between our three couples but she revenged herself.

MINERVA: Revenge has an honourable history.

MISCHA: Revenge has a primitive history.

MONTCRIEFF: Breast-feeding, staying up all night with it . . .

MISCHA: And with her revenge she betrayed us too.

MINERVA: Betrayed?

MISCHA: Yes, betrayed.

MONTCRIEFF: 'You'll never understand,' they say. 'I had the pain, you had the pleasure.'

MINERVA: God, you're self-righteous, Mischa.

MONTCRIEFF: I'd take *all* the pain for that miracle of birth.

MISCHA: *You* see self-righteous, I see outrage!

[MISCHA, *simultaneously with* MONTCRIEFF's *last speech, hurls words at* CLAIRE *underneath him.*]

MONTCRIEFF: Don't die, Leo. It's a waste of time.

MISCHA [*to* CLAIRE]: Betrayed . . .

MONTCRIEFF: Give birth to something . . .

MISCHA: . . . birth . . .

MONTCRIEFF: . . . money, gardens, cities . . .

MISCHA: . . . trust . .

MONTCRIEFF: . . . wine, food, clothes . . .

MISCHA: . . . love . . .

MONTCRIEFF: . . . theories, chaos – anything . . .

MISCHA: . . . friends . . .

MONTCRIEFF: . . . anything to give meaning to this helpless, weird and wonderful life!

MISCHA: . . . everything!

MONTCRIEFF: You hear me, Leo?

MISCHA [*to* MINERVA]: Betrayed!

MINERVA: Speak for yourself!

MONTCRIEFF: Birth!

MINERVA: Your friend is in pain, for God's sake.

MISCHA: Your friend has destroyed, for God's sake.

MONTCRIEFF: Give birth!

[*Lights out on all three areas of* VINCENT, LEO, *and* MONTCRIEFF.]

SCENE 12

The women are held as though paralysed by an explosion in their midst.

CLAIRE *especially is in a state of shock. On the verge of 'flipping'.*

The dust of revelation settles. They are not the friends they were when the play began.

Each is embarrassed. MISCHA *and* MINERVA *sit somewhere where they can pretend they are at ease.*

MISCHA: Perhaps a brandy?

MINERVA: Perhaps I should take up smoking again.

CLAIRE: Perhaps I should go home.

[*The atmosphere is tense. No one moves.*]

MINERVA [*to* CLAIRE]: *Is* Vincent destroyed?

CLAIRE: I don't know . . . I don't think so . . . perhaps . . .

MISCHA: He's been caught lying before three and a half million people, for God's sake.

CLAIRE [*with no conviction*]: He has charm . . . he can . . .

MISCHA: Charm? Charm? With every major politician watching?

CLAIRE: He'll plead human frailty –

MISCHA: They will devour him.

CLAIRE: – explain he was protecting the sensibilities of his mistress.

MISCHA: And what will his mistress explain?

MINERVA: That the man's a shit, a coward, an opportunist who placed career before other people's feelings – I hope.

[*Silence.*]

MISCHA: Claire?

MINERVA: Is she on trial here?

MISCHA: If we're to continue a friendship we've got to talk.

MINERVA: To say what?

MISCHA: To say why!

MINERVA: I don't think Claire needs to justify herself.

MISCHA: Justification is not the issue.

MINERVA: What is?

MISCHA: Values.

MINERVA: What values? Vincent employed Claire as his researcher, seduced her, used her, then dumped her as a threat to his political career.

MISCHA: Is that how Claire sees it?

MINERVA: How else can she see it?

MISCHA: Let Claire answer.

MINERVA: Maybe it's Claire's affair.

MISCHA: No. It's mine too. I introduced her to Vincent. She came with my recommendation and my blessing. I have a right to know.

MINERVA: What's there to know? She was a woman in love.

MISCHA: Which justifies all behaviour?

MINERVA: *Explains* all behaviour.

MISCHA: Explains what? Treachery?

MINERVA: You're talking reason, Mischa. Love is a pain, rejection is a pain. People in pain are not reasonable.

MISCHA: Perhaps we should parade the seductive myth of women's emotions. Those tender creatures who feel more deeply than men and can't be expected to use their heads.

MINERVA: That most definitely is *not* what I'm saying. I'm talking about pain right across the board. For both women and men. Pain is pain is pain is pain is pain.

MISCHA: Pain or no pain, I have a hard time reconciling love with betrayal.

MINERVA: And when love is withdrawn?

MISCHA: We don't love only because we're loved.

MINERVA: We love better, though.

MISCHA: But not less. I question the nature of a love that wants to destroy because love is withdrawn.

MINERVA: Then you've never met those women who rage, smash windows, break furniture, set fire to homes, make scenes in public, howl outside doors at night, put shit through letter boxes, poison the natural affection of children, parade them in the early hours before their father's mistress, threaten murder, suicide, and sometimes more than threaten.

MISCHA: Did *you* do any of those things when Montcrieff left *you*?

MINERVA: I wanted to.

MISCHA: But *did* you? *Did* you?

[*Silence.*]

Then why do you condone what Claire has done? Is it because she's done it for you, perhaps?

MINERVA: That's cheap. No, it's because he spat her out when she no longer suited his purpose. Crime and punishment. Someone wrote a book about it.

MISCHA: It is no crime to choose a new direction in life. That's everyone's right. If my new love wakes up one morning and decides to move out I will hurt to the core of my being but I *would* not, *could* not find it in me to punish him.

MINERVA: Say you don't know, dearly beloved, say cautiously, carefully, fearful of your unpredictable heart that you-just-do-not-know.

MISCHA: I know!

MINERVA: You can't know.

MISCHA: I can and do. What – to dare presume that he *had* to continue loving me? The arrogance of it! 'Me! Me! You must love only me!' I would be ashamed.

MINERVA: We are not talking of a man who loved but of a man who used. Callously used.

MISCHA: Well, let's look closely at that. 'Used'? Is that the word you'd employ, Claire? 'Used'?

MINERVA: All rejection makes you feel used.

MISCHA: Whose salary almost doubled? Who met some of the most illustrious minds of Europe? Who travelled to places undreamt of? Who's gained a wealth of experience, connections, influence?

MINERVA: The greater the pain of rejection.

MISCHA: Oh no! You can't have it both ways. Either her pain comes from being exploited or it comes from withdrawal of the good life.

MINERVA: Either way one feels used.

MISCHA: Used! An emotive word which blurs the truth.

MINERVA: Oh, and what is the truth, wise Mischa?

MISCHA: Neither dramatic nor consoling. Passion is ephemeral, an exotic plant with a short life-span. It chokes on its own succulence.

MINERVA: And love? Love? We all know about short-lived passion but what about love?

MISCHA [to CLAIRE]: Love? Let's look closely at that too. How did he break it to you, Claire? Coldly on the phone?

CLAIRE: No.

MISCHA: The inevitable, cruel letter of regret?

[CLAIRE *shakes her head.*]

MINERVA: How, then?

CLAIRE: Over dinner.

MISCHA: Face to face?

CLAIRE: Face to face.

MISCHA: Courageously face to face?

CLAIRE: Courageously face to face.

MINERVA: What does it matter how he told her? He told her! 'Over! Done! You've had your fun, it's the wife and children now.'

MISCHA: And had Montcrieff returned and said, 'It's the wife and children now,' you'd have opened your arms, blessed him, said he'd come to his senses and was an honourable man after all. Yes? No?

MINERVA: You are missing the point.

MISCHA: Oh, and what is the point, wise Minerva?

MINERVA: Love is a vow, in or out of marriage it's a commitment. A woman who loves surrenders herself totally, completely, utterly. It can't be treated lightly.

MISCHA: Who treated it lightly?

MINERVA: Vincent stopped loving a woman who passionately loved him.

MISCHA: Oh, so it *was* love? She *wasn't* used?

MINERVA: You're deliberately not understanding me. Used is what's left when loving stops.

CLAIRE: Loving didn't stop.

[*Both her friends turn to her.*]

MISCHA: Loving didn't stop?

CLAIRE: Loving didn't stop. He didn't stop loving me. He loves me still, I know. It's just that — it was that — I think that —

[*She is like one dazed.*]

— there was — such intensity. Of feeling. Of conversation. Of laughter. Of shared judgements and shared wicked joys. We mocked the same humbug, admired the same talents, marvelled at the same courage and integrity in colleagues. We generated each other's energy, built unspoken rhythms, gave each other space. I was dependable, discreet, undemanding. And then — one day — withdrawn! As if nothing had ever happened.

How could that be? We had come together as if by design. No doubts, no hesitations. Locked! Engaged! Instantly. Precision-made. An efficient machine to the world, an unexpected gift to ourselves. It was terrifying. Can't be true, we thought. Can't last. We'll be found out, caught. One of us will have an accident. A child will die. We'd have to pay for such happiness, surely. Surely we'd have to pay. No one deserves what the gods were bestowing upon us, we thought.

So what happened? I couldn't understand. The man who rejected me couldn't be the man I loved or who loved me, I reasoned. He was somebody else. What I did, I did to somebody else. I talked to the television researchers about somebody else.

That was right, wasn't it? That makes sense? Do you imagine I'd hurt the man I love?

[*She has gone over the edge.*
  Her friends move either side to comfort her.
  Fade.]

LETTER TO A DAUGHTER

a play in five parts with songs
for an actress who can sing

written for *Susanne Fuhr*

Sandefjord
September 1991

Letter to a Daughter had its world première in the Sanwoolim Theatre Co., Seoul, Korea, 20 March 1992.

ACTRESS	Suk-Hwa Yoon
Director	Young-Woong Lim
Set Designer	Dongwoo Park
Lighting Designer	Chongho Kim
Composer	Dong-Jin Cho

I am grateful to Professor Duk-Ae Chung of Seoul University, who heard me read this play to the British Council's International Cambridge Seminar in 1991, translated it immediately and proposed it to the director of the Sanwoolim Theatre Co.

NOTE

Music for the songs should be specially written by an indigenous composer.

PART ONE

MELANIE, *a singer of jazz and ballads. Aged thirty-five.*

In the darkness we hear her voice in song.

As the lights go up we find her in her study — work-room — surrounded by technical recording and play-back equipment, and all her little comforts, including an espresso coffee-machine for two.

She's listening to a song she's just written and recorded for herself to work on.

Strong, restless, unpredictable.

She is dressed in an old flowered silk dressing-gown. Flowing. Theatrical. Dramatic.

She is dramatic. Perhaps energetic is a better description.

Two actions are going to occupy MELANIE *throughout the play: the first — because she has been a nail-biter — is the painting of her nails as part of her battle to stop. (The removing and repainting must be paced out in rehearsals.)*

The second action will be fixing a fuse and rewiring a plug when the lights fail which, together with wet nails, will involve her in small physical contortions.

The five parts of the play will be punctuated throughout by song. A line of the letter, a mood, a reflection, will prompt one of her numbers.

We find her, therefore, listening to her tape and removing the old polish.

SONG ONE

I was Maiden-head Hunted

I was maiden-head hunted
From twelve years on

But twelve years on found no man
For this hot-headed maiden to sit upon.

The evening sky has a pink hue
As the day's shy sun lowers its gaze
His hills and my breasts sigh
And I wonder why I never understood men's ways.

My maiden-head has long since gone
Squandered with innocent waste
Upon the wrong long plea
That came into me with wanton haste.

The days are short, the maiden old
Her shy regrets fall upon stone
Who will look after the cooled hot-head
Now that the hot-headed maiden lives alone?

[*The song on the tape comes to an end.*]

MELANIE: Not bad. Not good but not bad. Perhaps good but not great.
    What's 'great' anyway? Who knows what's 'great' until long afterwards? Time makes things 'great'.

[*Re-thinks that.*]

Not true! You're sensitive? You *know* what's great.

[*Re-thinks that too.*]

Not true! I know lots of sensitive people who got it wrong. Sensitive, intelligent, knowledgeable – wrong! Should have known better. Wrong! I've sung them new songs which they should have recognized at once – wrong! And it's understand-able – if they were right all the time they'd be rich.

[*Pause.*]

Some of them *are* rich!
    Ah, Melanie, Melanie, Melanie! If you can't work it out for yourself, how can you work it out for your daughter?

[*She moves to her desk to look at a sheet on which she has been writing.*]

'My dear daughter, there comes a time in a young woman's life —'

Shit! That's a dreadful start. *You* didn't write that, you read it somewhere.

[*She sits at her desk to start again.*]

[*writing*] 'Daughter, mine. Some things are difficult to talk about and so I've decided to try and write you a letter instead —'

[*Stares at the sheet a long time.*]

As though writing was easier than talking! Just because you're not looking her in the eye doesn't mean the words come more easily. Matching words to thoughts is just as difficult whether someone's in front of you or not. Stringing notes is easier.

[*Thinks about that.*]

Perhaps you should sing her a letter on tape?

[*She tries.*]

[*singing*] 'Dear Babe . . .'

[*Stops. Tries again.*]

'Dear daughter, babe . . .'

[*Stops. Tries again.*]

'Dear daughter, babe,
A song for you
I have this song
To sing to you . . .'

[*Stops. Tries to continue.*]

'I have this song

To sing to you . . .'

[*Stops.*]

'To sing to you . . . to sing for you . . .'

[*Stops.*]

It's thinking that's difficult — not finding the right words or notes. *What* to say *that's* what's hard.

[*Sits to desk again. Attempts to continue writing.*]

'Dear Marike, the problem is — young women have problems!'

[*Stops. Disgusted with what she has written.*]

Did I *really* write that? [*self-mocking*] '. . . the problem is — young women have problems!' Cretin! Of course young women have problems. She knows young women have problems! She's a young woman with problems! In fact because she's smart, your daughter, she also knows *old* women have problems. [*in one breath*] Like her mother who isn't old she's only thirty-five but when you're thirteen anything over sixteen is old and twenty is middle aged and thirty is ancient and if you make it to thirty-five it's surprising to them you're still alive!

[*Looks down at her sheet again.*]

[*contemptuously*] 'Young women have problems!' Who *hasn't* got problems? Everyone's got problems! Young, old, rich, poor, the wise, the foolish, the beautiful, the ugly, the brave, the cowardly! No! Not the cowardly. The *coward* has no problems. He runs. Takes no risks. No risks — no problems. And God. He's the other person I know hasn't got problems. It's easy for him. All he has to do is forgive everybody. Lovely life! Rewarding! 'Wife batterer: I forgive you! Child murderer: I forgive you! Jack the Ripper, Genghis Khan, Adolf Hitler: I forgive you, forgive you, forgive you!'

[*Glances at her sheet.*]

'Young women have problems!' Oh boy, Melanie, what a pain in the arse you are. A great help! Mother? Millstone round her neck more like! Nothing to hand on! Stupid as shit!

[*She lets out a cry of frustration which builds and explodes –*]

'Dear Marike – your tits are growing!'

[*That arrests her. Makes her smile. Perhaps that's the way to begin.*]

'Dear Marike – your tits are growing. You told me so. "Don't touch me, Mother," you said, "I feel very tender there."'

[*Satisfied.*]

Good! Revealed in one! No pussy-footing! Straight to the point! That's the way everything should be.

[*Re-thinks that.*]

Not true! Sometimes it's cleverer to be devious. Sometimes it's even polite to be devious. Even amusing!

[*But –?*]

But not this time.

[*From here on she has no need to keep 'writing'. The letter will be constructed in her head.*]

'Dear Marike, your tits are growing. You told me so. "Don't touch me, Mother," you said, "I feel very tender there." Well, I won't touch you there, though take it from me – the tenderness will go. You'll get used to them. Soon you won't be able to *stop* touching them. You'll want *every*one to be touching them!'

[*She performs an amusing little 'scene' of the young girl who is trying to combine modesty with bravado, who is coy one minute, bold the next, retiring then – thrusting.*]

Wait! Who am I writing to? My daughter aged eleven or

my daughter aged fourteen or my daughter aged sixteen or my daughter aged twenty-one?

[*Thinks about it.*]

At twenty-one it's too late. A man could have destroyed her for life at twenty-one.

[*Thinks about that too.*]

Let's not be sexist about it – she could have destroyed her life with*out* anybody's help by twenty-one! Sixteen? If she hasn't got a mother's advice by sixteen she could be pregnant. Fourteen? [*considers*] Fourteen! A letter to my daughter aged fourteen.

So – [*continuing*] 'Soon you'll want everyone to be touching them. I can remember when I first saw mine growing. Sat in front of the mirror for hours, day after day, closing my eyes, covering them with my hands to feel if they were more of a handful, flopping them up and down, weighing them like melons.'

[*A mischievous thought* –]

I wonder if boys do the same thing.

[*She looks down between her legs, play-acting a little boy; then up at an imaginary mirror, eyes wide with amazement, then pleasure, then pride.*

Reaches for a ruler to measure 'it'. More pride. She shakes 'it' around a bit. Then, too violently, and puts her hands between her legs in mock pain.]

'Dear son. Your "ahem" is growing. You told me so. "Don't touch me there, it's tender . . ."'

No! No! Not possible! Thank God I have a daughter. What on earth do you *say* to boys? They don't understand what you're talking about until they're thirty, anyway!

[*Her lights flicker. She bends to a multiple plug adaptor, wiggles the wires until the lights steady.*]

Fix it! You'll end up in flames.

[*Looks at her nails.*]

One thing at a time. You've given up smoking, now you're trying to stop biting your nails. *Then* you'll fix the plug!

[*Continues cleaning her nails.*]

'And then came the day I had to buy my first bra. A light blue check thing it was. I was so excited. Really pretty, I thought. Long before I understood lace. And I looked myself in the eyes, very serious, very dramatic, as though God had given me the world to look after, and I said – you are a woman.'

SONG TWO

Said Woman, Said Child No More

Said woman
Said child no more
Said woman, said growing
Said change
And winds blowing
Away innocent confusions
Of day after day
Not knowing if I was coming or going
Said woman
Said child no more.

Little did I know how life shapes you away from dreams
Little did I know the wanton world weans you
On passions beyond your control and means you
For other things than spring's dewy dreams for you.

Said woman
Said child no more

Said woman, love yourself, love
Yourself
There is a wealth
For you
In this rich world waiting
To nurture you
Happy and healthy and glowing and wealthy
Said woman
Said child no more.

Little did I know we were all born with shadows
Little did I know each one has her terrors
Of failures, rejection, this world too large a place
For one woman's arms to protect and embrace.

Said woman
Said child no more
Said no more sugar and spice
Said all
The worthwhile loves
Land in your hand with their tagged price
Which you have to pay
Sooner or later
So learn never to make the same mistake twice
Be woman
Be child no more.

Said woman
Said child no more
Said woman, said growing
Said change
And winds blowing
Away innocent confusions
Of day after day
Not knowing if I was coming or going
Said woman
Said child no more.

PART TWO

PART TWO

MELANIE: 'Why, my sweet daughter, do I want to write this letter at all? Why don't I wait for you to ask me *questions*? So much advice is useless advice, as we all know to our cost. How do I know what it is you'll *want* to know or *need* to know in three years' time when you're fourteen?'

[*A worrying thought* —]

Perhaps it's not a letter to Marike aged fourteen but to Melanie aged thirty-five.

[*self-castigating*] 'Dear Melanie, you are thirty-five years old. Your life is a mess. How did this come about?'

Good! Revealed in one. No pussy-footing. Straight to the point!

[*taking pity on herself*] Oh, Melanie, Melanie, Melanie! Always unfair to yourself. It's not that your life's a mess it's that you're tired of who you are and you want to be someone else and you don't know if you've got it in you to change.

[*This is central to her state of mind.*]

Or if you've got anything inside you to change to!

[*Anxiety! Shakes herself out of it.*]

Stop talking about yourself. God! You're such a self-centred prima donna! You're supposed to be giving this time to your daughter and her tender tits!

'My dear Marike, you are a woman and I have things I want to tell you. Not to be read now but when you're fourteen. You are a woman and everyone will tell you that being a woman is hell and ecstasy but here's the first and most important thing I have to tell you: it's hell and ecstasy for everyone! Mostly hell. So no self-pity, no favours, no special pleading. There's only this: when God shared out ecstasy he decided men should have more than women, so he gave women to men and gave us men. [*Beat.*] Mostly! [*Beat.*] Don't ask me why; in fact 'why' is not something you should ever ask.'

[*Re-thinks that.*]

'Not true! You should *always* ask. Why? Why, why, why?'

[*Re-thinks that too.*]

'But not for everything. Why is the sky blue? Yes — the answer could be interesting. Why are people stupid? No point — it's a fact of life. Why did I do such and such? Yes — the answer could be useful for next time. Why is water wet? No point — it's wet! Starving people die, fire burns, fish can't fly — don't ask why. *Why* are people starving — *that* you can ask. And *who* set fire to the house — *that* you can ask. And why pain, why anger, why does he love me, why does he hate me? But fire always burns, water is always wet, and fish will never fly.'

[*Surprised, but pleased with herself.*]

That's quite good. Perhaps you're not as stupid as shit after all!

[*She considers what next to write. Hums. Perhaps a hint of the next song.*
The lights flicker again. She bends again to the adaptor, wiggles the wire, till the lights become steady.]

The wires are loose! Fix the bloody loose wiring!

[*But she doesn't. Continues with her nails.*]

'Now my dear daughter, here's the good news. You *wanted* to come into this world. Absolutely no doubt. The odds were against you but you fought like mad. How do I know? Here's the bad news – you weren't planned. I wore a coil, made love, and fell pregnant. You shouldn't have happened. The coil was supposed to give me freedom. And the doctor warned me: "Because you're pregnant you have to remove the coil or you may lose your baby." Never! Nothing was going to stop you. "I'm coming!" you yelled. "It's my time!" and you burst through, screaming fit to bring down the walls of Jericho.

'And how I loved carrying you. Once I knew you were inside me I wanted everyone to know. I couldn't swell fast enough. When my belly was still flat I used to arch my back and pretend you were just a few weeks away instead of eight months. As soon as the doctor told me you were coming I rushed out and bought smocks and flat sensible shoes. I was going to do everything right for you. Whatever the textbook ordered – I was going to obey. And did I, Marike? Go on, ask me. Did I?'

[*Her mood changes.*
She has a facility for talking herself up and down, into and out of moods.]

'Did I, hell! Nothing I hated more than flat, sensible shoes. No man would ever look at me again, I thought. And those smocks! Probably the most unsexiest things ever conceived – except for Bermuda shorts – and your mother was not going to be caught being unsexy! Being sexy was very important to your mother, it was what your mother imagined earned her a place in the world; not brains or personality or achievement but a firm bum, erect nipples, wet lips, flashing eyes, and sultry glances. A body moving healthily through the streets and glowing with promise. So it was high heels and tight skirts in no time at all! I'm telling you – I carried you around in my belly for nine months and fed my brains on fears of rejection. Developed a head like jelly. I *had* to stay one of the girls, one of the gang. I had to belong. At weekends I went berserk. Became a weekend hippy. Smoked grass and imagined I was living a glamorous life. But I hated grass. And I felt guilty. You've got this child in your womb, I yelled at myself. Grass can destroy its brain cells! It can give you cancer! It can create hormone changes! Then I'd argue with myself. Shit! It's only grass! Everyone smokes grass! I haven't seen anyone die of grass. Smoked! Drank! Danced! Opened my legs and humped up and down but nothing, nothing stopped you rocketing out of my abused body screaming! Screaming, flailing your arms, fisting everything in sight! Whooosh! Demanding life! Whooosh! Grabbing at the air with greedy hands – lungs like bellows.' [*She play-acts heavy breathing*.] 'Whooosh!

'And here's the second most important thing I have to tell you: firm bums, wet lips and sultry glances bring down upon you the idiot male population – all hands, hot breath and monosyllabic conversation. Achieve! Wear tight skirts but achieve! Trip along in high heels but achieve! Let your nipples stand erect but achieve! You grabbed air to breathe, now grab knowledge, skill, opportunity. Whooosh!'

[*Pause to remember.*]

'But not everything was right, and here's the third most important thing I've got to tell you. It's so important that perhaps it should have been the first most important thing I told you: everything you do has a consequence. Not necessarily bad, but as sure as night follows day follows night follows day – consequences follow actions. That's what it means to be thoughtful: to consider consequences. I didn't. You came out screaming but you had to go straight into an incubator. For a long time. And I cried. Boy! Did I cry. And to recompense you I swore I'd breast-feed you – and I did.'

[*Drifts into memory.*]

'And sang you to sleep with lullabies.'

PART TWO

SONG THREE

Lullaby – Kisses and Cream

She will give me kisses and the cream off the milk
And pull down clouds to warm my ears
She will touch my lips with a tongue of silk
And sing away my tears.

Do not make me weep with the look in your eyes
I will give you honey, little girl, and a bear
I will ask God for rainbows in the skies
And sunlight all year.

She will give me cuddles and sleepless nights
And moan with her long growing pains.
What will she dream these first nights?
She will call me her own name.

I will give you kisses and the cream of my time
And a penny to buy black sweets
And your wide laugh will last longer than mine
As you grow in the streets.

She will give me kisses and the cream off the milk
And reasons why she was born
And I will feel the touch of her tongue of silk
Long after her youth is gone.

SONG THREE

Alternative Lullaby – The Child Knows

And who will reach the gates?
The gates are there
The child knows.

A lifetime lived, a little loving done
But little love was left to reach the gates

The child waits
The child knows
The way the world goes, oh how the world goes.

And who will reach the gates?
The gates are there
The child knows.

The words were written, written long ago
And many times sung. Snow has touched the gates
The child waits
The child knows
The way the world goes, oh how the world goes.

And who will reach the gates?
The gates are there
The child knows.

Who'll give the key, teach how to plant the seed
She will not turn nor of her tears have need
The child sees
The child knows
But will not fear the way the world goes,
Oh how the world goes.

And who will reach the gates?
The gates are there
The child knows.

PART THREE

MELANIE: 'Not true! I *never* sang you lullabies.'

[*She is in a distressed state.*]

What the hell am I writing this letter for? What do *I* have to tell my daughter that could possibly be of any use to her? I'm trying to unravel the mess I made of my life, so what use can *that* be to her?

[*On the other hand –*]

Who says you have to be perfect before you can give advice?

[*Brightening.*]

Who's perfect? [*Pause.*] 'I never sang you lullabies but oh, what dreams I had for you. Before you were born of course. Four months old inside me and I was plotting complete lifetimes for you – from the cradle to the grave. And of course in each one you were famous. My daughter? Had to be! Famous and adored. I was your Walter Mitty. Actress! Surgeon! Astronaut! Ballet dancer! Poet! But not a singer. You must on no account be like me. Never like me.

'Crazy! I was a crazy pregnant mother. I was gorging myself on decisions, stuffing myself with certitudes, crippling your life with rules even before you were born. Crazy!'

[*Going easier on herself.*]

'On the other hand is it such a *bad* thing to have ambitions for your child? My problem was *no* one had ambitions for me.'

[*Recalls this, sadly.*]

'Oh, my parents loved me. At least my daddy did, only he never told me until after he'd had three glasses of wine and then he was all over me with his eyes. Used to worry my mother. Not that I was in danger from his affections, he was only ever an adoring father, but my mother could see emotions in his face that *she* could never arouse. His eyes announced he adored me, and it used to upset her. He was tender and I felt protected and it all used to upset her and I never understood why. Though sometimes . . . I saw expressions . . . made me wonder . . .'

[*A moment we shall never fully know the truth about.*]

'Here's a story for you. I shall never forget − I was about twelve − my father said to me, "Right, let's see if you're afraid of the dark." And he took me by the hand and he led me down into the cellar and he put me inside and he locked the door. And there I stood. For long, long minutes. Just me and the silence. No fear. No panic. No emotion. Just − what next, I thought? And then I heard my father's voice: "Well Melanie? Are you afraid of the dark?" And I replied: "I don't know, Daddy. I can't see anything!"

'He loved that. Oh how he loved that. Made him laugh! Laugh and laugh and laugh and laugh. Couldn't stop telling the story to his friends and neighbours and all the family. And every time he told it he laughed as though he was telling it for the first time. And the story grew. "I took Melanie down to the cellar and it was full of spiders . . ." Then it was full of rats! Then he switched the light on and off. Then he made ghostly sounds. "I left her for three minutes . . . for thirty minutes . . . for an hour . . .!" And he laughed! He had the kind of laughter made you want to laugh with him. Infectious. And bold. And I loved him. He was a father who didn't want his daughter to be afraid of anything. We went to the sea once and there was a huge storm and he stood with me in front of these big waves which were crashing towards us making the most frightening noise ever and he was shouting above it, "Don't be afraid of the elements . . . never be afraid of the elements. You hear those waves? Shout back at them, shout back, shout back . . ."'

[*She's shouting. Stops. Surprised. Collects herself.*]

'But he had no ambitions for me. He used to say, "I don't care if you drive a taxi as long as you're happy doing it." No ambition for me.'

[*It saddens her to remember. But she revives.*]

'So at seventeen I quit school without taking my finals and joined an academy to learn how to teach music to children. Three years. And that seemed all right to my daddy. Nothing wrong with that. Nothing special but – OK! A schoolteacher! Humble teachers sometimes taught children who became great men and women . . .'

[*Mind drifts . . .*]

'Just didn't give *me* much of a buzz, though. I like children but –'

[*Drift . . . drift . . .*]

'My daddy – your grandfather.'

[*Drift . . .*]

'I'm sorry you never saw him.'

[*Drift . . .*]

'Your grandfather – my daddy.'

[*Drift . . .*]

'If someone laughed at him, I used to cry. Cry. I used to cry if someone laughed at him.'

[*Drift . . .*]

'Drank too much!'

[*Drift . . . Drift . . .*]

'No. I never sang you lullabies.'

[*Shakes herself alert.*]

'Didn't play with you much, either. Or invent stories. Or read you other people's invented stories. Imagine! I trained as a music teacher for children and I used to make up stories and invent complicated musical games with them — but never with you! Invented nothing with my own daughter! And when I did do the things mothers should do — like knitting, making dresses, teaching you how to read — I didn't always succeed. I confess — I loved the idea of having a child of my own but I wasn't what you'd call a "natural" mother. Didn't come to me easily. In fact many would say it didn't come to me at all.'

[*Pause.*]

'But I tell you what I did do: I used to touch you a lot. It was the time everyone was touching. Be tactile, everyone used to say. If you touched someone it was a sign you cared for them. But I wonder. I was touched. They couldn't *stop* touching me, but I can't remember any of them really *caring* for me.

'And here's the fourth most important thing I have to tell you: select your peers. In fact perhaps it's *the* most important thing I have to tell you because if you get this wrong then anything else I tell you will go down the drain.

'Select your peers. Don't go with the herd. Don't look to be one of the gang. I know there's great comfort in a gang, in belonging, in being accepted but — resist it! A gang consists of people who are living their lives through each other. Ask me — I know! I was part of a gang. Always busy being what I thought would please the others, picking up their bad habits, thinking their thoughts, sharing their stupid prejudices, laughing at their mindless hatreds. We never questioned each other, we just stroked and confirmed each other's nonsense. "Right!" we'd say. "You've said it! Good for you! You've hit the nail on the head." We thought we were strong but we were all terrified of stepping out of line. Not one of us was independent. Not one of us had an opinion that was his own. And we intimidated each other. If one of us dared to say, "I don't agree! I don't think we should," out would come that dreary old cry: "Who does she think she is? Who — does she think — she is!"

'I think I hate that cry more than any other in the whole wide world. If anyone cries it out to you, Marike, you tell them: she thinks she's an individual! She thinks she can think her own thoughts! She thinks she can rise above the herd! You tell them that.'

[*Panic.*]

'No! Don't! They'll slaughter you! What advice am I giving you, for God's sake! This is a crazy letter. You have a "crazie" for a mother. Don't, whatever you do, don't stand above the herd. In fact don't even think of them as the herd. They are *not* a herd, a herd is cattle, dumb animals. They're not dumb animals. They're your brothers and sisters, your comrades in arms, your link to reality, your support system. Stay with them, for God's sake, or they'll tear you limb from limb.'

[*Panic turns to defiance.*]

'Then take the risk! Stand out! Fly! Perhaps you'll manage to fly out of their reach.'

[*The lights go out. We hear her voice through the dark.*]

Shit! Shit shit shit! See what happens if you leave undone things undone? Darkness! The light goes! You become blind! I should have seen to those loose wires months ago.

[*She rummages around in the dark.*]

Matches! Where are the fucking matches?

[*Finds them. Lights one candle. Goes off stage, bumping and cursing.*]

[*off stage*] The fuse box! Where's the fucking fuse box?

[*We hear clicking of mains being turned off.*]

[*looking for faulty fuse*] This one? No. This one? No. This one? Ah! Gotcha! [*Pause.*] I hate messing with electricity. It's a phobia. Some people have a phobia about heights, some people have a phobia about crowds, I have a phobia about fish bones and electricity. [*Pause.*] But you did it, didn't you, Melanie?

> [*She returns in the dark, still bumping and cursing. Lights three other candles, which immediately reveals to us that she has often sat in candle-light before.*
>
> *She looks for and finds a screwdriver. Unscrews the plug in order to rewire it.*]

'And here's something else I have to tell you, Marike, which is just as important as anything I have told you or am likely to tell you: don't put off until tomorrow what should be done today!'

> [*Long pause while she works.*]

'Because if you do it today and enjoy it you can do it again tomorrow!' [*Laughs.*]

'No, no, let's be serious. I'm your mother. Being frivolous is not allowed. It's important, this: don't procrastinate. Don't delay. If something has to be done, do it immediately or the dirt will accumulate. The shit will gather. The avalanche will fall. Tomorrow the sun may not rise. You'll forget what you wanted to do. Time will be lost. Life squandered. No one will wait. You'll lose friends. You'll lose loving, you'll lose all that precious kissing-time. The devil will catch up with you . . .' God in heaven, Mother! Enough! I get the message – procrastinate and the lights go out! God! She's a pain, my mother!

On the other hand candle-light is romantic.

> [*She's struggling still.*]

Grrrrr! I hate such fiddly things. Times like this I know why I need a man!

> [*Pause.*]

'My dear Marike, let me tell you a little bit about yourself. You know your most dangerous quality? You learn too easily. Everything comes to you without much effort. You don't have to work hard to remember things or to comprehend things. Me – I had to work hard to comprehend *anything*! Nothing came easily! And so I watch you and I worry for you because I see something that makes me fearful for your future. And it's this: anything that *doesn't* come easily to you, you reject. Anything that demands greater concentration – you turn away from. And if there's nothing else in my life which I can offer you as an example there's my discipline as a singer. Discipline! I rehearse non-stop. I go over a song again and again, worrying at it, to make it better, to make my voice reach out, to stretch myself. I don't possess a major major major talent but what's there I make work to the utmost.'

[*wildly declaiming*] TO – THEEEEEE – UTMOST!

[*At which point she bursts into an energetic but very, very difficult melody that takes her voice up and down between extreme registers.*

She looks very dramatic singing in the candle-light.]

SONG FOUR

Nothing Comes Easy

Nothing comes easy
Sing it again and again and again and again
Worry it, hone it
Trim it, dethrone it
Bring it before you
Try not to adore what you've chosen
Too often you've chosen
What's lifeless and frozen
Your darlings are dead

Get rid of them rid
Of them rid of them.
Sing pure. Sing pure. Sing pure.
Remembering
Nothing comes easy
Nothing sure, nothing comes easy.

Nothing comes easy
Look at the way that I worry all day
High note and low note
Wrong note and right note
Have I made it work
Is my talent in tune with my passion
Will I ruin career
With anxiety, fear
Can my discipline hold
Am I bold enough
Able to stand on a stage
And sing. And sing. And sing
Remembering
Nothing comes easy
Oh God, nothing comes easy.

Nothing comes easy.
Sing it again and again and again and again
Look at it, doubt it
Whisper it, shout it
Critics ignore you
Neglect or restore you, beware
Both their bile and their praises
Your life and your art each
Is a craft to be worked at
Worked hard at, worked hard at
Remember
Nothing comes easy
But nothing, nothing comes easy.

High note, low note
Wrong note, right note
Worry it, hone it
Trim it, dethrone it
Will I ruin career
With anxiety, fear
Can my discipline hold
Am I bold enough
Able to stand on a stage
And sing. And sing. And sing
Remembering
Nothing comes easy
Oh God, nothing comes easy.

PART FOUR

MELANIE *is exhausted. Flops in an armchair to continue fixing the wires into the plug.*

MELANIE: 'Why, you are asking yourself, is she writing all this to me? OK, so my tits are growing. Big deal! I'll get over it! What do I need such a long letter for? If I'd known I'd get all these pages of garbage, I'd have kept quiet about my tits growing. That's what you're saying as you read this letter. I bet!

'You're right! But I've got a confession to make. Your growing tits makes *me* think about growing up. *You're* facing a big change in your life – *I'm* facing a big change in my life.

'You've noticed, haven't you! Of course you've noticed. What else accounts for my short temper, my loud voice, my neurotic chattering, my creeping away into my room for hours on end? Poor Marike. What a lot you've had to put up with these last months from this crazie who creeps around your apartment.

'I sit watching television and I think, why are you watching television? Why aren't you doing something for your daughter? So then I feel guilty for neglecting you, for not being a constructive mum, for not shaping your talents, your personality. Guilts! And I get angry with *you* for making *me* feel guilty and suddenly I have *two* reasons for hating myself. And when I hate myself, boy, do I really hate myself! No one can hate me like I hate me! Everything comes back. I've got a memory like a sewer, all the smells of a rotten past rise up and I have to take a shower. You've noticed, I know. Sometimes I have to take a shower three times on a really bad evening and I can see you watching me. Frightened. And I hate frighening you, I really do, honest, just hate it. And it adds to my anger which adds to my guilt which adds to my hate which adds to my anger . . . I try hard to correct myself but I get like a child — I can *see* I'm doing wrong but I don't care. I just do not care!

'And oh, did I do a lot of things wrong!'

[*The wires are fixed in the plug. She plugs it in.*
Light!
She punctuates this next passage with the blowing out of the candles one by one.]

'I overestimated how much you could manage on your own.' [*blow*] 'I used to leave you alone to go on my singing gigs when you were only six years old. Six! I can hardly bring myself to confess it. Six! You hear of apartments catching fire and the children burnt to death while parents are out for a drink and that could have been you! Christ Almighty!' [*blow*] 'I go cold just thinking about it.' [*blow*] 'I was a monster! An irresponsible monster!' [*blow*]

[*She's agitating herself.*]

'Of course I always alerted the neighbours. I wasn't *so* irresponsible. And I'd rig up a rope at your bedside with a bell at the end of it so you could signal if need be, and they used to report to me how they could hear you brushing your teeth and singing to yourself — singing to yourself! To yourself! Alone! I left you alone! Oh God, Marike, forgive me.'

[*She's on the verge of tears but fights them back.*]

'Sometimes of course I took you with me. The guilt got so heavy I took you on tours with me. But — but —'

[*She struggles to confess this.*]

'— you were a burden! Let me say it — you got in my way. "Where are you going? How long for? When are you coming

266

back? Who are you going to see? What are you going to do? Why can't I come?" It drove me mad to think my movements, my desires, my every selfish need was thwarted by you. You made me feel like a dog on a chain! I had to be free! "I need my space!" I shouted. "No one is going to hold me back!" I raged. "This is my one and only life and I'm going to live it to the full!" Shouted, raged, scolded, and slunk off saturated with guilt like sweat, leaving you in your room in order to be with the others, always traceable, messages with reception to say where I was, but — this woman, this young woman with energy and appetites was not going to miss out on the fun, was not going to miss out on anything life had to offer and — oh my God, Marike, terrible things happened, terrible awful experiences, traumatic, which you'll never forget and I'll never forget and I will always feel guilty for them and — oh my God! Once I was drunk, so drunk . . .'

[*She can't bear to face the memory — and perhaps we don't need to hear it spelt out but can guess at it. She breaks down, weeping.*]

'Relationships? Minefields! Every relationship is a minefield.'

[*She's desperate to collect herself.*]

Quick, think of something good. You haven't been *all* bad in your life, remember something sweet, Melanie, sweet, kind, intelligent, something thoughtful that you've done.

[*She paces her room frantically, searching memory.*]

[*fast*] 'My dear Marike, we used to sing together in the car!' That's it! 'My dear Marike, we used to love to sing together when we drove to places. Loud, clear, in harmony, full of spirits, laughter, joy! Real joy! Those were really joyous times when we drove together to my gigs, singing at the top of our voices. And you had such a wonderful voice, my darling, you still have, and I wanted you to sing with the local

choir but you didn't want that. "I'm happy just to be singing with you, Mamma, you and me in the car. Just us!" And I listened to you. I respected your wishes. You had such large wise eyes when you were a child, I felt I wanted to give you responsibility, wanted you to grow strong, to become independent, self-reliant. I left you alone because —

[*Struggling* —]

NOT TRUE! Oh Christ! I must have done *something* right because *you* take care of *me* now. You do, and I love you for doing it. "Mother, you'll be late for your appointment . . . Don't forget the milk . . . You've got a ladder in your stocking . . . The keys, mother, you've forgotten the keys." Oh Marike — a child like you is like a gift of the gods!'

[*She breaks down a second time.*
The only way she can come out of her misery is to hum herself out of it.]

SONG FIVE

Child Like You

A child like you is a gift
I didn't recognize the gift
Till now
I didn't learn
I didn't earn the gift
Till now
And now I count the cost
Pray not everything is lost
Carry a heart tossed
With guilt
Mea culpa — guilt
Mea culpa — guilt
Child like you.

Everything I did was wrong
Even when I got it right it was wrong
Can we ever get it right as long
As love is such a strong
Emotion?

Mother like me can't be bad
I can't be accused of all bad
Take stock
You must not kill
You must not will away
Your rock
I am your rock hold fast
I'm all you've got to last
A lifetime till the past
Fades grey
Mea culpa – guilt
Mea culpa – guilt
Child like you.

Living means you must forgive
Giving love you learn to live and forgive
We cannot both despise and thrive
On lives of rich and strong
Emotion.

A child like you is a gift
I didn't recognize the gift
Till now
I didn't learn
I didn't earn the gift
Till now
And now I count the cost
Pray not everything is lost
Carry a heart tossed
With guilt
Mea culpa – guilt
Mea culpa – guilt

Child like you
Child like you
Child like you.

PART FIVE

MELANIE *makes herself two espresso coffees in her little Gaggia machine.*

MELANIE: God! I hope she's not like me.

    [*Disgust.*]

'Dear daughter, Marike, do–not–be–like–me!'

    [*Play-acting.*]

'What is it to be like you, Mamma?'

    [*Hesitant.*]

'Mamma? Mamma?'

    [*Finally.*]

'First I feel, then I think – *that's* what it's like to be me. Shoot first, ask questions later. Not the way to live.'

    [*Pause.*]

'But, daughter, I'm working at it. Thinking comes hard but I'm working at it. I'm trying to, how shall I put it? I'm trying to – reborn myself. How do you like that? Reborn myself.'

    [*She savours the word.*]

'The problem is – is it too late? Am I the prisoner of myself?'

    [*Thinks hard about that.*]

Now that would really be terrifying. That would really be a

nightmare to think that at thirty-five I had made my life, my habits, my attitudes, my expectations – a prison. Inescapable. On a train that would never stop and I couldn't jump off and it was all, all, all too late.

[*Shakes the terror from herself.*]

I can't believe that. I mustn't believe that. I refuse to believe that.

'My dear Marike, and here's the fifth most important thing I have to tell you: beware of emotions. Be emotional if you must but be aware of them. Emotions seduce. I fell deeply in love with myself being full of feeling. All hot air. Well, not all, but most. One of the easiest things in the world is to intoxicate yourself with your favourite image of yourself, and the image of myself that I fell in love with – because I thought it made *me* the most interesting, fascinating, deepest of deep creatures in the world – was the image of a magnificently erupting volcano. And friends around encouraged me – they enjoyed the fire, the sparks. Very colourful! Very dramatic!

'You see – your mother was born with this enormous energy. As you very well know I don't exactly disappear into the tapestry. But, my dear Marike, energy is a woman with two faces: one is violent and can destroy, the other is tender and can nourish. My energy was violent. It destroyed. Five times a year I'd go berserk, crazy, off the rails! And I'd show myself to the world as the arse-hole I really am not, believe me! Drinks, quarrels, betrayals! I'd break promises, turn up late, freak out in the middle of a gig. No one could depend on me. I was wild and unpredictable. Why? Sober upbringing, good hard-working family, sensible friends at school. Everything perfect. And even if it had *not* been perfect I wouldn't have blamed them because here comes the sixth most important thing I have to tell you: don't blame other people for what goes wrong in your own life. The only thing you can blame are your genes – and I don't mean the ones you wear! I did these awful things, I *watched* myself doing them, I *knew* they recurred again and again but I could do nothing about them and I never, never, never understood why. Somewhere inside me must be a gene that goes back God knows *where* to God knows *when* belonging to God knows *who* and *that's* a "why" you can't ever ask because a gene is a gene is a gene is a gene . . .'

[*Re-thinks that.*]

Christ! What am I saying? That's depressing! Didn't I just now declare, only a minute ago: I refuse to be a prisoner of myself?

[*Wrestles with fears.*]

The question is – the question is –

[*Her face lights up.*]

The question is: has every gene in my body been activated?

[*Relieved, she sips her second coffee.*]

Thank God for espresso! [*looking up*] Thank you, God, for espresso! I think I would die without my espresso.

[*Last gulp.*]

Probably die *because* of my espresso!

[*She is boiling to say something that is obviously difficult for her, but by now she is high and determined.*]

'Here, Marike, is my most difficult confession: I have never been in love. Can you believe it? Thirty-five years old, daughter of eleven, a "somebody" in the music profession, a public figure, my photo all over the place – I should have had the pick of men! From film star to politician, from tennis-player to oil-tycoon, from poet to lorry-driver. The pick! Nothing!

'Imagine me out there in the middle of the stage, my heart hanging out over the audience, some of the best instrumentalists ever, backing up my voice, and my voice in full throttle, pushing back the air, the sweat of effort flowing from every pore, pouring from every crevice. Passion! A mesmerizing energy drawing the attention of every man in the audience to every part of me, watching me, weaving their dreams around me, wanting me. And yet – I have never met a man *I* wanted. Isn't that strange? Don't you find that strange, daughter mine? There must be a reason.'

[*Thinks – what can it be?*]

'They say there are more interesting women in the world than men and – I don't know about the world – the *world*, I mean there's millions and millions in the *world* so we shouldn't generalize, but – in my experience, the women I meet, from all sorts of backgrounds, professions, countries, some have been married, some are single parents, some work hard at home, some at the top of their professions – nearly all of them tell me: they can't find a man! Not a really kind, gentle, tender, intelligent, imaginative, interesting, supportive, thoughtful, respectful, educated, courageous, chivalrous, witty, thrilling, thrilling, thrilling man.'

[*Dry irony –*]

'Perhaps we're asking too much!'

[*Pause.*]

'Oh, they can find a man to sleep with. It's never difficult to find a willing body – but a man to *love*?'

[*She holds the word in the air.*]

'Love?'

[*Long, long pause.*]

'Perhaps I feared loss? Perhaps I feared getting too close to someone I might lose. Close but not too close! Hold me but not too tight! Take your pleasure, give me some in exchange – then go! Poor men! My lips must have told them: your kisses don't claim me! They must have felt they were making love to a hedgehog!'

[*She is gently amused.*]

'Perhaps we should only expect three of those qualities.'

[*Considers this.*]

'But which three? Interesting, chivalrous, kind? Imaginative, witty, gentle? Thoughtful, thrilling, courageous? It's a problem.'

[*Enthusiastic.*]

'*You* select, Marike. Look at my list and select which three qualities you would want in a man before you could love him. Add to my list and then choose. Do you want to be made to laugh, made to think, to be cared for, to care for? Do you want gentleness, firmness, reliability, unpredictability? Do you want someone more intelligent, less intelligent, of equal intelligence? Make a long list then choose – three qualities.'

[*Mood changes.*]

'And then forget them! For here's the seventh most important thing I have to tell you: love has nothing to do with anything you dream or plan or decide for yourself. It makes no sense *when* it happens, *where* it happens, *how* it happens, or with *whom* it happens – which of course is a very good reason for avoiding it like the plague!'

[*Bitter!*]

'I know what you're thinking. You're thinking – Mother, if you've never been in love how do you know these things? Well, the eighth most important thing to tell you is: use your reason as much as possible but don't expect reason from human nature.'

[*Bitter, bitter!*]

'My dear daughter. I am not sure this letter is going to be much help to you!'

[*Desperate.*]

God in heaven! There must be something useful I can tell her after thirty-five years of a life.

[*Determined.*]

'My dear daughter. Here is the ninth most important thing I have to tell you: men are the products of their mothers. Blame them for nothing. "Wrong" is its own gender — neither male or female. Like stupidity, tyranny, kindness, generosity, and love itself — each its own gender, neither male or female. You like cooking? Cook! You like knitting? Knit! You want to be an astronaut? Be one! Study and take off! Don't live by dogmas. Sweetness is not the prerogative of women. Me — I love cooking, hate knitting, am terrified of flying. Your tits are growing whether you like it or not; you're a woman whether you like it or not; your instincts will be feminine whether you like it or not. Neither good nor bad. Follow them, don't fight them. Only one important thing — the tenth: don't let anyone abuse you. And that's another thing has its own gender — abuse. I've known many women as well as men who got high on abusing others — so be a woman, but don't be smug!'

[*Surprised.*]

'Say! How about that? I think — is it possible? — maybe — maybe — your mother's found another gene . . .?'

[*She goes to the tape-recorder, rewinds. We hear the song she's been rehearsing 'Song One — I was Maiden-head Hunted'. As it's playing, she talks.*]

'My dear Marike. I wish I could see your future. Your teacher and your friends tell me how special you are.

'But when I kiss you goodnight in bed I can feel — your neck is stiff. Your aunts look at you and they say to me:

"That one is in tune with herself! *There's* a girl full of harmony." But in the middle of the night I can hear your teeth grind with anxiety . . .

'My dear daughter, Marike. I have been meaning to write to you for some time . . .'

[*She turns off the vocal part of the song and takes over, live, singing just with her instrumentalists.*

She's working, changing things as she goes along. Work on the song absorbs her.

The lights go down on a singer in full voice.]

BLOOD LIBEL

a play in four parts

with music needing to be composed

commissioned for the opening of the
new Norwich Playhouse

Blaendigeddi
September 1991

A man may start by wishing for truth without going the right way to arrive at it, and may end by embracing falsehood till he cannot bear to part with it.

Augustus Lessopp, DD, from the introduction to
his translation, together with Montague Rhodes James,
from the Latin of *The Life and Miracles of St William
of Norwich* (1896)

CHARACTERS

HERBERT DE LOSINGA, bishop, founder of the Church of
   Norwich, aged 60

WILLIAM, a skinner's apprentice, aged 12

STRANGER, aged 35

THOMAS OF MONMOUTH, monk of Norwich, aged 48

ELVIVA, mother of William, aged 28

WENSTAN, farmer, father of William, aged 32

WULLWARD, priest, father of Elviva, aged 50

HETHEL, sister of Elviva, aged 29

GODWIN, priest, husband of Hethel, aged 35

MATHILDA, daughter of Hethel, aged 16

PENITENT, aged 50

PRIEST OF HAVERINGLAND

SKINNER, William's employer, aged 35

JOHN DE CHEYNEY, Sheriff of Norwich, aged 50

ELIAS, Prior of the Church of Norwich, aged 60

DOM AIMAR, Prior of St Pancras, aged 50

MAUDE, maidservant to Jewish household, 50

AELWARD DED, citizen of Norwich, aged 50

THEOBALD, monk, Jewish convert, aged 35

1ST VOICE
2ND VOICE
3RD VOICE
1ST MONK
2ND MONK
3RD MONK, rabble-rouser

Those upon whom miracles were worked

EDMUND
CLARICIA
MURIEL
RADULFUS
STEPHEN
OLD WOMAN
WALTER
COLOBERN
ANSFRIDA

NOTE

Although there are 34 characters, only 11 actors are needed. Of course the more actors used the greater will be the impact of the crowd scenes.

SUGGESTED GROUPINGS

Actor A	BISHOP HERBERT DE LOSINGA THEOBALD PENITENT	Actor E	SHERIFF JOHN DOM AIMAR AELWARD DED COLOBERN
Actor B	STRANGER WENSTAN 3RD MONK STEPHEN	Actor F	WILLIAM WALTER
		Actress A	ELVIVA 2ND VOICE CLARICIA
Actor C	WULLWARD PRIEST OF HAVERINGLAND SKINNER 2ND MONK RADULFUS	Actress B	HETHEL MAUDE 3RD VOICE MURIEL
Actor D	GODWIN 1ST VOICE 1ST MONK EDMUND	Actress C	MATHILDA OLD WOMAN ANSFRIDA

THOMAS and ELIAS cannot be doubled with any other character.

PRODUCTION NOTE

There is no interval.

All actors are on stage throughout, as though they have assembled to listen to one another tell the story — a familiar theatrical device but one belonging to the nature of the play, which attempts to piece together the story of a crime about which there are only a few inconclusive facts. It is as though they, the actors, are witnesses and jury both.

Only one scene they do not watch: the rape scene. When this occurs they turn their backs on it.

From Scene 3 onwards THOMAS OF MONMOUTH takes control of the play. He is on stage continuously — sometimes writing in his cell, sometimes haranguing, sometimes watching and urging, driving, driving the play forward to its 'hosanna' finale like a latter-day preacher at a revivalist meeting.

MUSIC

The 'Hymn to St William' needs to be specially composed.

I suggest 'religious music' based on traditional church music should also be specially composed for scene-linking, background and ceremonial moments.

TRANSLATIONS

The opening sermon 'On the Birthday of the Lord' by Bishop Herbert de Losinga (c. 1050–1119) was transcribed and translated from the Latin by Edward Meyrick Goulburn, DD, Dean of Norwich, and Henry Symonds, MA, Rector of Tivetshall and late precentor of Norwich Cathedral. Published by James Parker & Co. (1878).

Although there is no interval the play is divided into four parts.

PART ONE: The story as it was told, with a few added
               suppositions.

PART TWO: The first witnesses present their evidence and are
               countered by Prior Elias.

PART THREE: Brother Thomas of Monmouth presents new
               witnesses with additional evidence.

PART FOUR: We hear of the miracles and rejoice.

PART ONE

The story as it was told, with a few added suppositions.

ACT ONE

SCENE I

Pulpit, Church of Norwich, c. AD 1110. *Bishop* HERBERT DE LOS-
INGA *is delivering a sermon.*

HERBERT: Like a stream of brimstone are the fiery troubles of
this present life; but Christ is with you; the Virgin is with
you; the holy angels are with you; and he who fights before
such witnesses as these may fix his thoughts only on victory.

I will relate to you a circumstance, brethren, which I
learned from a faithful report. There was a certain city of the
Greeks in which Christians and Jews dwelt mingled with one
another. Thence sprang familiarity and common dealings.
The language of both was the same, while their religion
differed. The children of the Jews were taught the learning of
the Christians, and thus the sap of truth was by degrees
distilled into the tender minds of the Jews, whence it came to
pass that on the holy Day of Easter, a Hebrew boy among his
fellows and those of his own age approached to the Altar and
received the Holy Communion. When the rites of the sacred
solemnity had been performed, the Hebrew boy returned
home and with childish simplicity disclosed to his mother that
he had received a sacred portion from the Christian Altar.

Then the mother, stirred with a woman's fury, went to her
husband, declared to him what had passed, and kindled in the
father of the child madness and cruelty. Whereupon this most
unnatural father heated a furnace, and threw his son into the
midst of it, into the live coals and raging flames, and in his
madness sealed up the mouth of the furnace with stones and
cement. The mother's bowels of compassion were moved,
and she yearned over her dying child; she cried out in her
rage, ran to the Christians, and disclosed that cruel and

horrible tale to the ears of mourning friends. The Christians fly to the furnace, and more quickly than it takes to say it, break open the mouth thereof, and drag out the boy alive and safe whom they had supposed to have been burned within. They wonder and rejoice and render due thanks to the Divine Presence. They ask the boy how he had escaped, and by whose protection he had overcome the flames of the furnace. To which he replied, 'The Lady who sitteth above the Altar of the Christians, and the Little One Whom she cherishes in her bosom, stood around me and, stretching forth their hands, hedged my body round and protected me from the flames and fiery coals, so that I felt no burning but only the refreshment and comfort of a frame which could take no harm. By His fostering care therefore I escape unharmed from the furnace, Whose most sacred Body I received at the Altar of the Christians.'

Forthwith there followed a most just vengeance on the heads of the Jews; and they who would not believe in the Incarnate Word were all alike burned in the aforesaid furnace.

Behold, brethren, Christ everywhere protects His own fellow-soldiers, and suffers no one to perish whom He hath foreknown and predestined to be a partaker of His Heavenly Kingdom. He calls those whom He hath predestinated; He predestinates those whom He hath foreknown; and in the foreknowledge of God no change or alteration can be made.

Let us be born again unto our Saviour, Who was on this day born; and walking in the newness of life let us forget those things which are behind and reach forth unto those which are before, cleaving to Christ, abiding in Christ, enjoying Christ, Who, with the Father and the Holy Ghost, liveth and reigneth, God for ever and ever. Amen.

SCENE 2

Thorpe Wood on the edge of Norwich, 1144.

WILLIAM, *a skinner's apprentice, is walking alongside a malevolent-looking* STRANGER, *who seems to be accompanying him somewhere.*

The STRANGER *has become agitated. He stops. Confronts a surprised* WILLIAM. *Begins to rape him.*

The boy screams, is gagged and dragged off.

From the direction the boy has been taken there grows a glow into an intensely bright, ethereal light.

As the light grows there grows with it a swelling sound of mob voices.

VOICES: The Jews! The Jews! The Jews! The Jews! The Jews! The Jews! The Jews! THE JEWS!

The rape, the light, 'The Jews, the Jews':
this sequence will be repeated every so often throughout the play.
NOTE: *The rape must be distressing but not graphic, its impact made with the simplest of actions and sounds rather than with long, drawn-out visual violence.*

THOMAS's *cell. He writes at his table.*

THOMAS: April 27 in the year of our Lord 1172. Twenty-eight years after the event, twenty-eight years of argument against those who would deny his martyrdom, twenty-eight years of miracles which prove his sainthood, I, Thomas of Monmouth, the least of your monks, sendeth greeting and all due obedient service to His Holiness the Reverend Father and Lord William, by the grace of God, Bishop of Norwich.

Here beginneth the Prologue concerning the Life and Passion of Saint William, the Martyr of Norwich.

[*He stands to harangue an imaginary adversary, using those who sit around, listening.*]

But before I proceed with my testimony hear me you wordy gabblers driven against me by malice or envy; you who with saucy insolence and insolent sauciness contradict all that which I know to be true and will prove to be true. I will pierce you with the spear of satire and restrain you with the curb of reason because I can no longer put up with it. I cannot! I have testimony! And it shall be written down!

SCENE 4

The house of ELVIVA *and* WENSTAN, WILLIAM'*s parents.*
ELVIVA *is pregnant and in the company of her husband and her*
father, WULLWARD, *a priest.*

ELVIVA: The dream was about you, father, you an' a fish. I were
standin' in a road, you by my side, an' I saw at my feet, there
as I bent my eyes, a fish, a luce it were. An' it hed twelve fins
on each side, all red, like they were splashed with blood. An' I
say to you, surprised wi' wonder, I say, 'Father, I see a fish,
but how do it come here and how do it live in so dry a spot?'
An' you say to me, you say, 'Take up the fish, Elviva, take it
up and put it on thy bosom.' An' I do just that. Like you say I
should. An' that fish lay there an' you know what? That
grew! That moved and grew and grew till I couldn't hold it
on me no more, an' suddenly – an' this were what were really
strange, father – suddenly, it slipped out through my sleeve
and it grew wings. Yes, it did! The fish grew wings and flew
away, up and up, passing through the clouds and into heaven
which open to receive it.

Weren't that a strange dream? That *were* a strange dream.
So now, father, you've always told me what my dreams
mean. Since I bin a gal, look, you told me. Tell me now.

WULLWARD: That dream mean you'll give birth to a child
what'll be special by the time he come of twelve years old.

ELVIVA: How so, special?

WULLWARD: Special. Special. I can't be no more precise'n that.

ELVIVA: Special handsome? Special strong? Special brave? Special
clever?

WULLWARD: Special holy. You talked of heaven in your dream,
didn't you?

WULLWARD: Special holy. You talked of heaven in your dream, didn't you?

ELVIVA: Well?

WULLWARD: About a fish that flew from your bosom up into heaven?

ELVIVA: Heaven, well?

WULLWARD: Well, your child will be honoured in heaven.

ELVIVA: Honoured in heaven!

WULLWARD: Twelve fins mean twelve years.

ELVIVA: My son?

WULLWARD: Up there with the highest.

ELVIVA: Honoured in heaven.

WULLWARD: Rejoice, daughter, that your son, my grandson, is goin' to be raised to this pitch of glory.

SCENE 5

Candlemas Day, 1132.
   House of ELVIVA *and* WENSTAN.
   ELVIVA *gives birth.*
   A feast! In celebration! Music!
   GUESTS: HETHEL, GODWIN, WULLWARD, *a* PRIEST, OTHERS.
   In the midst of the festivities enters a PENITENT, *his arms shackled in chains, begging for alms.*
   He's given a drink and food.
   While eating, he notices ELVIVA *nursing her child and stretches out his arms to be allowed to cradle the baby.*

WENSTAN: Give William to the man doing penance – a holy child to a holy state.

ELVIVA [*holding back*]: What's your penance for, old man?

PENITENT: The worst a man can do. Struck my son in anger.

WENSTAN: Narthin' wrong wi' a trashin' now and then.

PENITENT: Crippled him.

ELVIVA: For doin' what? What could a son hev done was so awful?

PENITENT: If I'd've thought on it hard and wise – narthin'.

ELVIVA: Narthin's not much to do so much penance for.

PENITENT: For disagreein' wi' me – struck him for that! For my son using his own head, which I asked him to do since time, look, an' when he did I struck him. Don't reckon you'll let me hold that babe now, will you?

WENSTAN: Any man big enough to own up guilt can hold my child.

   [*The infant,* WILLIAM, *is handed to the* PENITENT.
      Soon, after some rocking, his chains fall off. The GUESTS *are amazed.*

The PRIEST *steps forward to pick up the chains.*]

PRIEST: Glory be to God, he's given us a sign. I'll hang these holy chains in my church in Haveringland. A memory for those now and those to come.

[ELVIVA *takes back her child.*
The PENITENT *falls to his knees before her.*
Other GUESTS *follow.*]

ELVÍVA: Don't do that. No, don't do that. Thaas a daft thing to do. Don't –

SCENE 6

A SKINNER's *yard.*
   WILLIAM, *aged twelve, is an apprentice of four years standing.*
   SKINNER *and* WILLIAM *stand before a table on which lies a pile of skins.*

SKINNER: The Jews hev a good nose for a skin and a good nose for a bargain, an' they like you. They respect skill an' learnin', an' they know a craftsman when they see one, I'll give 'em that. But you bin seen goin' in an' out too often an' that ent safe. They beint normal like us Christians, they be Jews. Remember!

WILLIAM: They be Jews but they spoil me well enough.

SKINNER: More'n any other I've sent to deal wi' 'em they spoil you rotten.

WILLIAM: Well, ent that good?

SKINNER: Thaas very good. For you thaas good, for me thaas good, an' because you're the skilled o' the lot thaas good for them. But them's strange, wi' their prayers and loud goings on at festival times, an' the secretive way they keep theirselves to theirselves. People what hide hev secrets to hide. So take my advice, visit them on business but no more'n that.

WILLIAM: They tell me I'm their friend.

SKINNER: Thaas 'cos they need all the friends they can get 'cos no one don't much like them. But you're too good-natured and too trusting, which it don't do no good to be in this life. Specially with Jews around.
   Now, smell them skins. Run your hand over them.

[WILLIAM *runs his hands over the skins – sensuously.*]

WILLIAM: Good for patchin' up an' rough work but no more.

WILLIAM: Good for patchin' up an' rough work but no more.
   [SKINNER *ruffles the boy's hair.*
      WILLIAM *smiles the most charming of flirtatious smiles at his employer.*]

SKINNER: I think you should've bin a gal. You're too pretty by half.

   [WILLIAM *takes off his apron, puts on his jacket. Packs tools in his satchel. He's ready to leave for his lodgings and friends.*]

SCENE 7

Outside the SKINNER's *workplace.*
  WILLIAM *is confronted by a* STRANGER, *nervous and agitated.*

STRANGER: There you be. I bin searchin' for you here there and
  everywhere.
WILLIAM: Who are you, mister?
STRANGER: I bin sent for you.
WILLIAM: Sent? Who sent you for me? I ent never seen *you* these
  parts.
STRANGER: But I've seen *you*. Many a time. I was told, see, to
  make inquiries 'bout you, to follow you an' to watch you.
  An' I done all that.
WILLIAM: Watch me? Follow me? What for?
STRANGER: For good things, that's what for. Boy like you?
  Only good things.
WILLIAM: What good things?
STRANGER: To take you off into the service of William, Arch-
  deacon of Norwich.
WILLIAM: Archdeacon of Norwich? You're hevin' me on a
  lead.
STRANGER [*angry*]: Listen! I don't make jests. [*quieter*] I'm his
  cook, see. I need the help of a young'un what's got sense an'
  good legs 'cos there's a lot of standing around to do in a
  kitchen. An' you've got good legs, I can see that. Fine legs.

  [*He squeezes* WILLIAM's *thighs and calves.*]

WILLIAM: But I got a job. Skinner's apprentice.
STRANGER: An' thaas all you'll ever be! But wi' me? In the
  Archdeacon's service? There's a ladder there, do you see a
  ladder in the skinner's yard?

[WILLIAM *hesitates*]:

He's waitin'. The Archdeacon said bring him at once. The boy's bin talked about. Soon everyone will want his skills an' intelligence an' sweet nature. Oh, I see it! Sweet nature. Sweet, sweet, sweet! Come –

[*He puts his arm round the boy's shoulders.
WILLIAM draws away.*]

WILLIAM: You must ask my mother first, though.

STRANGER: Straight way! Well go now. 'Brng him at once,' the Archdeacon said, 'or they'll all be after him.' But I'm first. Ha! Got here before the lot on 'em!

SCENE 8

ELVIVA's *house*.
ELVIVA, WILLIAM *and* STRANGER.

ELVIVA: But he've a job already. 'Prentice to the skinner.
WILLIAM: Skins smell.
STRANGER: Listen to him.
ELVIVA: Skins've served you up till this day.
WILLIAM: Skins've served the skinner.
STRANGER: Listen to him.
WILLIAM: Him's rich, not me.
ELVIVA: One day you'll be skinner, you'll be the rich'un.
WILLIAM: Who needs so many skins?
STRANGER: Listen to him, listen to him!
ELVIVA: Skins'll always be needed — gloves, jackets, hats, boots.
　　An' look at all the patchin' up the Jews call on you to do for
　　the stuff them unfortunates hev to pledge 'gainst loans.
WILLIAM: The Jews have a good nose for a skin an' a good nose
　　for a bargain. There's no future there.
STRANGER: Right, bor! There's never any future with the
　　Jews. Stay away from them. Your mother's right — they live
　　rich lives off the lives of unfortunates. Stay away from the
　　Jews.
ELVIVA: Now's the time I need your father. [*to* STRANGER] Died
　　when the boy was three. Brought up three on 'em alone,
　　look, an' hed to make all the decisions meself.
STRANGER: Then let me help you decide this time, woman. First
　　— cook's help. Then — a cook! Next — a clerk to buy and stock
　　up. Then — a steward. Then Chamberlain p'raps. An' then, if
　　he save prudently, he can purchase his own appointment.
ELVIVA: That do sound like a good future for you, boy.

STRANGER: Now I see where his brains come from as well as his pretty looks.

ELVIVA: I got neither o' those but I do know about preparing for the future. I see to it that he can read an' write for the future; an' I worked hard on the land so's all our sons had a future.

STRANGER: An' here's more for your future.

[*He takes coins from a purse. Attempts to press them into her hand.*]

ELVIVA: No, I can't take them.

STRANGER: For the future.

ELVIVA: Wait till after Easter.

STRANGER: Not for thirty pieces of silver!

ELVIVA: I won't decide till Easter's passed.

[*He again offers the coins.*]

STRANGER: For the future. Some shillings from the Archdeacon who tell me: she'll be anxious for him, his mother, 'cos she be a good an' anxious mother.

ELVIVA: Well you go, son, an' you look an' work a little, an' if that beint anythin' you're happy with, you leave. Remember the dream I hed what your grandfather give meanin' to. You're blessed. An' that mean you can turn your hand to anythin'.

STRANGER: Blessed! Blessed! Indeed blessed. Come.

SCENE 9

The rape.
  The light.
  'The Jews! The Jews!'

SCENE 10

GODWIN's *house.*
But first, THOMAS *from his cell.*

THOMAS: And you out there who don't believe the testimonies
I've assembled, who doubt the signs I've recorded, who don't
believe the witnesses I believe, you who don't believe me, call
me presumptuous – I know you! You're those who delight in
others' misfortune, you're those saddened by success. Disappointed with no evidence for slander, aren't you? Eager to
find fault, unwilling to praise, prompt to disparage – I know
you! Well hear me: your idle barking wearies the air! You
claim religion but have none. You deny divine mystery
because it's happening *now*! Only that which is passed are you
able to accommodate. Only what *age* sanctifies do you sanc-
tify. Well hear me – I have testimony!

[GODWIN *relates his story to a stunned* HETHEL.]

GODWIN: The first to see it was the nun, Lady Legarda, she what
lives like a beggar an' tends the sick for the good o' her soul.
She see this light, 'like a ladder to heaven' she say, two shafts
from the ground up, an' it make her wonder. 'What did the
Lord want me to know?' she ask herself. So she walk with her
attendants towards it, prayin' that he'd direct her in the right
direction. An' he did! An' there he were, William, at the root
of an oak, dressed in narthin' but his jacket an' shoes, his head
shaved, an' full o' stab wounds which ravens was a peckin' of.
She didn't knowed that were Elviva's boy, but she knew she
was lookin' at a boy what was special. 'A person o' merit,' she
say, an' she go home rejoicing an' she tell others.
HETHEL: I knowed something dreadful were goin' to happen.

GODWIN: Next come the Bishop's forester, Henry O' Sprowston. He see the light too, an' he was making towards it when a peasant stop him an' say to come look quick 'cos he'd seen the body of a boy.

HETHEL: I just knowed it!

GODWIN: 'Brutally slain,' Henry tell his wife. 'Stripped an' stabbed an' gagged an' bruised.' He call a priest to bury him but the priest say to wait till Easter is passed.

HETHEL: I knowed somethin' dreadful were goin' to happen 'cos I hed this dream last night.

GODWIN: But no one could stop the rumour spreading, an' crowds an' lads went looking 'cos it's one o' the sad things o' this life that a dead body is like a side-show at a fair. An' they see him, the dead boy, their friend, William. An' they tell his brother, Robert, an' you know the rest.

HETHEL: About Jews.

GODWIN: We go to verify an' we verify: their friend an' our nephew.

HETHEL: I knowed somethin' dreadful were goin' to happen 'cos I hed this dream last night – about Jews.

GODWIN [suddenly interested]: Narthin' more?

HETHEL: They were chasin' me.

GODWIN: More, woman, more. You know dreams is important for knowin' the truth.

HETHEL: An' you know I can't never remember my dreams, only the sensation o' them – happy, sad, fearful. I wake up laughin', cryin' or terrified but I don't ever remember why.

GODWIN: Someone must tell his mother.

HETHEL: Me, I suppose.

GODWIN: You're her sister.

SCENE II

ELVIVA's *house*.
   HETHEL *is with her*.

HETHEL: An' the nun, Legarda, see these ravens tryin' to settle
   on his body but they couldn't settle.
ELVIVA: Oh, William.
HETHEL: They kept tryin' to peck at his head but they couldn't
   peck.
ELVIVA: My best beloved.
HETHEL: They kept tryin' to settle an' peck at his poor ole head
   but they kept slidin' off.
ELVIVA: Oh, William, my best beloved.
HETHEL: An' when she see that, the nun knew! She *knew*, look.
   This was a special boy. Your son William was no ordinary
   boy, he was special.
ELVIVA: My best, best beloved –
HETHEL: Well let me tell you my dream the other night –
ELVIVA: Loved by everyone.
HETHEL: Saturday before Palm Sunday the Lord see fit to give
   me – an ignorant woman – a forewarning of all what was to
   come, 'cos he tell me, I heard him say in this dream, that soon
   I'd lose one o' my dear ones.
ELVIVA: Justice!
HETHEL: One I loved more'n any o' the others.
ELVIVA: Justice!
HETHEL: It were a dream about Jews.
ELVIVA: I want justice for my boy's dyin'.
HETHEL: They were chasing me.
ELVIVA: Who'll gi' me justice for my boy's dyin'?

HETHEL: I was standing in the high street of the market place
and suddenly the Jews come upon me from all sides an'
surround me an' – but I can't remember narthin' more.

SCENE 12

ELVIVA *in Norwich market place.*
CROWDS *around her.*

ELVIVA: An' she try to flee, my sister. In this dream – which she remember from beginnin' to end it were so vivid – she try to flee from the Jews, but they seize her an' break her right leg with a club, an' tear it away from the rest on her body, an' off they run, carrying it away wi' them. True! A true vision!

1ST VOICE: An omen!

ELVIVA: Justice!

1ST VOICE: That were an omen, woman.

ELVIVA: Who'll give me justice 'gainst the Jews?

1ST VOICE: An omen 'bout your poor son, William.

ELVIVA: They seduced him wi' false promises o' gain in high places. A man come an' he tell me he were cook to the Archdeacon who wanted my son to work for him.

2ND VOICE: What work?

3RD VOICE: Dyin' work!

1ST VOICE: Jews' work!

> [*The* CROWD *huddle and exchange inventions and exaggerations.*]

2ND VOICE: Did you hear the story how he was found? A heavenly light directed a holy woman to the place.

3RD VOICE: Thorpe Wood. They find him in Thorpe Wood.

1ST VOICE: Ravens peckin' at his head.

3RD VOICE: Tryin' to peck, *tryin'*!

1ST VOICE: But she see a light over the body an' out of it come

a figure with thorns on his head, an' he speak to her an' he
say: 'This boy do I want at my side in heaven.'

2ND VOICE: An' here's a thing – when his uncle an' family went
to identify him an' they dig to reach him the earth move,
look! It move!

3RD VOICE: He were alive!

2ND VOICE: No, he were dead when they got to him but it
were a spirit in him sayin', 'Be comforted! I be goin' to
heaven in peace.'

3RD VOICE: An' here's somethin' else – when they reach his
poor body which should've smelt o' the dead – it didn't!
Instead there come the perfume o' spring flowers. Spring
flowers an' fragrant herbs, look!

ELVIVA: An' did I tell you? When I were pregnant wi' him
I hed this vision of a fish with twelve fins either side?
splashed wi' blood? which I suckled at my breast till it
grew wings and flew to heaven? Twelve fins! All bloody!
Like my blood-splashed boy were only twelve year
old.

1ST VOICE: An omen!

ELVIVA: Justice! Who'll give me justice 'gainst the Jews?

[3RD MONK, *who has been part of the* CROWD, *stands upon a
barrow as orator/rabble-rouser.*]

3RD MONK: Who are the hereditary enemies of the church?

CROWD: The Jews!

3RD MONK: Who are the money-lenders?

CROWD: The Jews!

3RD MONK: Who is not in debt to the Jews?

CROWD: No one!

3RD MONK: Who allows wives to be their business partners?

CROWD: Jews! Jews!

3RD MONK: Christian doctors use herbs for their medicine but
which doctors use blood?

CROWD: Jewish doctors, doctors of the Jews!

3RD MONK: Who tries to corrupt and convert our vulnerable

youth to their beliefs? Who are the clever-tongues, the know-alls, the richest who dwell in stone houses while we live in wattle, wood and mud?

CROWD: The Jews!

3RD MONK: Who arrogantly challenges Christian doctrines, preaches against our images in church, chastises us for our trust in miracles?

CROWD: Arrogant Jews! Know-all Jews!

3RD MONK: Who condemned our Lord to the cross?

CROWD: The Jews! The Jews! The Jews! The Jews! The Jews! The Jews! The Jews! THE JEWS!

[SHERIFF, JOHN DE CHEYNEY, *appears.*]

SHERIFF: Who touches the Jews answers to me. The Jews are the property of King Stephen and I'm King Stephen's man. Go to your homes and pour sense over your senseless tempers. There'll be no blood-letting while I'm Sheriff of Norwich.

[THOMAS *takes over.*]

THOMAS: And who was this Sheriff of Norwich? John de Cheyney. Sheriff John, who, when the Synod called for the Jews to come and answer the accusations made against them, advised them not to attend and hid them in his castle till the just wrath of the people settled into Christian peace and reason. But oh, he was punished. By his own testament, which I obtained from his servants after he had passed away, at the very moment when he protected the Jews, the very moment when he opposed Christian law – at that very moment, look! he began to suffer from internal haemorrhage. The vengeance of God!

And let that be a warning! To those hard and slow of heart to believe that the Jews perpetrated this crime in scorn of the Lord's Passion and the Christian law – let Sheriff John's bleeding be a warning. There will be blood for blood!

PART TWO

The first witnesses present their evidence and are countered by Prior Elias.

Easter 1144. The synod: an ecclesiastical council-meeting presided over by ELIAS, *Prior of the Church of Norwich. Among those present are ecclesiastical functionaries, including the priest,* GODWIN; DOM AIMAR, *Prior of St Pancras, visiting;* ELVIVA, HETHEL, MATHILDA. GODWIN *rises to address the assembly.*

GODWIN: Very Reverend Lord an' Father, Prior Elias. May that goodness of your'n which everyone here abouts know, make you bend your ears to what tis I, your humble priest, Godwin, have to say by way o' complaint and accusation. May the reverend assembly also o' my brethren an' fellow priests, who I see before me attending this present synod, also bend their ears. For what I hev to say is sad an' bitter an' I'm angry, so all must forgive me my simple an' direct words.

Your fathership know, an' I don't 'spect tis a secret to most o' the rest on you, that a certain boy, a very little boy, a harmless innocent little boy, were treated in the most horrible manner in Passion Week an' found dead in Thorpe Wood, an' up to this day, look! he've hed no Christian burial. He were a cousin to my own children an' because of kindred ties he were very dear to me. So what I relate will p'raps make a fond uncle cry. You'll hev to forgive that too.

His name were William. He were only twelve. He'd been stripped, his head shaved, stab wounds in his side, his skin scolded wi' boiling water, an' his mouth gagged wi' a wooden gag which, very reverend brother, I hev in my hand, look. A gag! To stop him from screaming. To gag up his poor ole cries. The cries of an innocent lamb. William. Twelve year old.

Now, brethren, who could do this? Who do you know among the good townsfolk of Norwich could carry out such a terrible crime? An' which other crime in history do it remind you of? A bloody head, from a crown of thorns? A stab wound in the side? Is there any *Christian* you know could carry out such a bloody thing? Who did it once? An' who've done it agin and agin in mockery o' the first time they did it? You'll know which crime I'm thinkin' of. That don't need me to name it. Eleven hundred an' forty-four years ago – once. Eleven hundred an' forty-four years later – once again!

The Jews! I accuse the Jews! Enemies of the Christian name. Shedders of innocent blood. An' I can prove their guilt. Facts! so's you can judge for yourselves, so's you can add to what you know 'bout Jews an' their practices an' what they must carry out on days specified.

An' because that do concern me when my neighbour's house go up in flames therefore I dare bend your ears and lay before you my complaint, sure that you'll find justice for the sister o' my wife, the mother o' the boy, William.

[ELVIVA *steps forward*.]

ELVIVA: An' he says, 'I'm cook to the Archdeacon, and his reverend sir wants your boy William in his kitchen to work for him, look.' 'No!' I say. 'He've got a job,' I say. But William argue 'cos he weren't so happy sellin' skins to Jews. An' this mysterious stranger wooed me like the cunning serpent make Eve eat the apple, an' I'm a woman alone, sirs, wi' no man to help me make decisions, an' poor wi' it. So's when this devil, sent by the Jews, offer me money, my resolve weaken. I let my son go, a poor innocent – an' don't I regret that, oh! I do so regret that. But he were supposed to hev gone to the Archdeacon, look, an' blame-fool, me, I listen to him!

[HETHEL *steps forward*.]

HETHEL: An' in this dream which come to me like a vision, the Jews seize me an' tear off me leg an' run wi' it an' I hear this voice say to me, it say: 'Through the Jews will you lose a part

o' your family that you love dearly.' 'Cos I lost me leg, see.
They ran off wi' me leg like they ran off wi' me nephew.
True! Well, thaas what dreams is for, ent they, to tell you the
truth?

[MATHILDA *steps forward.*]

MATHILDA: So, after this mysterious stranger persuade my aunt
to let him take William to work for the Archdeacon's kitchen,
they visit us. The stranger an' my cousin. They don't stay
long 'cos he were in a hurry, weren't he, the stranger? 'We be
goin' off to work at the Archdeacon's kitchen,' say Cousin
William to me. 'Wish me luck and gi' me blessin's.' Which
'corse we did 'cos he were a lovely boy an' we love 'im. But
we don't trust *him*. Him! The stranger. He look evil an' ugly,
an' so my mother tell me to follow them. 'Follow them,' she
say to me, 'follow them an' see where they go.' An' I did. An'
they went into a Jew's house an' shut the door an' I don't see
my cousin not ever agin.

[ELIAS *stands to question them.*]

ELIAS: Young woman –
MATHILDA: Mathilda.
ELIAS: Mathilda. This mysterious stranger. Could you tell us –
was he a Jew or a Christian?
MATHILDA: Like I say, he were evil-lookin' an' ugly, sir. He
must've been a Jew.
ELIAS: Must he? Look around you, Mathilda. Look. Some forty
faces. Carefully. Is every face you see beautiful?

[MATHILDA *is fearful and hesitant.*]

Answer me, young woman. Look at every face and tell me, is
every face you see a sweet and saintly face?

[*She is silent.*]

And you followed them, you say? That's not an easy thing, to
follow someone without them seeing you. Is it something you
do often? Follow people?

[*She is silent.*]

Something you do well? You're an expert follower?

[*Silent still.*]

And did he look back, this mysterious stranger? This man who was on such a cruel errand, an errand that he knew would bring great punishment upon himself and his people, did you observe him taking every precaution to ensure no one was following him to see where he was going?

[*Silent still.*]

Or was this a stupid Jew who imagined there was no danger and so he walked boldly forward with not a glance back, thus making your difficult task of following him easier?

[*Silent still.*]

And the house, the Jew's house. Could you say exactly which one it is?

[*Silent still.*]

If we took you to the street could you point with absolute certainty and say – in there they went, Prior Elias. That one! The mysterious stranger and my Cousin William. That one. Without a doubt, that one. Could you?

[*She is silent still, and moves away.*
    He turns to HETHEL.]

And you, woman, with your dreams. Do you dream often?

HETHEL: Every night, reverend sir.

ELIAS: Every night. And what did you dream last night?

HETHEL: Oh, I can't remember that, reverend sir.

ELIAS: I understand. I too often dream but can rarely remember my dreams. What about the night before, can you remember that?

HETHEL: Oh no, sir. That I can't. The truth is I dream every night but I remember narthin'. I only ever remember the

sensation o' them — happy, sad, fearful. I wake up laughin',
cryin' or terrified, but I don't ever remember why.

ELIAS: But this dream, about the Jews seizing you and wrenching
your leg from your body and running off with it down the
high street by the market place, this one you remember in
every vivid detail?

HETHEL: Oh yes, sir, I do, I do! Every vivid detail.

ELIAS: Remarkable. Possible, I suppose, but remarkable.

HETHEL: It come from God, see, sir?

ELIAS: Ah. Yes. God. But I have a question has been nagging at
me ever since I heard the story. Perhaps you can help me
answer it. This mysterious stranger — his was a terrible errand.

HETHEL: Terrible indeed, sir.

ELIAS: Planned, calculated, evil.

HETHEL: Evil indeed, sir.

ELIAS: First he found the boy and seduced him.

HETHEL: Like the serpent seduced Eve, sir.

ELIAS: But the boy, being well brought up and responsible,
insisted that his mother be asked for her permission first.

HETHEL: An' that were the right and proper thing to do, sir.

ELIAS: And so they went to his mother and the mysterious
stranger bribed and seduced her.

HETHEL: Like the serpent seduced Eve, sir.

ELIAS: And that was that.

HETHEL: That was that, sir.

ELIAS: He had his boy for the Jews.

HETHEL: Hed 'im, sir.

ELIAS: Evil.

HETHEL: Evil indeed, sir.

ELIAS: And he took him straight there. To the Jew's house.

HETHEL: Oh no, sir. He bring the boy first to me.

ELIAS: I forgot. He brought the boy to you.

HETHEL: My nephew wanted my blessing.

ELIAS: A blessing to work in a kitchen?

[*She is silent.*]

Does a nephew require an aunt's blessing to work in a kitchen?

[*She is silent.*]

And the mysterious stranger, a Jew perhaps, commissioned to bring a Christian child to be ritually slaughtered, agreed to let himself be seen a second time and run the risk of being followed just in order to allow his victim to get an aunt's blessing? Why would such a scheming, evil messenger do that, I wonder?

[*She is silent, and moves away.*
    ELIAS *turns to* ELVIVA.]

And you, mother of the poor boy, you allowed your precious son, in return for money, to go off with a man *he* did not know, *you* did not know, and now of whom no trace can be found?

[*She is silent, and moves away.*
    One by one everyone in the assembly has moved away, leaving only three: GODWIN, ELIAS *and* DOM AIMAR.]

[*to* GODWIN] And did you actually *see* a crown of thorns?

[GODWIN *realizes he is not believed. He moves away, angry, vengeful-looking.*
    DOM AIMAR *confronts* ELIAS.]

DOM AIMAR: That was an engaging but unfair spectacle, Brother Elias.

ELIAS: I know it, Brother Aimar. I don't know how you administer *your* priory at St Pancras but I will not have superstition replace true faith in mine.

DOM AIMAR: What you call 'superstition' many of us would argue is the honest faith of a simple flock.

ELIAS: I have heard such arguments.

DOM AIMAR: Do I detect contempt in you, Brother Elias?

ELIAS: I have heard that said too. Yes, I do not confuse a duty to care with a need to admire those I must care for.

DOM AIMAR: Since, then, you doubt there exists conclusive

evidence of Jewish culpability I have, as prior to prior, a proposition. Sell me the body of the boy.

ELIAS: That's not a holy thing either for you to propose or me to consider, Brother Dom Aimar.

DOM AIMAR: Everything that enables the church to survive and carry out its work is holy.

ELIAS: A dubious ethic and one I don't really think you believe. Besides, the body is not the possession of the church.

DOM AIMAR: Not yet.

ELIAS: Nor ever will be while I'm prior.

DOM AIMAR: Ah, you may have contempt for those in your care but you're a wily church administrator, Brother Elias. You know full well the value of what's in your possession. God's placed a martyr in your hands and you know his price. Had I been in your place I'd not have sold a martyr either.

ELIAS: You and my bishop, both. Ebolard also argues that the boy be named a martyr. 'It'll bring pilgrims!' he cries.

DOM AIMAR: He cries wisely.

ELIAS: He cries shamelessly.

DOM AIMAR: Pilgrims bring money in the hope of miracles.

ELIAS: A shameless fool!

DOM AIMAR: I see that like me you too quarrel with your bishop. Good with souls, inept with accounts. But mark me, Elias, you have a treasure on your doorstep.

ELIAS: A martyr is not a martyr unless he die for his religion. Not suffering but *why* he suffered is what lays claim to martyrdom.

DOM AIMAR: Precisely!

ELIAS: Precisely what? The boy William was murdered, I strongly suspect, by a mad and cruel stranger for cruel obscene desires of the flesh.

DOM AIMAR: But prove it was the Jews, you prove a martyr.

ELIAS: It cannot be proven. Besides, such spilling of blood goes against their teachings.

DOM AIMAR: That is not what the Christian world knows.

ELIAS: Then the Christian world is ill-informed.

DOM AIMAR: Humility, Elias, humility.

ELIAS: It goes against all reason. The Jews have no normal freedoms here. They're the property of the King, who taxes them at a whim. They're clever and rich, for both of which they're hated and resented. They're small in number —

DOM AIMAR: Thirty thousand —

ELIAS: — *three* thousand. Why should they risk such crimes?

DOM AIMAR: Your priest, Godwin, thinks he was murdered by the Jews in mockery of our Lord's suffering.

ELIAS: My priest, Godwin, is a greedy, ignorant and superstitious man who has made mischief before. He thinks wrong!

DOM AIMAR: But supposing that for once in his life he thinks right?

[ELIAS *is a sick but passionate man.*]

ELIAS: Somewhere you will read that to drink dried menstrual blood will induce the menstrual cycle, that to eat three lice between bread will cure colic, that to prevent the bursting of a dam a child must be buried alive, that to immure a human being in its foundations will ensure the building stands.

And if you read the books of early Christian sects you will find *them* full of blood rituals, the sacrifice of babes and the eating of their parts. Whereas turn to Leviticus, turn to Deuteronomy and you will find such sacrifice most strictly forbidden to the Israelites.

The ecumenical councils pass edict after edict declaring such belief in Jewish slaughter false, yet such belief persists. I am tired of the ignorance and stupidity of the simple flock. The simple flock chooses superstition for which it needs no learning. I am tired, yes, and full of contempt. Jesus was a Jew steeped in the knowledge of the wisest laws. Law, learning, mercy, wisdom — these are the pillars of the Christian faith. They represent all that I cherish in this damned existence, they are the only hope for hopeless mankind, they are what formed my life and what in life I informed. I will not bow to the fevered intoxications of illiterate monks who love more their image before God than God's meaning to the world.

[DOM AIMAR *is not impressed. A cynic, he ignores* ELIAS's *words.*]

DOM AIMAR: Think on it. A precious treasure on your doorstep, Elias. I would guard it most diligently.

[ELIAS *is troubled.*]

Murdered by the Jews. [*Pause.*] In mockery of our Lord's suffering. [*Pause.*] As an insult to Christ. [*Pause.*] Think on it.

[DOM AIMAR *leaves.*
   Three MONKS *approach* ELIAS.]

1ST MONK: Bishop Ebolard has granted us permission to transfer the blessed boy's body to our cemetery.

ELIAS [*angered*]: So, you appealed to the bishop, a man terrified of his own shadow, when you knew I was against the translation?

2ND MONK: We don't think you understand how strongly we feel about the martyred child, Brother Elias.

ELIAS: I understand your feelings only too well — you want to bask in the unholy light of an unholy relic.

3RD MONK: We want to bring glory to our church, Brother Elias.

ELIAS: You'll bring shame instead.

1ST MONK: We respect and venerate you, Brother Elias —

ELIAS [*mocking*]: Brother Elias! Brother Elias!

1ST MONK: — but many of us believe the boy to be a martyr to our faith.

ELIAS: And there are many, thank God, who believe him to be a poor murdered child.

2ND MONK: The signs cannot be denied, Brother Elias.

ELIAS: Signs! Signs! What signs?

3RD MONK: The signs of a ritual murder as it is known the Jews commit in mockery of our Lord.

[*The sounds of a requiem mass.*]

ELIAS: And would the Jews strip and batter and then hang a

child in the open to be gawped upon by every and any passer-by?

[*The* MONKS *leave to pick up a coffin, which they take in procession round and round the stage, followed by a crowd carrying lighted candles.*]

[*Over the singing*] It is presumptuous to maintain that which the church universal does not accept.

[*He is ignored.*]

I will not allow you to honour upon earth him whom it is not yet certain that God has glorified in heaven.

[*He is ignored.*]

There is much mischief and foolishness in this church and I . . .

[*But* ELIAS *is a sick man. He cannot sustain his anger.*
As the procession and singing continue, THOMAS *steps forward with his book.*]

THOMAS: And still they slur his name and fame. Let them listen, then, those who slur the fame of the most gloriously named martyr. Let them listen, those who persecute him by making light of him, who deny his sanctity, who do all they can to stop the spread of his renown. Let them listen, those who say we are mad — for we have testimony! We have certain testimony that he was slain by Jews as is their custom on the day of Passover. The nature of his wounds proves it. We have testimony that the Jews perpetrated this crime in scorn of Christian law and the Lord's Passion. And it is testimony unknown by Elias or Godwin or Elviva or Hethel all those eight and twenty years ago. Listen!

SCENE 14

The rape.
  The light.
   'The Jews! The Jews!'

PART THREE

Brother Thomas of Monmouth presents new witnesses with additional evidence.

SCENE 15

An old maidservant, MAUDE, *sits carding wool, talking to* THOMAS *as he writes.*

MAUDE: They called me Maudie the Maidservant an' I worked long an' I worked hard for the Jews, cleanin' an' serving an' mendin' an' runnin' their errands on days their religion forbade *them* do it. I can't say they was good to me nor can't I say they was bad. But this I can tell you – they was strange.

First they treated the bor kindly. Fed 'im an' fussed 'im like they always did, for they'd taken a shine to his sweet nature. Then things change. From bein' angels one minute they become devils the next. Strange. Like I say, strange.

They'd come back from their synagogue, Passover-time that were, an' they was still singin' what hymns they hev to sing in that strange language o' theirs, when suddenly they seize hold o' the bor as he were eatin', an' some hold him from behind while others push into his jaws what they call a teasel – a kind o' gag which they tie round the back o' his neck as tight as they can.

Next they git a rope an' make four knots in it. Round his head it go an' under his chin an' round his neck tight as ever it can be so's the knots press into his forehead an' temples an' his poor ole throat.

But that weren't enough for them, no, that it weren't! They hev to shave his head, look, then they hev to prick it, prick his poor ole scalp wi' thorns so's the blood come horribly out an' then – an' this is what git to me, what really upset me – they tie him to a cross an' nail one foot an' one hand, the right one I think that were, an' then they push a knife into his side so's there was even more blood all over the place an' you should've seen their hands. Covered in blood! An' they was crying out these very words, I remember them word for word: 'Even as we condemned the Christ to a shameful death, so let us also condemn the Christian. Lord an' servant in like punishment so's they can feel the pain of *our* reproach as we feel the pain of *their* reproach.' Word for word! As God is my witness.

Oh, there was a commotion in that room, I can tell you. Every Jew fighting with the other tryin' to do the worst they could to the poor ole thing. But they got frightened, see. Blood all over the place. They got scared.

'Bring boilin' water!' they yell at me. 'Quick, boilin' water.' So I rush up an' rush down to boil them the water they ask for, thinkin' they wanna clean up the mess they was makin' so's no one would notice the horrible things they bin doin', but no! That *ent* what they wanted boilin' water for. Know what t'were? To throw over the bor to stop the bleeding! Scalding water! To stop the bleedin'! Well, that fair upset me. It did. But what could I say to anyone? The Jews was my livin'. An' what they pay were poor 'nough, but *I* were poor, too!

You ask me how I know all this? I'll tell you how I know all this. 'Cos when I bring them water an' they hev to open the door a little, I see wi' one eye through the chink in the door. Didn't last long. They open an' close the door in a small second 'cos they was afeared I might see the terrible things they done, but I see all I need to see. In that small second. Through the chink in the door. All what I tell you.

[THOMAS *rises*.]

THOMAS [*reading from his book*]: Thus then the glorious boy and martyr of Christ, William, dying the death of time in reproach of the Lord's death but crowned with the blood of a glorious martyrdom entered into the kingdom of glory on high to live for ever. Whose soul rejoiceth blissfully in heaven among the bright hosts of the saints, and whose body by the omnipotence of the divine mercy worketh miracles upon earth.

[*Looks up at his listeners.*]

Presumption? Am I to be accused of presumption for keeping up the memory of a saint whom the world does not know and the church does not celebrate? Then who is *not* presumptuous? Of few saints can it be said that the whole Christian world knows them. Whom Rome honours, does Gaul and Britain equally accept? Or is the famous name of our most Blessed King and Martyr Eadmund, or the Glorious Confessor Cuthbert, equally well known to the people of Greece or Palestine?

Listen, then, our testimony continues. The Jews, having carried out their cruel mockery of Christ upon the saintly child, now had a martyr's body to dispose of.

SCENE 16

AELWARD DED *is dying.*
From his death-bed he tells his story to a MONK.
It is the year 1149.
THOMAS *is at his desk, writing.*

AELWARD DED: Not all my wealth nor all the respect given me as a worthy citizen of Norwich could help relieve my pain.

So I thought: Aelward Ded, you must visit the holy churches of the city. Pray there. Do what good deeds you can. Perhaps the Lord will hear you and take pity and ease the pain of your last years. I took my servant one evening. A pilgrimage through the night. I walked from one church to the next, asking God to forgive my sins and distributing alms to the sick and the poor who were sheltering in God's houses.

And as I was making my way from the Church of St Mary Magdalene to St Leonards Church, along the edge of Thorpe Wood, I came across two Jews known to me, riding their horses deeper into the wood. Why? And more, it was the holy day of the Adoration of the Cross, a day when Jews usually dare not leave their houses. And more, across the neck of one horse was a sack. On such a day where could they be going?

I was curious. So I dismounted and walked up to them and touched their sack with my right hand. Inside was a human form. Well, they fled! It was obvious I'd surprised them because they fled in terror. Into the thick of the wood. But I did nothing. My suspicions were aroused but my pain and my devotional task pressed upon me and I alerted no one, nor to my shame did I myself take action.

THOMAS [*reading from his book*]: But the enemies of the Christians, being alarmed and in despair, determined to make advance to

John the Sheriff, who had been their refuge and one and only protector. 'Look you,' they said, 'we are placed in a position of great anxiety, and if you can help us out of it we promise you a hundred marcs.' And John the Sheriff was well pleased with so many marcs.

AELWARD DED: The next I knew I was summoned by the King's Sheriff, John de Cheyney. Upon oath he made me swear never to divulge in my life-time, or at least not until the point of death, what I knew against the Jews. And I *had* to. I had to swear it. He forced me.

[*Pause.*]

I am upon the point of death.

MONK: But John de Cheyney died three years ago. Why did you not tell us then?

[AELWARD DED *rises in his bed in anger, able only to make the gurgling sounds of a dying man.*
Dies.]

THOMAS: Whoever attributes to me the sin of presumption, whoever charges me with rashness, let him come forward with his babble and jabber and I will answer him. Lo! by the sling of my lips I will crash through the shameless forehead with the smooth stone of the word – for I have testimony!

And what is his babble and jabber? It is this, look you. [*mocking voice*] 'It is very presumptuous to maintain that which the church universal does not accept, and to account holy that which is not holy.' Babble and jabber! 'It is rash to honour so magnificently upon earth him whom it is not yet certain that God has glorified in heaven.' Babble and jabber!

Testimony! I have testimony! Listen – the testimony of testimonies. Brother Theobald. Once a Jew now a convert to the army of the Lord.

SCENE 17

THEOBALD, *monk of Norwich, talks and sews a church vestment meanwhile.*

THOMAS *writes.*

THEOBALD: For that I was once a Jew – no! For that I was *born* a Jew. Distinctions. Important to make distinctions. I was born a Jew but in my *heart* I could never have been one because I came so easily to Christ. No! Not easily. I cannot say that. Hard. I struggled. For what can be worthy that comes easily? So, for that I was born a Jew and therefore grew up with Jews, I am familiar with their teaching, with their laws, and with their holy rituals. Not a scholar, I must add, it would not be true to say I was a scholar, to my regret and shame, for I was scorned harshly for being slow in the school where Talmud was taught and argued over. I learned poorly and argued feebly and was laughed at for that. So, though not a scholar, I was privy to their teaching, to their laws and to their holy rituals and – oh, I've already said that, forgive me, I repeat myself. It is a failing. Yet another which they scorned me for. No! Not scorned. Mocked. Scorn can be ignored. Mockery is withering. Distinctions. Important to make distinctions. I try hard to make distinctions in this life. And fail. Mostly.

So. The Jews' teachings.

It is laid down in the writings of our fathers, *their* fathers, that the Jews, unless they regularly shed, each year, the blood of a Christian child in some part of the world in scorn and contempt of Christ then they will never obtain their freedom nor could ever return to the land of their fathers. Christ's death had shut them out from their own country and made them slaves in foreign lands, therefore must they avenge their sufferings on him.

So, the chief rabbis, who live in Spain, where they are held in high esteem, assemble every year in the city of Narbonne and cast lots for all the countries which the Jews inhabit; and whichever country the lot falls upon then the chief Jews of that country's capital city must cast lots again for the city in which the fulfilment of this terrible duty must be imposed.

[THEOBALD *knows this to be a lie.*
He speaks faster, as though to get it over with quickly.]

So. In that year when William, God's Glorious Martyr, was slain, the lot fell upon the Norwich Jews and all the synagogues in England signified consent that the wickedness should be carried out here. I know all this because at the time I lived in Cambridge, a Jew among Jews. The commission of the crime was no secret to me.

[THEOBALD *suddenly and abruptly becomes exultant, in the grip of religious ecstasy. An escape from his sense of guilt.*]

But oh, oh, oh! In the process of time, as I became acquainted with the glorious display of miracles which divine power carried out through the merits of the Blessed Martyr, William, I became afraid, afraid, afraid! And my conscience burned guilt in me like coals of hell and I forsook Judaism and turned to the Christian faith, brothers, to the love of the Lord Jesus Christ.

[*He swoons away.*]

SCENE 18

A sick ELIAS *wearily listens to a haranguing* THOMAS, *who at first is writing in his book.*

THOMAS [*writing*]: But the struggle to raise our martyr to his rightful place in the minds of many was long. And as so often in the history of our faith it is those who should know better who are the prevaricators.

ELIAS: You are referring to me, Brother Thomas.

[THOMAS *rises to him.*]

THOMAS: Sometimes I think we are weighed down by too much learning —

ELIAS: There cannot be too much learning.

THOMAS: — too much thought —

ELIAS: There cannot be too much thought.

THOMAS: — too much learning and too much thought lead to doubt —

ELIAS: To wisdom.

THOMAS: — leaving no room for faith.

ELIAS: Faith without wisdom is superstition. I will not have superstition in my church.

THOMAS: And revelation? What place has revelation in your church?

ELIAS: What is revealed to you this time, Brother Thomas?

THOMAS: Testimonies! By the grace of God! I have testimonies of a wondrous revelation given me by the grace of God.

ELIAS: And who am I to deny God's grace?

THOMAS: Oh, you confuse me, Brother Elias.

ELIAS: But with God's grace all will be wondrously revealed. I'm waiting.

THOMAS: With the blessing of the late Bishop Ebolard, may he rest in peace, who sanctioned it, the holy body of our martyr was transferred from Thorpe Wood to the monks' cemetery.

ELIAS: Where it should have remained.

THOMAS: A poor resting place for so great a martyr.

ELIAS: His martyrdom is not proved.

THOMAS [*pressing ahead*]: But heaven was not satisfied or happy with so poor a resting place for so glorious a martyr.

ELIAS: His martyrdom is not proved.

THOMAS: And so the body was permitted burial in the Chapter House.

ELIAS: Where I believe it should remain.

THOMAS: The resting place of Saint William of Norwich should be by the high altar of the Church of Norwich.

ELIAS: His martyrdom is not proved and sainthood cannot be conferred.

[*This is a battle of wills between a relentlessly fervent monk with a cause and an ailing, weary sceptic.*]

THOMAS: Listen to me, Brother Elias, listen how in a dream I saw standing beside me a venerable old man with grey hair clothed in episcopal robes who roused me with his episcopal staff, saying: 'Arise, brother! and make haste to bid my beloved son, Elias, Prior to the Church of Norwich, that he must announce to your new Bishop William from me: "Remove that precious treasure which the brethren keep hidden away in their Chapter House. Obey not my paternal order and they will lose that treasure to the great harm of their church. For those relics, unless soon placed safely by my high altar, will be carried off by a thief who now stands on the threshold of a deliberation, led on by hope of gain. Wherefore, brother, when thou risest in the morning, neglect thou not to carry my paternal orders to those my sons whom I have named."'

Then, as I inquired who was making this announcement, he answered: 'I am that Herbert who, by God's grace, founded this Church of Norwich.'

[THOMAS *awaits a response as one who has dealt an unbeatable trump*].

ELIAS: I believe not one word you utter, Brother Thomas, but I am a dying man and the clamour for this poor boy to be declared martyr and named saint grows beyond my control. As Prior my responsibility is order. If I deny the claim, the clamour will become conflict. Therefore let his body be transferred into the church —

[THOMAS *is triumphant, jubilant, and rudely interrupts.*]

THOMAS: — beside the tomb of Blessed Herbert himself! Oh yes! It will be done. God has blessed you with wisdom, Brother Elias. It will be done! To be buried in the church is the Glorious Martyr's rightful place. The sweet saint has found his home. It will be done! And you mark, Brother Elias, you mark how all of England will travel to his tomb. Mark! His fame will spread far and wide. It will be difficult to hold back all the pilgrims. Swarms of them! Tides of them! Knights will compete with one another to endow the church. And there will be miracles! Mighty works and miracles!

[*Music!*
    The air is thick with jubilation.
    Four MONKS, *including* THOMAS, *carry a coffin to the centre of what has now become the interior of the Church of Norwich.*]

PART FOUR

We hear of the miracles and rejoice.

The interior of the Church of Norwich.
  Over the coffin is placed a sepulchre which dominates our attention.
  CROWDS *of* PILGRIMS *form a queue. Each has a different ailment.*
  The sounds of ailing and religious fervour mix with the music.
  With THOMAS *urging them, guiding them, saluting them, they one*
by one list and enact before the sepulchre their miraculous cures.

THOMAS: Mighty works and miracles!

EDMUND: I, Edmund, monk of Norwich, troubled with a most terrible toothache, I touched the sepulchre with my suffering face and straightway the swelling disappeared. Glory be to God and the Blessed Martyr!

CLARICIA: I, Claricia, wife of Gaufridus de Marc, for years kept pain in my knees till the fame of the Excellent Martyr reached me and with the support of my husband and sons I approached his holy sepulchre with my bare knees and immediately I felt soundness through the bones of my body. Glory be to God and the Blessed Martyr!

THOMAS: Mighty works and miracles!

MURIEL: I, Muriel de Setchy, bled without pause till I offered two candles covered with my tears, knelt, prayed and kissed the sepulchre of the Martyr and then oh then the Grace of the Lord's pity came down upon me and I ceased to flow. Glory be to God and the Blessed Martyr!

RADULFUS: I, Radulfus, nephew to Prior Elias, had an infant son sick to death. Advice was given to my wife that we should cause to be made a candle the length and breadth of our little boy –

THOMAS: The blessed saint was born on Candlemas Day and he loved candles. Everyone had to bring a candle –

RADULFUS: — the length and breadth of our little boy to be offered to St William for the restoration of our little boy's health. Which we did, straightway, and laid it at the sepulchre of the Holy Martyr. And when we returned, lo! he was well. Our boy was safe and well. Glory be to God and the Blessed Martyr!

STEPHEN [*a very old man*]: Stephen, me. Old Stephen. Oldest of the Norwich monks. I couldn't sleep. Neither day nor night for three days. Closed my eyes but stayed awake till my head rocked and throbbed and I was fit for nothing but howling. So I upped and supplicated and devoted and prayed and this here is what I said:

[*He kneels before the sepulchre.*]

'Oh holy Lord William! If it is true thou art of so great estimation and sanctity in the presence of God, grant me thy servant some rest that I may recover the power of sleeping which I have lost.' And it happened. There and then. My eyes became heavy. My head lost its neck. My rocking, my throbbing, my howling stopped. I slept! They tell me – like a child. Not a snore! Glory be to God and the Blessed Martyr.

THOMAS: Glory be! My William's fame spread! Who came with coin and candle was not denied his miracle. I know, because by this time I was the Blessed Saint's secretary.

SCENE 20

GODWIN's *house.*
  A bowl of holy water on the floor.
  An OLD WOMAN *has come for a miracle cure.*

OLD WOMAN: And is it true, you dip it in holy water an' you drink it an' you get better?

GODWIN: This is the martyr's gag, old woman. Wi' this they plugged up his cries for help. You won't find no more holy relic than this.

OLD WOMAN: You've helped many, they say.

GODWIN: They keep a comin' for help an' I'm a man o' pity.

OLD WOMAN: Then gi' me your pity and help this poor old'un, for I've pains and aches fit to kill me they've bin wi' me so long.

GODWIN: And what d'you bring for offerins?

OLD WOMAN: You see I'm poor.

GODWIN: You're not so poor you can't bring me a hen.

OLD WOMAN: From where in heaven's name?

GODWIN: In heaven's name no one's *that* poor.

OLD WOMAN: Believe me, reverent Godwin. *That* poor.

GODWIN: You 'spect me to heal you for narthin'?

OLD WOMAN: Narthin's all I got, look, you can see.

GODWIN: I'm lookin' and I can see clothes on your body, shoes on your feet, an' flesh what's bin fed on your bones.

OLD WOMAN: You and the Blessed Martyr are my only hope.

GODWIN: Did the tailor gi' you clothes for narthin'? Did the cobbler shoe you for narthin'? Did you get your bread for narthin'? Did you?

OLD WOMAN: All what I had left I spent on doctors what do me no good.

GODWIN: Then nor can't the martyr heal you for narthin'.

OLD WOMAN: But I'm in pain.

GODWIN: Well you listen to me, woman: he that gives not what he prizes gets not what he asks. So if you want your pain eased you go get me a hen.

OLD WOMAN: May God judge between us.

GODWIN: He will, I can assure you.

OLD WOMAN: An' may the merciful martyr St William treat you as you've treated me.

GODWIN: He were my nephew. Him and me understand one another well 'nough, so don't you be worryin' yourself 'bout that, old dear.

[*She leaves, weeping.*]

SCENE 21

Return to interior of the Church of Norwich.

THOMAS: Mighty works and miracles! True testimonies! And
mark this well: he who would accuse me of stamping falsities
as truths, or of dressing up facts with fiction, is guilty of
sin!

[THOMAS *allows his intimidation to sink in.*]

And if among you are those who still doubt, then hear this.

[*A young man, of subdued cockiness, steps forward. He is a
natural sceptic who has been cowed.*]

Yes! Your turn! Tell them.

WALTER: I, Walter, sometime servant of our dean at Norwich,
well – me – I –

THOMAS: Tell them! Tell them! Or surely William will come at
thee again!

WALTER: I doubted.

THOMAS: Only doubted?

WALTER: Doubted, mocked, made fun of all what I heard.
Whenever I was told another miracle I'd imitate the sufferer.

[*He pauses. Frightened to continue.*]

THOMAS: Well show us, show us!

WALTER [*showing us*]: 'Cured! Cured! I be cured! Once my head
was back to front an' then I give a candle to the saint an' look!
I don't need to walk backwards no more! Glory be to God
and the Blessed Martyr!'

[*Pause.*]

Things like that.

[*Pause.*]

THOMAS: Yes? Go on. Tell them.

WALTER: An' then, one night, as I was sleepin', William come at me in a terrifying shape an' he asked me, 'Why do you make fun o' me an' mock me?' An' 'corse, in the dream I were scared sick. Couldn't speak. An' when he said, 'Follow me,' I couldn't follow. So he had to drag me, to a cave, an' he ask me, 'Whose cave is this?' So I tell 'im: 'Thaas yours, sir, yours, where you live.' Well it were his, werenit? His in the wood, Thorpe Wood, where he was found? So he says to me, he says, 'Enter!' Well, I thought I was goin' to drop dead in the middle o' me own dream an' that would've bin a rum thing. But howsomever I didn't, I stay alive, an' he pushed me inside his cave an' bor! he set about me. He had this great big cudgel an' he cudgelled me black an' blue an' bruised every limb. An' when I woke — an' this were the strangest part on it — when I woke I was smartin' with the pain! As though it'd actually happened, look! Well, you don't find me mockin' an' makin' fun no more, that you don't.

THOMAS [*prompting him*]: So everyone should learn from your dream?

WALTER: So everyone should learn from my dream.

THOMAS: Glory be to God and the Blessed Martyr.

WALTER: Glory be to God and the Blessed Martyr.

THOMAS [*triumphant*]: Mighty works and miracles!

[*Last — a young couple,* COLOBERN *and* ANSFRIDA, *clinging to each other with acute shyness.*

As they speak we hear, low at first, the sound of singing. It grows. A hymn of praise to St William. A triumphant choral work by the end.]

COLOBERN: My name be Colobern —

ANSFRIDA: — and mine, Ansfrida —

COLOBERN: — husband and wife — wi' a son —

ANSFRIDA: — a lovely child, sweet-natured —

COLOBERN: — what were dumb.

ANSFRIDA: Dumb! Seven year!

COLOBERN: From birth.

ANSFRIDA: He understood —

COLOBERN: — but made no sounds.

ANSFRIDA: Well, it happened like this, one night —

COLOBERN: — the two on us asleep —

ANSFRIDA: — we have a dream.

COLOBERN: The *same* dream!

ANSFRIDA: Together, look!

COLOBERN: A reverend man he come to us an' he say —

ANSFRIDA: — tomorrow you must take your son to William's sepulchre —

COLOBERN: — with a candle!

ANSFRIDA: The same dream, look!

COLOBERN: The two on us!

ANSFRIDA: So we go —

COLOBERN: — the bor with the candle in his hand —

ANSFRIDA: — and we pray.

COLOBERN: A long time.

ANSFRIDA: By the sepulchre.

COLOBERN: An' suddenly our bor he turn to us an' he say —

ANSFRIDA: — he say, 'Home now, let's go home now.'

COLOBERN: He were talking!

ANSFRIDA: Like he'd always been talking.

COLOBERN: An' we wept.

THOMAS: And we who stood by watching wept as well and gave praise to our Lord who had done great things by the hand of his Holy Martyr, William.

> [*There is a tumult of voices. Many want to reach the sepulchre.*
>
> *All now is spoken against the background of activity and music.*
>
> ELIAS *hobbles into view.*]

ELIAS [*protesting*]: This church was not erected to be a pilgrim's way.

THOMAS: From far and wide they came, with candles and coins.

ELIAS: It is a house of prayer, peace, reflection!

THOMAS: And the Church of Norwich grew rich from gratitude. Sing! Sing out!

ELIAS: The boy William must be moved from here.

THOMAS: The boy *martyr*! *St* William.

ELIAS: He will be deemed saint when the evidence is conclusive.

THOMAS: The evidence *is* conclusive.

ELIAS: Oh, Brother Thomas, your fervour is too intense for me.

THOMAS: You confuse me, Brother Elias. Why do you resist? We have been blessed with a saint. Miracles have been performed. Mighty works and miracles! Listen to the testimonies.

ELIAS: If such miracles are listened to, then I fear for the faith.

> [*He falters.*
> MONKS *go to his aid.*]

ELIAS: There is a chapel to the north side of the church. It was once used specially for the worship of Holy Martyrs –

THOMAS: – God be praised –

ELIAS: – transfer his body there. Pilgrims can approach without risk –

THOMAS: – sing! Sing out!

ELIAS: There must be peace inside the house of God.

THOMAS: Sing praise to the saint of Norwich. Let William hear your voices praise him, praise him, praise him!

> [THOMAS *has conducted the litany of miracles, whipping up fervour and ecstasy.*
>
> *All loudly sing the triumphant hymn of praise as the sepulchre and coffin are raised to be translated for the last time inside the Chapel of Martyrs.*
>
> *The last procession moves off.*
> *The hymn ends.*
> *The stage is empty.*
> *Silence.*]

SCENE 22

The sound of WILLIAM'S *scream.*
The light.
'The Jews! The Jews!'
The light dies.
Blackout.

WILD SPRING

a play in two acts

written for *Brenda Bruce*

Blaendigeddi
15 August 1992

CHARACTERS

Three characters to be played by two actors:

GERTRUDE MATTHEWS, a well-known actress, who ages from 44 to 59

SAMSON MARTIN, black, aged 19, a theatre car-park attendant

KENNEDY PHILLIPS, black, aged around 30, theatre-company manager

Both male parts to be played by the same actor

NOTE

The reason for suggesting one actor to play the two male roles is in order to give one actor a challenge. But it is not essential to the meaning of the play.

Also, for companies outside the UK where there is no black community the play will be as effective, with minor modifications, played to represent any group of outsiders, for example: Arabs in France; Turks in Germany; gypsies everywhere!

TIME AND PLACE

The play, except for one scene, is set in London over a period of fifteen years.

ACT ONE is set in 1976

ACT TWO is set in 1991

SETTINGS

. . . the childishly egotistical character of her acting, which is not the art of making you think more highly or feel more deeply, but the art of making you admire her, pity her, champion her, weep with her, laugh at her jokes, follow her fortunes breathlessly, and applaud her wildly when the curtain falls. It is the art of finding out all your weaknesses and practising on them — cajoling you, harrowing you, exciting you — on the whole fooling you . . .

– George Bernard Shaw on Sarah Bernhardt,
from *Dramatic Opinions and Essays: Volume 1*

ACT ONE

SCENE I

Spring 1976.

Actress GERTRUDE MATTHEWS (*we will call her* GERTIE), *with her back to us, is performing Lear's Fool to an unseen audience (Act III, Scene 2).*

Music is building through it.

GERTIE:

> This is a brave night to cool a courtezan.
> I'll speak a prophecy ere I go:
> When priests are more in word than matter;
> When brewers mar their malt with water;
> When nobles are their tailors' tutors;
> No heretics burn'd, but wenches' suitors;
> When every case in law is right;
> No squire in debt, nor no poor knight;
> When slanders do not live in tongues;
> Nor cut-purses come not to throngs;
> When usurers tell their gold i' the field;
> And bawds and whores do churches build;
> Then shall the realm of Albion
> Come to great confusion:
> Then comes the time, who lives to see 't,
> That going shall be us'd with feet.
> This prophecy Merlin shall make: for I live before his time.

[*Music at its height.*
  Lights down.]

363

SCENE 2

GERTIE's *dressing-room. Sound of applause. The play has ended.*

GERTIE, *petite, pugnaciously pretty, enters from the room where she has been disrobing; only the Fool's cap on her head remains from her costume. The rest is underwear.*

She is buoyant, bubbling. Pours herself a whisky.

She talks to her unseen dresser, Lottie, in the other room, through which comes a general backstage buzz.

GERTIE: My God, didn't they love all that tonight. A woman playing the Fool! They'll go home and tell their family and friends, 'Do you know, the Fool was played by Gertie Matthews, a woman! Fantastic!'

[*in front of the mirror*]

Sharp! Sharp, sharp, sharp!

[*to Lottie*] That's it, Lottie. I won't be needing anything else. Don't hang about. See you tomorrow.

[*Closes door. Turns down tannoy. Starts to take off make-up. Singing:*]

When that I was and a little tiny boy,
With hey, ho, the wind and the rain . . .

No! Stop that, Gertie! You can't carry the play around with you everywhere. Leave it alone, on stage, wash it out of your hair.

[*singing*]

I'm gonna wash ole Shakespeare out of my hair
I'm gonna wash ole Shakespeare out of my hair
I'm gonna wash ole Shakespeare out of my hair
Gonna send him on his way

[*closing her eyes*] If I close my eyes I can see everything that's wonderful about being alive.

You're in good spirits tonight, Gertie. What's happened? [*Pause.*] I'll give you three guesses. [*Pause.*] You've been asked to take over the company. God forbid! Confront actors' egos all day every day? [*Pause.*] You've discovered your mother is not really your mother, you were adopted. Ha! Wouldn't *that* change my life. [*Pause.*] You're going to be laid tonight. Wrong again! That would put me in very high spirits indeed, but all the men are dead as far as I can make out. Or emigrated. [*Pause.*] What, then? [*Pause.*] I'll tell you what then, you were stunning tonight, that's fucking what then. You were one hundred per cent in tune with your Fool and you knew it and they knew it and you knew they knew it, and they knew you knew and they loved you and you loved them and everybody loved everybody and it was electric and fantastic. Fan-fucking-tastic. [*Pause.*] Gawd! That's terrible! To be so dependent upon praise. To be so dependent upon the praise of an audience for your happiness – that's a shameful confession. Just a little love and admiration from anybody and you're anybody's!

[*Make-up is off. Contemplates herself in the mirror.*]

'You walk like a crab,' said my ballet teacher when my mother took me to classes, aged eight. 'I hope you don't dance like one.' *Do* I walk like a crab?

[*She stands and walks slightly sideways.*]

I suppose I do. But not on stage. On stage, Gertie Matthews, you're something else. Crab off stage but on stage – goddess!

[*Knock on her door.*]

Enter!

[SAMSON MARTIN, *black, the theatre's car-park attendant, pokes his head round the door, catching her in a 'goddess' stance.*
Her deified posture and scant dress startle him.]

SAM: Sorry, Miss Matthews. I'll come back.

GERTIE: It's OK, Sam. I may be half undressed but by the same token I'm half dressed.

[*She reaches for an old, exotic dressing-gown.*]

SAM: I thought you'd be finished, miss, so I brought your car keys.

GERTIE: You knew very well I wouldn't be finished, the applause is still ringing in our ears. Come in, sit down, pour yourself a whisky and prepare to listen to a lecture I'm going to give you.

SAM: I keep telling you, Miss Matthews, I don't like whisky.

GERTIE: What *do* you like?

SAM: I keep telling you, Miss Matthews, I like Coke.

GERTIE: Take a Coke, then, and listen. You didn't come to give me car keys. You normally give me my car keys as soon as you've parked the car – for which I'm very grateful because the car-park is meant for the audience not the players so I hope you do it very surreptitiously –

SAM: What's 'surreptitiously', Miss Matthews?

GERTIE: Stop that! How many times must I tell you don't play ignorant you're not good at it so I hope you do it very surreptitiously because I don't want you getting into trouble on my account. No! You came to share my company. You've got good taste – you like me. I've got good taste – I like you. We like each other. *You're* too young and *I'm* too old for this to be passion but let's be grateful for small blessings and try to be honest with one another.

SAM: I *was* being honest.

GERTIE [*ignoring him*]: My mum made *me* a liar because she didn't let me go out with the friends I liked, so I learned to lie like a chameleon. But you and me –

SAM: I *was* being honest.

GERTIE: You weren't.

SAM: I was.

GERTIE: You weren't.

SAM: Was.

GERTIE: Weren't.

SAM: Was.

GERTIE: Weren't.

SAM: Was.

GERTIE: Wasn't.

SAM: 'Wasn't'?

GERTIE: Yes. Wasn't. What's wrong with 'wasn't'?

SAM: Sounds funny.

GERTIE: Wasn't — was not.

SAM: You 'was not' being honest?

GERTIE: Didn't they teach you at school about the fun of playing with words?

SAM: Might've done. I wasn't listening.

GERTIE: You listened well enough to know 'wasn't' was incorrect.

SAM: I didn't *know* it, it just *sounded* wrong.

[*She goes into the other room to change.*]

GERTIE [*off stage*]: And the other reason for being honest is that the English mostly aren't, and if you want to get on in this cold and hostile society you've got to build a reputation for honesty.

SAM: Are you always honest, Miss Matthews?

GERTIE [*off stage*]: No! Do you think I'm crazy? I'm a woman, an actress, and white. As a woman if I were honest I'd never be able to hold a man; as an actress I get paid not to be honest; and being white *I* can get away with murder — but as you're black —

[*peeps round door*]

— you *are* black aren't you?

SAM: No, miss, I just haven't washed.

GERTIE: Oh sharp! Sharp, sharp, sharp!

[*Returns to continue changing.*]

But as you're black you've got to be twice as virtuous.

[*Long pause before she reappears.*]

Christ! I do talk nonsense, don't I? It's all more complex than that.

SAM: What does 'complex' mean?

GERTIE: Will you please *stop* that? You know perfectly well what 'complex' means. Pretending you're a car-park attendant! Do you enjoy the image of yourself as a 'car-park attendant'? People are always creating an image of themselves which they fall in love with and then can't get rid of. I'm encased in this image my mum inspired, bless her.

SAM: What image is that, Miss Matthews?

GERTIE: 'Don't you go thinking *you've* got talent, Gertie, it's just God's gift.' Not a bad image to fall in love with, modesty.

SAM: If it's true.

GERTIE: Sharp, sharp, sharp! But in your case it's not. You've confused modesty for self-denigration — don't you dare ask me what 'self-denigration' is — and if you're not careful, Sammy-son, Samson, you'll persuade yourself you can't be anything else but a car-park attendant. Frozen! For the rest of your life! Car-park attendant! Unable to discard it, even though God might have wanted you to be an astronaut. I, on the other hand, get paid for falling in love with countless images of myself which I can later discard. Where was I?

SAM: 'It's all more complex than that.'

GERTIE: Thank you. It's all more complex than that.

[*Pause.*]

What's more complex than what?

SAM: Needing to be twice as virtuous because you're black.

GERTIE: Oh yes. Did I say that?

SAM: 'Fraid so.

GERTIE: Well, it's *some*times true. The point is: there are no rules in life. One or two laws, like 'Thou shalt not kill'; or 'Fall off Big Ben and you'll hurt yourself'. But no rules. You make life up as you go along. You lie to those who can't take the truth

or don't deserve the truth, but when you find special friends,
like me, you're honest. Understood?

SAM: And can I lie to protect others?

GERTIE: Only if those others deserve protecting.

SAM: What if they're friends who've done wrong?

GERTIE: That's a moral dilemma you'll have to face yourself. I'm
no philosopher.

SAM: What's 'a moral dilemma'?

GERTIE: If you keep asking stupid questions I'll hit you.

SAM: I'm only a car-park attendant, you know.

GERTIE: Stop weeping for yourself. Now, my friend, I must
rush. My son's waiting to be tucked up and kissed to sleep and
then I've got a dinner date with colleagues who need me to
organize a committee for good works and I'm a good organ-
izer who loves being needed so off I go and why don't you
come and have Sunday lunch with me one day so's you can
get to meet Tom.

[SAM *seems uncertain.*]

He's only a mongol, not a vampire.

SAM: Cor! You don't half make jokes about strange things.

GERTIE: It's called 'black humour' – a way of surviving.

SAM: How old is he?

GERTIE: Seven. Now *he's* my passion. You'll love him. Everyone
does. Will you? Sunday lunch? See how the other half lives?

SAM: You're always making me do things I shouldn't be doing.

GERTIE: 'Shouldn't'?

SAM: You get me to eat food I ain't never eaten before, you get
me to see plays which make my friends laugh at me, you buy
me ties I don't have the shirts to go with. You even make me
read books! When I leave you and go home I don't know
who I am.

GERTIE: Join the club!

SAM: I'm serious.

GERTIE: OK. You're a car-park attendant. I'll try to remember
that. You were born to be a theatre car-park attendant. Come
for Sunday lunch and I'll make you hamburgers and chips.

SAM: I mean, it's not right to make someone what they're not.

GERTIE: It's worse to *imagine* you're someone you're not. I've got to go.

SAM: I mean, it's all right for people like you, Miss Matthews, you're famous, you're needed, you know where you're going.

GERTIE: Yes, and I've got to go there, Sam. We'll talk later.

SAM: I mean you don't know what it's like to —

GERTIE: I know very well what 'it's like to' but I've got to go. Sunday lunch. Hamburgers and chips. No pâtés. Promise.

[*She leaves.*

SAM *looks around. He loves the atmosphere of dressing-rooms.*]

SAM: She trusts you, Sam. You could pinch her watch which she's forgotten. [*Pockets her watch.*] You could steal this antique coffee-cup which'd fetch a bob or two. [*Pockets cup.*] I bet this old print is worth something. [*Slips it into his overalls.*]

[*imitating her*] 'My mum made *me* a liar because she didn't let me go out with the friends I liked, so I lie like a chameleon. But you and me —' She's always talking about her mum. 'My mum was a manipulator . . .' 'What's a manipulator, Miss Matthews?' 'My dad was hungry for affection but my mum was emotionally parsimonious . . .' 'What's "parsimonious", Miss Matthews?' 'Gertie hasn't got looks, said my mum, but she's got character . . .'

She has too. Aren't you lucky I like you, Miss Matthews? [*Returns print.*] Aren't you lucky I'm your friend, Miss Matthews? [*Returns cup.*] Aren't you lucky you can trust me, Miss Matthews? [*Returns watch.*] I've got a mum too, and she tell me, 'You steal, boy, and you end up messing your only life. And don't think 'cos I'm your mum I'll come running to bail you out, 'cos I won't.' So, Miss Matthews, we both got mums.

[*He says it in such a way that we're not certain.*]

[*closing his eyes*] If I close my eyes I can hear my head thinking.

[*He places the Fool's hat on his head. Preens himself. He's no actor but he's heard the lines many times.*]

This is a brave night to cool a courtezan —
I'll speak a prophecy ere I go . . .

'You steal, boy, and you end up messing your only life.' Good ole Mum.

[*He makes a joyful leap in the air, kicking his feet together.*]

You enjoy being trusted don't you, Sam boy?

[*Another leap.*
   Sound of applause.
   Taking off hat, he bows.
   The applause belongs to —]

SCENE 3

An award ceremony.

GERTIE *stands before a microphone, clutching a statue. She's crippled with embarrassment to have won.*

GERTIE: Well. What do I say? I know — that's what everyone asks: 'What do I say?' and then everyone thanks everyone. And I do. Everyone. Thank them . . . Oh dear — you can tell I didn't expect to win, I'm not prepared. Bit strange really. This. Such a coveted award. Just for playing the Fool. I should have lots of them if that's all it takes.

[*Waits for laughter.*]

I don't know . . . I'm . . . I'm . . . honoured. You all know that. It's more than honour, though, isn't it? If we're truthful it's also vindication. Your work and your faith have been vindicated. You've proved them wrong. Them! Those loving doubters. My mum, bless her, she meant well, but my mum used to say 'Gertie hasn't got looks but she's got character.' 'Character.' So, I win awards playing the Fool. Ha! Yes. Well. Vindicated. And justified. You hold something like this in your hand and you feel your existence is justified. As though you've earned the air you're breathing. I'd better stop now — I'll get even sillier or weep. Thank you.

[*She offers an unexpected and sweet curtsy.*
  Applause.
  Over it comes the voice and laughter of a mongol child. It's a moving and joyful sound. Mixed in with it is GERTIE'S *voice.*]

SCENE 4

GERTIE's *dining-room. Mixed styles, elegant, orderly. Full of memorabilia.*
SAM *is at table. Lunch is finished.*

GERTIE [*off stage*]: Enough now, Tom. You've played with Sam
and it's time for a sleep. Yes yes yes of course I love you. Yes,
I know, and you love me. Sing to you? But I can't leave Sam
all alone out there. [*calling*] Sam, you all right for a minute?
SAM: Fine, Miss Matthews.
GERTIE [*off stage*]: Have some more ice-cream cake if you want.
[*to Tom*] OK now, Tom. Just once. Promise if I sing it that
you won't ask me to sing it again. Just once. Promise?

[GERTIE *sings Feste's song from* Twelfth Night, *Act V,
Scene 1.*]

When that I was and a little tiny boy,
With hey, ho, the wind and the rain,
A foolish thing was but a toy,
For the rain it raineth every day.
With hey, ho, the wind and the rain,
For the rain it raineth every day.

[*While she sings the remaining verses off stage,* SAM *executes
some t'ai chi movements. Slow, surprising and beautiful.*

GERTIE *has obviously succeeded in singing her son to sleep
because she's backing out of his room with the last lines. A
touching scene: singing mother with her back to us,* SAM,
oblivious, doing his Chinese exercises.

*She turns and watches him a while until he realizes the
singing has stopped. He turns and sees her watching. He's
embarrassed.*]

GERTIE: I thought you were only the car-park attendant.

SAM: I'm the car-park attendant what can do t'ai chi, en I?

GERTIE: Can you teach me some movements?

SAM: Easy.

GERTIE: Go on, then.

SAM: Now?

GERTIE: Never put off till tomorrow what can be done today, my mum used to say. Pretty stupid saying I thought, but not always.

SAM: Try this.

[*He demonstrates an elementary movement. She follows. Another. She follows. A third. She follows.*]

GERTIE: I think I could become attached to this.

[*She repeats them on her own a number of times, talking meanwhile.*]

I didn't know anything was wrong with him for ages. He was just weeks old when I adopted him and the silly buggers in the adoption centre hadn't seen it. We took one look at each other, Tom and me, and fell in love. Couple of months later I took him for a routine check-up to our doctor who said nothing to me – because of course I was only the mother, a woman – but he rang my husband. 'You've adopted a mongol child.' Chilling news chillingly delivered. Chilled my husband. Chilled him for days. Then one morning at ten o'clock, two hours before a dress rehearsal of *Three Sisters*, he blurted it out. 'We've adopted a mongol child.' Buggered up rehearsals, I can tell you. Halfway through I broke down and the director yelled at me, 'I know you've had heartbreaking news but thank your lucky stars you've got your work so GET ON WITH IT!'

SAM: Why did your old man tell you on the day of a dress rehearsal?

GERTIE: Well you may ask. *I* never understood. But then there were a lot of things I didn't understand about my husband.

Of course our doctor was furious. He wanted to write letters all over the place but it was too late – we loved Tom too much by then.

[*She stops her t'ai chi movements.*]

Cor! Reveals muscles you didn't know you had. [*Pause.*] So, I never go anywhere without seeing him every night to sleep. Sleeps a lot, does Tom. Very energetic awake, very still asleep. [*Beat.*] Wadja think? Didn't you love him?

SAM: Yeah. But *I* don't have to be with him all the time.

GERTIE: I *can't* be with him all the time. Costs a bomb for a nanny. [*Pause.*] What do you see when you close your eyes?

[SAM *does so. Thinks about it.*]

SAM: Dying images of what I saw just before I closed them!

GERTIE: Will you never give a straight answer?

SAM: What you taking such a friendly interest in me for?

GERTIE: Friends don't ask questions like that. Friends know they're friends.

SAM: 'Friends', Miss Matthews?

GERTIE: I think it's about time you called me 'Gertie'.

SAM: I like calling you Miss Matthews.

GERTIE: Suit yourself.

SAM: Friends? Me nineteen you forty-four?

GERTIE: How did you know my age?

SAM: I didn't. You just told me.

GERTIE: Oh sharp. Sharp, sharp, sharp!

SAM: You ain't doing good deeds, are you, Miss Matthews? Me black, you white?

GERTIE: Yes. Of course I'm doing good deeds. What's wrong with good deeds?

SAM: People should do what makes them happy, not what makes them look good.

GERTIE: Good deeds *make* me happy and I *like* looking good! Jesus, what's got into you, Sam?

SAM: My mum always told me, 'Beware of Good-Deed-Doers.'

GERTIE: Well, mums are a mixed blessing. We all know that.

SAM: You do a lot of good deeds?

GERTIE: Can't do enough of them. You ask me, I'll do it. Makes up for all the bad deeds I do.

SAM: Bad deeds? You?

GERTIE: You really probe, don't you?

SAM: Not bad for a car-park attendant you mean?

GERTIE: A car-park attendant!

SAM: Well, some's got it and some ain't.

GERTIE: Haven't.

SAM: Haven't.

GERTIE: And you – haven't.

SAM: To be what? See me acting? See me painting? See me being an architect, a doctor, a lawyer, a politician, a deep-sea diver?

GERTIE: The alternative is being a car-park attendant?

SAM: If I can't be any of those things . . .

GERTIE: A car-park attendant! Nice image to fall in love with.

SAM: Aren't you in love with *your* image? Good-Deed-Doer?

GERTIE: Probe *and* hurt. Yes. I enjoy the image of myself being useful. Nothing useful about being an actor. Once you know you can do it you just go on doing it. The audience applauds, goes home, and you're left wondering what you did. Played a role. Someone else's words. Someone else's image.

SAM: Which you fell in love with!

GERTIE: Oh sharp. Sharp, sharp, sharp!

SAM: For a car-park attendant.

GERTIE: That really is a chip and a half on your shoulder.

SAM: Got lots more where that came from.

GERTIE: How fortunate you are. Wish I had a few chips to lean on. I've got nothing to complain about and no one to blame.

SAM: Except your mum.

GERTIE: Mums are always a good stand-by for off-loading blame. Problem with my mum was she taught me to blame myself. For everything. 'Don't annoy people, don't contradict them, don't ask favours, don't lose your temper, don't complain, don't bang doors . . .' She made me feel I had to apologize for the air I breathed.

She was tiny. Very tiny. And strong. Gave my poor dad a

rough ole time – worked for a boot and shoe factory as a commercial traveller. Hated it. I only ever saw him when he came home at weekends, so Mum and I went twice a week to the pictures and I spent the rest of my time imagining I was Doris Day or Marlene Dietrich. They were second cousins, you know. Mum and Dad, that is, not Doris and Marlene. Dad thought she was a saint. Not Marlene, Mum. She only married him to please *her* mum. Mum's mum, that is, not Marlene's. [*Beat.*] You do know who Marlene Dietrich and Doris Day are, don't you?

[SAM *nods his head but says 'no'.*]

How do you do that?

[*She shakes her head but can only say 'no', nods it and can only say 'yes'.*]

I can't do it.

[SAM *gives another demonstration, shaking and nodding his head and saying the contrary word.*]

Stop it! Makes me dizzy.

SAM: Go on telling me about your mum.

GERTIE: 'The only person in the world worth loving is your mother.' Subtle! Never understood the possibility you might meet someone else. And as for sex. 'It's all disgusting, and women never enjoy it!'

SAM: Learned about it from books did you?

GERTIE: Books? *Books?* There *were* no books in the house. You weren't supposed to *read*. I joined Boots library and read under the bedclothes with a torch. No books, no conversation, no social conscience, no sex. Just guilts. There was so much I shouldn't do that I did and lied about, it was such a don't-do-this-or-that upbringing that I was riddled with guilts. And so if anything goes wrong I know it's me who's made it go wrong. You may have noticed – I walk like a crab, as though there's always something to avoid. You're lucky. You're black. You can blame everybody for everything. I've got no

377

one except myself to blame, at which I am an expert, believe me. So you stay a car-park attendant, Sam, you can blame a car-park attendant's life on a whole number of things. Cosy. Try to be something more you might fail then you'll have to blame yourself. Not so cosy.

SAM: You *are* a talker, aren't you, Miss Matthews?

GERTIE: Thank you.

SAM: I like listening to you.

GERTIE: Thank you.

SAM: Even though you don't always make sense.

GERTIE: Thank you.

SAM: Why don't I always make sense, Sam?

GERTIE: Why don't I always make sense, Sam?

SAM: I'm glad you asked me that, Miss Matthews. Your mum made you feel everything was your fault, right?

GERTIE: Right.

SAM: She was wrong to make you feel everything was your fault, right?

GERTIE: Right.

SAM: But you think I should try to be more than a car-park attendant so that if I fail it can only be my fault, right?

GERTIE: Right.

SAM: So your mum was wrong to make you blame yourself, but you're right to want me in a situation where only I can take the blame, right?

GERTIE: Right.

SAM: How can two contradictory situations both be right?

GERTIE: Because that's life.

SAM: You don't let me get away with nothing.

GERTIE: Anything.

SAM: Nothing.

GERTIE: If I *don't* let you get away with nothing it means I *do* let you get away with something. So – anything.

SAM: See what I mean?

GERTIE: Oh sharp. Sharp, sharp, sharp!

SAM [*shaking his head*]: Oh yes, yes, yes.

GERTIE: Stop that! Stop it!

A beach.
  High winds. Raging sea. Exhilarating. Near by — a rock.
  GERTIE's *voice calling above the sound.*

GERTIE [*off stage*]: Sam! Sam! Don't get too near. An unexpected
  wave could grab and drag you down to old Davy's locker.

  [*She appears on the rock, warmly dressed for gales.*]

  Blow, winds, and crack your cheeks! rage! blow!
  You cataracts and hurricanoes, spout
  Till you have drench'd our steeples, drown'd the cocks! ★

  [*Pause to call again.*]

Sam! Sam!

  You sulph'rous and thought-executing fires,
  Vaunt-couriers of oak-cleaving thunder bolts,
  Singe my white head! And thou, all shaking thunder,
  Strike flat the thick rotundity o' the world!
  Crack Nature's moulds, all germens spill at once
  That make ingrateful man!

  [SAM, *similarly dressed and with a haversack, has appeared*
  during this and stood, as audience, looking up.
      They must shout at each other to be heard.]

I should have played Lear, not his fool. Wadya think?
SAM: As a king or a queen?
GERTIE: A queen. Queen Leah and her three sons. Question is —

★ *King Lear*, Act III, Scene 2.

would a queen have been as stupid as a king and not recognized the sweet honesty of her youngest son?

SAM: Women's intuition, right!

GERTIE: If *my* youngest son told me, 'I love you according to my bond, no more no less,' I'd know exactly what he meant.

SAM: Which is why the old bard made Lear a man, didn't he? Have a woman – there'd be no play.

GERTIE [*referring to the high winds*]: Exhilarating, isn't it?

SAM: Yeah. Wild.

GERTIE: Help me down.

> [*He does so.*
> *From the haversack he withdraws a groundsheet and lays it in a sheltered part of the rock.*
> GERTIE *dips into the haversack for a hip flask and a Coke. They sit to drink.*
> *The sound of the elements fades.*]

GERTIE [*referring to brandy*]: I knew this would come in handy.

> [*She unscrews and pours.*]

SAM: When did you know you was going to be an actress?

GERTIE: When I was three years old I announced, 'I, Gertrude Matthews, am going to be a fairy.' Cheers. [*Drinks.*]

SAM: Cheers. Simple as that? [*Drinks.*]

GERTIE: Nothing's as simple as that. I caught double pneumonia at two and lost the use of my legs. Had to be taught to walk again. Doctor advised dancing lessons. Pah-poum! Start of brilliant career.

SAM: 'I, Gertrude Matthews, am going to be a fairy.' Sounds easy. 'I, Samson Martin, am going to be a –'

GERTIE: A what?

SAM: Well, not a fairy, that's for sure.

GERTIE: A car-park attendant. We know.

SAM: Yeah. I forgot. 'I, Samson Martin, am going to be a car-park attendant.'

GERTIE: In sickness and in health, for better or for worse . . .

SAM: Till death do us part.

GERTIE: Amen.

SAM: So, you decided to be a fairy. What then?

[*Long pause.*]

GERTIE: When I close my eyes [*she does*] I can see Palmers Green. The tiny, dreary, two-up two-down behind the curtains of which, wrote the poet, are people living out their lives of quiet desperation. I don't think my mum knew she was doing that but when I close my eyes I can smell the acrid smell of the kitchen range which she'd painted silver. She *was*. Quietly desperate. Nothing pleased her. She found *joy* in no one and no thing.

There *was* a time when she got excited. The early days. When I close my eyes I can see Dad frantically making props and Mum sewing on sequins for my first dress in my first public appearance – Miss Milligan's Dancing Display. But there was this girl called Renée Harmer, 'the Harmer Girl', and when I close my eyes I can hear Mum saying, 'If only you smiled like the Harmer girl. Renée Harmer is so pretty. You watch the Harmer girl, *she'll* go places.' Practised like the furies, but it wasn't enough for my mum.

When I close my eyes I can see photographers flashing. I can see Mum taking my make-up off with margarine. I can hear the compliments of anyone who was anyone in North London. And all ending, every Saturday, year in year out, eating raisin sandwiches and drinking cocoa.

When I close my eyes I can see my dad painting. Landscapes. That's all he wanted to be – a landscape painter. He was a dreamer with never enough talent to make his dreams come true but just enough sense never to wake up.

When I close my eyes I can see every blister like a medal, feel every headache like tokens of triumph.

[*Long pause.*]

What do you see when you close *your* eyes?

SAM: When I close my eyes [*closes them*] – hills. Purple hills. Behind me. In front – a beach. All sand. No stones. No stones and no people. I'm lying flat on my back. Bermuda shorts, pattern from playing cards – red diamonds, black spades, red hearts, black clubs. My eyes are closed. Suddenly – I feel a snake. Crawling over me. Up my leg, my sides, under my armpit. It stays there. Curled up and snug. I'm terrified. Can't move. Can't open my eyes. Hours pass. Hours and hours and hours. It's night. I can hear the tide getting closer. And closer. And closer. Water's touching my feet. Covering my legs. I've got to move. I've *got* to. I move. The snake bites. I die.

[*Long pause.*]

GERTIE: Try again.

SAM: When I close my eyes – screaming. Dad beats Mum. Mum beats sister. Sister beats me. I beat brothers. Blood. When I close my eyes – blood and screaming. No one listens. No one to no one. Screaming. Blood.

GERTIE: Too purple. Too pretentious. Try again.

SAM: When I close my eyes –

[*With eyes closed he struggles.*]

– when I close my eyes –

[*Struggles more.*]

– when I close my eyes –

[*Struggle turns to distress as though he were an epileptic, which he's not.*

GERTIE *feels she must hold him or he'll explode. He nestles in her arms, calmed.*]

When I close my eyes I'm all feeling. Can't see *anything* really. Can't think anything either.

GERTIE: Maybe you *hear* instead? Family voices?

[*He thinks about this.*]

SAM:

'Where you going, Mum?'
'Out! Away from you bloody lot.'

'Don't go, Mum. I'll keep them quiet.'
'What, this brood? Quiet? Not till hell freezes over.'
'Where you going, Dad?'
'Out.'
'Out where?'
'Just out! Anywhere but here.'
'Don't go, Dad. We'll paint the living-room.'
'You all give me grief, you know that? Grief!'

GERTIE: Feudin' family, huh?

SAM: Nah! Everybody loved everybody, only nobody loved themselves.

GERTIE: Unlike the English who hate each other and love only themselves. And even then not much.

SAM: Not true. Some of my best friends are English.

GERTIE: Like me?

SAM: Yeah. Like you.

[*He kisses her lightly on the lips. It's a moment.*]

I've never had a white woman.

GERTIE: You're not having one now.

SAM: You mean that's it? One kiss?

GERTIE: You can have another if you like, even a third if you promise not to catch fire, but nothing more.

SAM: Wrong colour?

GERTIE: Wrong age.

SAM: I don't think you're too old.

GERTIE: Thank you. But I think you're too young. Find someone your own age.

SAM: I don't like young girls.

GERTIE: It's time to go, Sam.

SAM: All they think about is sex.

GERTIE: Disgusting.

SAM: I like women who've lived.

GERTIE: Weather-beaten, you mean. On your feet.

SAM: This the brush-off, then?

GERTIE: Don't be dramatic.

SAM: Did I tell you my mum died?

GERTIE [*sympathetically*]: Oh, Sam.

SAM: My dad won the premium bonds. Hundred thousand pounds. Ran off with the lot. Broke my mum's heart. Gave her cancer.

GERTIE: You're lying.

SAM: We never heard from him again.

GERTIE: You mustn't lie about such things, they come true.

SAM: Sent me off the rails, I can tell you.

GERTIE: I'm not listening to your lies. They upset me.

SAM: Started robbing Paki newsagents and pushing white girls around.

GERTIE: I think there's a storm coming up.

SAM: They nabbed me in the end. Three years' detention.

[*No response.*]

Where I found God.

[*No response.*]

Joined the Salvation Army when I came out.

GERTIE: Are you going to stop?

SAM: Are you going to kiss me?

GERTIE: This spring's getting too wild for me. My mother always warned – spring! Beware the wild spring. I'm going.

SAM: Kiss?

GERTIE: Oh sharp. Sharp, sharp, sharp!

[*She offers her lips to him.*
He kisses her lightly, not wildly.
The wind howls and only the sea is wild.]

SCENE 6

SAM's *bed-sitter. He's ill in bed. Caught cold by the sea.*

GERTIE *in a chair at his bedside. He's just finishing a plate of soup she's made and brought to him.*

GERTIE: The Scots swear by it. Broth. Scotch broth. My husband's mother taught me how to make it. *She* wasn't Scottish but her husband was. [*Beat.*] My husband's father. [*Beat.*] She was his second wife. [*Beat.*] My husband's step-mother. [*Beat.*] Don't try to work it out. [*Beat.*] The only thing she ever *did* teach me. Didn't rate me very high, my stepmother-in-law. Said I was the dullest thing on two legs.

[*He's finished the soup.*]

SAM: Great. Thanks.

GERTIE: *You* don't think I'm the dullest thing on two legs, do you?

SAM: What's this full of foolishness you are?

GERTIE: Are you Caribbean-talking to me?

SAM: Me don't wan' no foolish conversation wi' you.

GERTIE: Me *what*?

SAM: Me tink time's come we talk de trut.

GERTIE [*attempting it*]: You're no capable of talking de trut, mun.

SAM: You'd make a rotten black woman.

GERTIE: So would you.

SAM: Jesus Christ! I ain't never been so ill.

GERTIE: Have you taken your temperature?

SAM: What with?

GERTIE: Funny you should ask. It so happens that here in my bag . . .

[*She draws out a thermometer.*]

Now, you know what you can do with this, don't you?

SAM: Under my tongue?

GERTIE: Not this thermometer.

SAM: Under my arm?

GERTIE: Not this thermometer.

SAM: You don't mean —?

GERTIE: I do mean!

SAM: But that's rude.

GERTIE: And accurate.

SAM: You're corrupting me.

GERTIE: Do you want to live or die?

SAM: There's more than one way of dyin', ya know.

GERTIE: Oh sharp —

GERTIE and SAM [*together*]: — sharp, sharp, sharp.

SAM: *You* do it.

GERTIE: Not so likely. It does *not* befit our relationship.

SAM: What if you were a nurse?

GERTIE: Well I'm not a nurse. I'm an actress.

SAM: Act nurse to me.

GERTIE: Not even if you were Juliet in drag.

SAM: It could be your most rewarding role.

GERTIE: Will you stick this where it counts so's we can know how hot you are?

SAM: I don't need no thermometer up my arse to tell me how hot I am. I *know* how hot I am. I'm *very* hot. I'm so hot I'm burning underneath these blankets. [*Lifts them.*] Feel.

GERTIE: Sa–am!

[*She thrusts thermometer into his hand and discreetly turns away.*
He runs a finger down her back. She shifts forward out of reach.
Comic scene as he wriggles to find 'the entrance'.]

SAM: Oooh, it's cold. [*wriggles*] I can't find it. Where is it? I've lost it. [*wriggles*] Ah. [*Finds it. Pushes.*] Mmmmm. [*Beat.*] Nice.

GERTIE: That day out by the sea. You weren't dressed warmly enough.

SAM: Which is why I needed to be kissed –

GERTIE: Only twice.

SAM: – which is why I caught cold. Denied the warmth of your passion.

GERTIE: Passion is rare, to be offered sparingly.

SAM: To husbands.

GERTIE: That's right.

SAM: Surprised your mum ever let you get married.

GERTIE: On my wedding day I caught her looking dramatically out of the window –

SAM: Little drama-queen was she?

GERTIE: That was her! 'You all right, Mum?' I asked. 'I'm all right,' she replied. 'It's just that now you've left me my life is over and I don't think I'll be alive next year.'

SAM: Great send off.

GERTIE: She meant well.

SAM: Happy marriage was it?

GERTIE: Ups and downs.

SAM: What were the downs?

GERTIE: His secretary moving in.

SAM: I'm sorry.

GERTIE: Don't be sorry. She said she'd never been so well looked after.

SAM: Did you ever get happy again?

GERTIE: You're getting very personal.

SAM: What are friends for?

[*Pause, as she considers.*]

GERTIE: The last six months of Gerry dying were the happiest. Poor Gerry. Had to wait to die to be happy. He wanted to get back into theatre directing after running a TV company but no one wanted to know. Went cap-in-hand to theatres in the sticks – turned down! After being so famous, one of the early TV personalities – turned down.

SAM: Tough.

GERTIE: Very tough.

SAM: What did he do?

GERTIE: Opened a pub. I did the cooking.

SAM: Famous actress cooking in a pub?

GERTIE: I was given some of the best roles of the season and I cooked in between rehearsals.

SAM: Mrs Everybody were you?

GERTIE: One and a half years later he was dead. One year out of work, year and a half running the pub – dead! And the six months nursing him in the hotel were the happiest.

SAM: Happiest? Nursing the dying?

GERTIE: Probably because I was needed! Needed to be part of a company, needed to be part of a family. Needed to be needed.

SAM: How could you play leading roles, look after Tom, cook pub food, and nurse a dying man, for Christ's sake?

GERTIE: Piece of cake. Boring just being an actress.

SAM: You *do* see yourself as Mrs Everybody, don't you?

GERTIE: That thermometer –

SAM: Mrs Ordinary Everybody!

GERTIE: – should be boiling by now.

SAM: It's called inverted snobbery.

GERTIE: Give!

[*Another comic scene as he pretends he can't find it.*]

SAM: Oh! Where is it? Where'd I put it? I've lost it. Help! I've swallowed it.

[*She turns abruptly to him. He holds it up. She holds out her hand for it.*]

SAM [*handing it to her*]: Cor! You're taking risks, aren't you?

[*She peers.*]

GERTIE: You've got a temperature all right. Hundred and one point one.

[*She goes off.*]

388

Sound of tap running.]

[*voice off, bossy*] You'll stay in bed for a week. I'll bring you food and hot lemon drinks and you'll sweat it out. I'll change your sheets, wash your pyjamas, and bring you books to read. I'll also speak to the office to make sure you don't lose pay. You'll be better than new before you can say Ginger Rogers.

SAM: I thought it was Jack Robinson.

[*She returns with a wet flannel.*]

GERTIE: I don't know who Jack Robinson is.

SAM: I don't know who Ginger Rogers is.

GERTIE: I may be older but you're not *that* much younger. Here, lie still with this on your forehead.

[*He lies back. He's really very weak.*]

SAM: I'm grateful, Gertie.

GERTIE: Hush.

SAM: Serious now. I had a rotten mum. Not rotten, she just didn't know how to be a mum. Which is strange if you think about it. It's usually the black mums who know how to be mums while the black dads don't know how to be dads. But my dad's all right. Works as a ticket inspector on the Underground.

GERTIE: And your mum?

SAM: She really is dead. Only not from cancer. And there was no hundred thousand pounds either. [*Pause.*] Mmm! This is lovely.

GERTIE: The flannel is cooling.

SAM: It's not the flannel, it's being looked after.

GERTIE: Don't be maudlin.

SAM: What's 'maudlin'?

GERTIE: Saaaammmm . . .

SAM: Well, I reckon some of the best things in life are maudlin − like love, having babies, ice-cream, being looked after . . .

GERTIE: Hush, you'll tire yourself out.

SAM: Cor, I suddenly feel — whacked, weak. I've *never* felt so weak. I just want to sleep. Sink into the bed, close my eyes and sleep.

GERTIE: Then close your eyes and sleep, darling.

SAM: They're so heavy.

GERTIE: Don't fight it. Close them.

SAM: Couldn't keep them open if I wanted to.

GERTIE: Sleep.

SAM: It's the middle of the afternoon.

GERTIE: Sleep.

SAM: When I close my eyes . . .

GERTIE: Sleep.

SAM: Goodnight, Mrs Ordinary Everybody.

GERTIE: A car-park attendant indeed!

SCENE 7

GERTIE'S *dressing-room in half-light.*
   But first, off stage, GERTIE *as Lady Macbeth (Act II, Scene 2).*

GERTIE'S VOICE:

> *That which hath made them drunk hath made me bold:*
> *What hath quench'd them hath given me fire. — Hark! — Peace!*
> *It was the owl that shriek'd, the fatal bellman,*
> *Which gives the stern'st good-night. He is about it.*
> *The doors are open; and the surfeited grooms*
> *Do mock their charge with snores: I have drugg'd their possets,*
> *That death and nature do contend about them,*
> *Whether they live, or die.*

> [*Voice fades.*
>   *Silence.*
>   *Applause. Lights up in dressing-room.*
>   SAM *enters backwards, followed by a dazed* GERTIE. *She's wearing Lady Macbeth's nightdress.*)

SAM: You were fantastic tonight. Fan-fucking-tastic.
GERTIE: I know it.
SAM: Best ever.
GERTIE: I know it, I know it.
SAM: Why? Out of nowhere. Just like that. Why?
GERTIE: I don't know.
SAM: I've never seen such an audience. They were —
GERTIE: — electrified. I know it.
SAM: Why does it happen?
GERTIE: I don't know.
SAM: *How* does it happen?
GERTIE: I don't know, I don't know.

SAM: You must know.

GERTIE: You're asking questions, Samson Martin, which touch on the deepest mysteries of life. Don't!

SAM: I want to know.

GERTIE: I don't want to think about it. Something like that happens you don't ask questions, you get down on your knees and you give thanks.

SAM: Then how do you know how to do it again?

GERTIE: You don't! And when you think you do, you fail.

SAM: Well, you don't do *nothing*. You don't go out with your fingers crossed.

GERTIE: You rehearse.

SAM: Yeah. We know all about rehearse, don't we? Actresses rehearse and rehearse and ask deeply serious questions and look deeply, deeply thoughtful – nothing! Zilch!

GERTIE [*insisting*]: You rehearse.

SAM: You're frightened to admit the truth aren't you, Mrs Everybody?

[*No response.*]

Mrs Ordinary Everybody.

[*No response.*]

Some people 'ave got it and some people ain't!

GERTIE: Haven't.

SAM: And you'd like to think that everybody's got it 'cos you like thinking we're all one happy family. But we ain't.

GERTIE: Aren't.

SAM: Some is and some isn't. Some 'ave and some 'aven't. Am I right, Mrs Everybody? Mrs Everybody! Mrs Ordinarybody! Mrs Ordinary Everybody. All that modesty stuff. [*mocking*] 'I don't know where it comes from. I just go out there and do it. It's not me, really. I want to thank the director and my designer and my husband who stood by me and the carpenter and –

GERTIE: – and God –

SAM: – and God –

GERTIE: — and the car-park attendant —

SAM: — inverted snobbery! You ain't just ordinary everybody. Your mum made mischief. You're Mrs Special Body. *You've* got it, *they* 'aven't.

GERTIE: Don't you talk to me about 'special' and 'who's got it' and 'who hasn't', Mr Car-park Attendant, Mr Wet-rag, Mr Window-wiper, Mr Wheel-changer!

SAM: I haven't got it!

GERTIE: That's right. You're black. I forgot. [*Beat.*] A car-park attendant indeed! Get off my back and go to college.

SAM: To do what?

GERTIE: How the hell should I know? All I know is I'd prefer you to use your intelligence on a tough professor instead of hitting poor little me over the head with it. I've had a great night. I'm the toast of the company. You should be showering me with care and loving kindness.

SAM [*contrite*]: Bloody hell. I'm sorry. After such a performance. Rotten of me. Sorry.

[*Pause.*]

GERTIE [*calling to her dresser*]: Lottie? You can go, love. I'll chuck the nightdress into my own wash. See you tomorrow.

SAM: You roared like a bull.

GERTIE: How about 'raged like the possessed'?

SAM: How about 'delivered like a demon'?

GERTIE: How about 'shone like the sun'?

SAM: How about 'erupted like a volcano'?

GERTIE: How about 'flashed like a falling star'?

SAM: You mean 'shooting star'?

GERTIE: Do I?

[*Pause. Reflects on that.*]

Stars have to fall some day.

SAM: Some do, some don't. Like some 'ave got it and some ain't. [*Beat.*] Haven't.

[*Phone rings.* SAM *answers it. Listens. Holds out phone to* GERTIE.]

For you. Nanny.

[*She suddenly seems frightened. Doesn't take it. Cups her hand over receiver instead.*]

GERTIE: What does she sound like?

SAM [*uncomprehending*]: What?

GERTIE: Her voice. What did it sound like? Light? Heavy?

SAM: I don't know. I didn't listen. Strict. Like nannies.

GERTIE: She's not a strict nanny. Oh God!

[*She moans, sits.*]

SAM: What's happening?

[*She takes the phone.*]

GERTIE: Nanny? [*listens*] Confirmed? [*listens*] I'm coming.

[*Blackout.*]

SCENE 8

TOM's *bedside.*
  GERTIE *there.*

GERTIE: I'm sorry, Tom. Some things I could do for you, some
I couldn't. Some things I can help, some I can't. But Mum
will look after you. That's what mums are for aren't they, to
look after their children, be there, run around for them? And
there's no doubt I run around for you. Got me running
around all over the place, haven't you, on the end of your
little string? I shouldn't let you do it, you'll grow up spoilt
and impossible. You're not very possible now, are you, poor
ole fellow? God made you only half possible. Wonder why he
did that? Got tired halfway, did he? Do you think he did that
with most of us? Got tired halfway? Feels like it sometimes,
that I'm only half made. It's all right when I'm up there on the
stage being wonderful and loved and admired, but there's the
rest of the time.

　　Still – the rest of the time is you, isn't it? Thank God for
you, Tom. Acting and looking after you go well together.
There's only half of you and only half of me, which makes a
good fit I'd say. Wouldn't you? So don't close your eyes,
Tom, stay awake with me. I need you. To fit the other half.
You'll make him stay, won't you, God? I mean, I know you
work in mysterious ways, but don't be too mysterious. Not
all the time. I mean – give yourself a break, throw a little
light on things now and then, I've got to understand something . . . Don't be mean about meaning, there's a good God.

SCENE 9

Rehearsal room.
    GERTIE *rehearsing Gertrude in* Hamlet (*Act III, Scene 4*).
    SAM *watching.*

GERTIE:

> *Alas, how is't with you,*
> *That you do bend your eye on vacancy,*
> *And with th' incorporal air do hold discourse?*
> *Forth at your —*

> [*She's interrupted by 'the director'.*]

Yes, James? [*listens*] Why do you want me to make a question of the *whole* line? [*listens*] Yes, I know she's bewildered, but I think you'll get the right emotion if you get the meaning first, and *I* think Gertrude is asking Hamlet why he's talking to the air. 'Th' incorporal air' is what I should go for. [*demonstrates*] Hamlet asks her, 'Alas how is't with you?' She responds:

> *Alas, how is't with you,*
> *That you do bend your eye on vacancy,*
> *And with th' incorporal air do hold discourse?*

Your way it's — well, listen:

> [*Demonstrates, applying the questioning tone on each of the three lines.*]

> *Alas, how is't with you,*
> *That you do bend your eye on vacancy,*
> *And with th' incorporal air do hold discourse?*

I think it comes out too — heavy. But can I finish it please? I don't think I've ever had a chance to deliver this speech through to the end without you interrupting me.

[*The combination of her anguish over* TOM *dying and irritation with the director gives extra depth to her rendering of the passage.*

She delivers it as though asking TOM *to 'sprinkle cool patience' and not look at death.*]

Alas, how is't with you,
That you do bend your eye on vacancy,
And with th' incorporal air do hold discourse?
Forth at your eyes your spirits wildly peep,
And, as the sleeping soldiers in th' alarm,
Your bedded hair, like life in excrements,
Start up and stand an end. O gentle son,
Upon the heat and flame of thy distemper
Sprinkle cool patience. Whereon do you look?

[*It was moving. Waits for her note.*]

Did you? Yes, well, I'm feeling a little sad today, perhaps that helps. [*listens*] Oh, nothing serious. Just one of those days. It'll pass. [*listens*] What a strange question. *Every* actor thinks there's more than one way to deliver a line. [*Pause.*] But to tell you the truth, now you ask, I'm not certain. I think, oh dear, I'm not sure I can say this, you'll disagree violently, but I have this horrible suspicion there's probably only *one* right way to deliver a line and all the time we're struggling to find it — that one right way. And we think each time we do it differently, each time another actor is doing it differently, that we're giving a different 'interpretation'. But we're not. It's not really interpretation, is it? We do it differently because we can't *help* doing it differently — we are each of us different and in our different ways we're struggling to find the one right way to deliver it, to get the line into focus. A bit like life — we struggle to find the one right way to live it, to get it in focus, get back to paradise. Never succeed of course. Paradise is unattainable and life's always out of focus, isn't it? But that doesn't stop us aiming for paradise, focus, the one right way. [*Pause.*] Can I tell you a story – perhaps it's time for a break?

[SAM *brings her a chair to sit on.* GERTIE *may or may not sit on it.*]

I was at a dinner once, not theatre people but – others. A mixed crowd – writers, business people, media – and I happened to say to my neighbour at the dinner table just what I've said now, that there's probably only one right way to deliver a line. And this neighbour, a businessman, turned abruptly on me and said, 'Well I think that's the biggest load of nonsense I've ever heard.' Rude and abrupt. No discussion, just insult. It hurt, I can tell you. So I shut up. Went silent. Sulked probably.

And the hostess could see something was wrong, so she asked what had happened. And the whole table went quiet and turned to us. Terrifying. But I thought: I'll try something out. And I told them. 'This man,' I said, 'this gentleman on my right here, we were having a discussion about acting and I put it to him that there was probably only one right way to deliver a line, and he said –

[*She imitates an exaggeratedly apologetic man.*]

'Well I think that's the biggest load of nonsense I've ever heard.' At which he protested, saying, 'No, no! I didn't say it like that. I don't have a pathetic nature.' 'Oh, of course,' I said, 'you said it like this.'

[*She imitates an exaggeratedly loud and aggressive man.*]

'Well I think that's the biggest load of nonsense I've ever heard!' At which he protested again. 'No, no! I didn't say it like that either. I don't have a belligerent nature.' 'Oh, I'm sorry,' I said. 'Do you mean there's only one right way you delivered your line?'

[*She allows this to sink in.*

Despite the intensity of her anecdote her mind is elsewhere.
The 'director' is questioning her.]

[*listening*] Yes, something *is* wrong. Tom is dying. Leukaemia.
[*listening*] Yes – in *very* mysterious ways.

SCENE 10

TOM's *bedside*.
GERTIE *there*.

GERTIE: *O gentle son, upon the heat and flame of thy distemper, sprinkle cool patience. Whereon do you look?*

Not at death, Tom. Don't take any notice of the old Reaper. He's looking for ancients. Those who've lived a long life, those who are tired. Not you, Tom. You've got ages and ages and ages and ages. I've got plans for you. Plans you'll like. Travel to weird and wonderful places. Don't go from me, lovely boy. Behave, now. I don't want to be a lonely old woman.

SCENE 11

A crematorium.
  Hum of people.
  Music: Adagio from Mozart's string trio, E flat 'Divertimento'.
  GERTIE *comforted by* SAM.

GERTIE: I think I wanted to be a mother more than anything
   else. So many miscarriages. Thought the fault was mine, like I
   always think the fault was mine. Our doctor offered to test us.
   Gerry refused. So I went when I still had some of him inside
   me. She showed me what was under the microscope. Gerry's
   were flat out, exhausted, mine were up there dancing. [*small
   laugh*] Poor Gerry. I didn't tell him. We just adopted Tom.
   [*Pause.*] Oh Tom, Tom, Tom.

   [*Pulls herself together.*]

Do you realize – if I evaporated at four in the morning I'd not
   leave a hole in anyone's life?
SAM: I'd –
GERTIE: Don't say *you'd* miss me. And if you did you'd soon get
   over it.
SAM: What about –
GERTIE: What about no one! There's no one. You blacks and the
   Jews have hundreds of aunts and cousins all over the place.
   I've got no one.
   Do you know, when my dad died he said to Gerry, 'Don't
   let Mum swallow up Gertie any more.' Poor Dad. I only got
   to know anyone was there in his last months. It's always the
   last months. I didn't even know what his politics were? I just
   knew he used to stand up at night in the living-room when
   the National Anthem played on telly. [*Pause.*] What made me

think of that suddenly? This solemn atmosphere, I suppose.
[*Pause.*] Poor Gerry. Glad he's not alive for this death.

[*They share a smile.*]

SAM: Want to hold my hand?
GERTIE: What, with all that lot watching?
SAM: They'll understand.
GERTIE: They won't! But who cares. Just for a minute.

[*He holds out his hand and she takes it.*]

Oh, I'll recover. We all do. Survive and recover. Problem
with me is I feel guilty about it. Everything pains me, even
surviving. Terrible affliction.

[*Suddenly, as though struck with divine revelation, but really
she's flipped.*]

He's alive. Tom's not dead, he's alive. I know it.
SAM: Gertie, easy now.
GERTIE [*Shouting to 'Funeral Director'*]: Open his coffin!
SAM: Gertie, don't do this.
GERTIE: I know he's still alive. I want his coffin opened.
SAM: You're upset, Gertie.
GERTIE: I feel it. I want his coffin opened.
SAM: It's a loss, Gertie, we know, and you're probably more
shocked than you realized . . .
GERTIE: I want his coffin opened.
SAM: Gertie! Be sensible! Tom's been screwed down four days
now. He can't be alive.
GERTIE: And what if he is?

[*She waits for that awful possibility to sink in.*]

What, what if he is? My boy. Depending on me. My son,
waiting for his mother to rescue him? My child. What if he
is?
SAM: It's just not possible, Gertie. It doesn't make sense.
GERTIE: And how will I feel for the rest of my life if I don't
make certain?

[*She leaves.*
SAM *sinks to his knees on the hassock.*
Nothing but the low hum of people and the music.
A drained GERTIE *returns, joins* SAM *on her knees.*]

GERTIE: I don't believe in God. Why am I on my knees?
SAM: You're saying goodbye, ent you.

[*She is weeping.*
Fade.]

ACT TWO

SCENE I

Fifteen years have passed.

   GERTIE, *with her back to us, is performing Lear's Fool to an unseen audience.*

GERTIE:

> *This is a brave night to cool a courtezan.*
> *I'll speak a prophecy ere I go:*
> *When priests are more in word than matter;*
> *When brewers mar their malt with water;*
> *When —*

> [*She dries.*]

  Yes?

PROMPT [*off stage*]: *When nobles are their tailors' tutors —*

GERTIE:

> *When nobles are their tailors' tutors;*
> *No heretics burn'd, but wenches' suitors;*
> *When every case in law is right;*
> *No —*

  Yes?

PROMPT [*off stage*]: *No squire in debt —*

GERTIE:

> *No squire in debt, nor no poor knight;*
> *When —*

  Yes?

PROMPT [*off stage*]: *When slanders do not live in tongues —*

GERTIE: *When slanders do not live in tongues —*

[*She dries again. Freezes.*
She turns to face us — terror struck.]

SCENE 2

GERTIE'S *dressing-room.*

She sits before her mirror, trembling violently.

She attempts many things to control herself. A drink — it spills. A cigarette — she coughs.

GERTIE [*to her dresser*]: No, I'm all right, Lottie. You can go. Yes. I'm sure.

[*Deep breathing — coughs even more.*]

I am not going to cry. I *am* not.

[*Begins to wipe off make-up.*]

'You look so ugly when you cry.'

[*The remains of prettiness linger about her eyes.*

KENNEDY, *a black company manager of around thirty, enters with a tray of food kept warm by a silver hood; a pot of tea and its accoutrements.*

He pours out tea. Hands her a cup. It rattles in her hand. He holds her firm. As he's holding —]

GERTIE: When I was three years old I announced, 'I, Gertrude Matthews, am going to be a fairy.'

KENNEDY: Ambitious from the word go.

GERTIE: Double pneumonia at two. Had to be taught to walk again. Doctor advised dancing lessons. Good exercise. A year later I announced, 'I, Gertrude Matthews, am going to be a fairy.'

KENNEDY: Can I let go now?

GERTIE: You can try.

[*He lets go. The trembling recommences. He takes hold again.*]

At eight I started ballet lessons with a famous ballet mistress who told me I walked like a crab. 'You walk like a crab, I hope you don't dance like one.' Insults! They've never stopped.

KENNEDY: Tell me when I can let go.

GERTIE: 'Don't you go thinking *you've* got talent, Gertie,' my mum used to say. 'It's just God's gift.'

KENNEDY: I'm letting go.

GERTIE: She was probably right.

KENNEDY: You do talk nonsense, don't you?

[*He lets go.*]

GERTIE: There! You see? Another insult.

[*Hands trembling again.*]

KENNEDY [*again taking hold*]: Maybe you invite them.

GERTIE: I married a man whose stepmother told me I was the dullest thing on two legs. Did I invite that?

KENNEDY: Jealousy.

GERTIE: 'Gertie hasn't got looks but she's got character.' Did I invite that?

KENNEDY: She said you had character.

GERTIE: 'If only you smiled like the Harmer girl. Renée Harmer is *so* pretty. You watch that Harmer girl, *she'll* go places.'

KENNEDY: I'm letting go.

[*He does so.*]

There. Better.

GERTIE: I learned that it *was* possible to do more than one's best, but it was never quite good enough for my mum.

[*She drinks. Puts down cup, exhausted.*]

My understudy's good, isn't she, Mr Phillips?

KENNEDY: Very good. Why do you ask?

[GERTIE *has learned how to protect her vulnerability with bawdy humour.*]

GERTIE [*evading an answer*]: Why don't we go out for dinner tonight?

KENNEDY: Gertie, will you stop making passes at me?

GERTIE: Why should I? The spring is coming. I feel wild stirrings.

KENNEDY: Here, I've bought you half a bottle of the best Bordeaux.

GERTIE [*cod Slav accent*]: I want your body.

KENNEDY [*cod Slav accent*]: Well, I don't want yours.

[*She pulls open her dressing-gown, flashing her breasts.*]

GERTIE: You sure, Mr Phillips?

KENNEDY: They're very nice, yes, now put them away and eat your steak.

GERTIE: If you don't want my body why do you look after me, buy me expensive wine, hang around as though I were a bitch on heat?

KENNEDY: Because as company manager I'm paid to look after you, and because you're a great actress from whom I learn something each night.

GERTIE: Like how to dry?

KENNEDY: Every actor dries at least once in their life.

GERTIE: But not twice a week. Look –

[*She holds out her shaking hand.*]

– can you tremble like that?

KENNEDY: Of course I can.

[*He holds out his hand. It trembles.*]

GERTIE: You're just acting.

[*Drinks deeply.*]

'Just acting.' Are you aware, Mr Phillips, that society normally uses the name of our profession as a term of abuse? 'Oh, ignore her, she's just acting!' Are you aware, Mr Phillips, that every night I go out there in front of an audience and pretend to be who I am not? Are you aware, Mr Phillips, that if I did that in public life I'd be shunned, vilified, called a humbug, a fraud, a sham, a fake, a liar, but up there, made up, lights bright, someone else's words of wit and brilliance, I can dissemble to my heart's content, it's acceptable, no one gives a toss. What is despised in a person *off* stage I am deceiving an audience to praise *on* stage. And the more convincingly I deceive the more they praise. They even pay for it. Are you aware of all that, Mr Phillips? Audacious, huh? What other profession do you know where the professional exposes herself to the ridicule of disbelief, the ignominy of dismissal, the humiliation of being seen through, and makes that her *raison d'être*, her justification for existing, eh? What other profession?

[*Her make-up is off. Her face is 'naked'. She pulls her hair to stick up, defiantly making herself unattractive.*]

Come to bed. I have such delights to offer you.

[GERTIE *from here on will change, make up, occasionally cut her food and feed it to* KENNEDY. *He loves her sufficiently to ride her flippancy and address her serious side.*]

KENNEDY: You are not asking your audience to praise your acting . . .

GERTIE: You could demand whatever you desired.

KENNEDY: You are not saying to an audience, 'Look at me, aren't I a clever actor.'

GERTIE: Even lie on top if you like.

KENNEDY: Be serious! You miss the point of acting.

GERTIE: Oh, I do, do I? After twenty-five years of giving my all, I miss the point of all I gave?

[*She goes off to shower, conversing from there.*]

KENNEDY: You're asking an audience to listen, think and feel about what it is your *character* says, thinks and feels.

GERTIE: Through an actor!

KENNEDY: Yes. *Through* an actor. But the theatre is not *about* actors, any more than medicine is about doctors. Medicine is about saving life, acting is about representing life.

GERTIE: Artificially!

KENNEDY: Everything human beings do, except bodily functions like eating, sleeping and you-know-what –

GERTIE [*lasciviously*]: Oh yes, I do, I do, I do know what –

KENNEDY: – everything other than the above mentioned could be called artificial. Words, signs, songs, dance – they're all artifacts for representing selections from the real thing, which is life itself.

GERTIE: Oh sharp! Sharp, sharp and sexy.

KENNEDY: I've never thought it either useful or helpful to describe what we do as acting.

GERTIE: A thinking man is so sexy!

KENNEDY: We represent. We employ a skill, a skill to represent selections in the life of –

GERTIE: – a Fool!

[GERTIE *reappears in a bathrobe.*]

Pa-poum!

[*Sits before mirror to make up.*]

GERTIE: Why do I dry as Lear's Fool? What is there about that speech?

KENNEDY: Lists! The speech is a list. Meaning – drives, pulls you along. In a list it's easy to get lost.

GERTIE: It's not just the drying, it's the fearing. And it's not just the fearing, it's the fear of fearing. It's the putting yourself up there when the 'believe-in-me' is gone. Everything goes out of your head. Your body is paralysed. Terror! It's to do with being caught out. If you dry then everybody suddenly knows you've been 'just acting'. Blood drains from you and in its place shame seeps like poison through your whole system. I've often stood in the wings and thought, I'm not going out there, I can't do that show again tonight. And I've wanted to lock myself in the dressing-room. And I think – when will that day come, locking myself in – when is it going to be me?

[*Long pause. Mood changing.*]

Ha! There was this actor who'd made up a set of seven lines for when *he* dried in a Shakespeare role.

Aye, my Lord, yonder Hereford cometh
And Shrewsbury too. And York hath mounted
And will shortly come. Behold is yonder
Basingstoke your favourite forsooth
And Cornwall calls thee home to rest.
Look, sire, Somerset and Dorset too
And Surrey, aye, and Buckingham . . .

By which time he'd either remembered the lines or his colleagues had fed him.

[*Both are convulsed.*]

KENNEDY: The counties, thank God for the English counties.
GERTIE: Look, sire, Somerset and Dorset too . . .
KENNEDY: And Surrey, aye, and Buckingham . . . [*laughter*]
GERTIE: They could be made to fit anything.
KENNEDY: Not *anything*, surely. Histories, maybe, but what if he dried in *Romeo and Juliet*?
GERTIE: Romeo, Romeo – [*Beat.*] – and Somerset and Dorset too . . .
KENNEDY: And Surrey, aye, and Buckingham . . .

[*They have difficulty stemming their laughter.*]

GERTIE: Tell me about your mum for a change.
KENNEDY: My mum? Married at seventeen, had five children, and when the youngest was fourteen said goodbye to us all and went off with a dark stranger. It was as if she'd just been given the charge of us for a short while until the time came to give us back. Though who to, we never found out. She rings one of us now and then but we don't see much of her. Strange lady. Laughed at everything and seemed to understand nothing. When we meet she looks at us as though she's trying to remember who we are.
GERTIE: What about poor old Dad?
KENNEDY: Poor old Dad is a very bewildered, incompetent

bricklayer who works non-stop for builders with no standards. His wife going off with a dark stranger bewildered him; his children's ability to thrive and survive without either of them bewilders him; and the builders who continue to employ him bewilder him.

GERTIE: You feel close to your people?

KENNEDY: My *what*?

GERTIE: People! I said 'people'. [*to an imaginary neighbour*] I did say 'people', didn't I?

KENNEDY [*sardonically*]: Which 'people'? My family 'people' or my black 'people'?

GERTIE: Oh dear. Have I asked the wrong question? Soorreeee!

KENNEDY: I once got into a fight at school defending a white boy against the overwhelming odds of three black boys who turned on me and screamed, 'Where are your roots, black boy? Don'tcha know where you belong? Roots, man, roots! Remember your roots!' To which I replied, 'My roots are anywhere intelligence is.' Having said which, they laid me out flat as a slab for the dead.

GERTIE: Complicated.

KENNEDY: Complicated.

GERTIE: So from whence your desire to act?

KENNEDY: Don't know. My Dominican great-grandfather is purported to have been seduced by a runaway cancan dancer who'd pinched her ageing lover's silver.

GERTIE: Say that again.

KENNEDY: My Dominican great-grandfather is purported to have been seduced by a runaway cancan dancer who'd pinched her ageing lover's silver.

GERTIE: Complicated.

KENNEDY: Complicated.

[*She's provocatively putting on her grip stockings.*]

GERTIE: Nice legs?

KENNEDY: Gorgeous.

GERTIE: Yours if you play your cards right.

[*He parries her bawdiness as usual.*]

KENNEDY: Gertie –

GERTIE: Sounds ominous.

KENNEDY: – do you think I have a talent for acting?

[*Long pause.*]

You paused too long. I have no talent for acting.

GERTIE: It's not that you have no talent for acting, it's that . . . well . . . you act as though you don't really want to.

KENNEDY: It shows?

GERTIE: Know what I think?

KENNEDY: I didn't think it showed.

GERTIE: I think you should apply to run a theatre.

KENNEDY: And yet I desperately want to act.

GERTIE: Become a producer!

KENNEDY: Or perhaps I should be directing. Or writing. Or –

GERTIE: Producers have the power.

KENNEDY: I've thought about it.

GERTIE: Don't think, do!

KENNEDY: It so happens I'm good with money.

GERTIE: See! Not a qualification for acting.

KENNEDY: I actually do understand money.

GERTIE: So go out and get rich and make me your mistress.

KENNEDY: I'll confess something –

GERTIE: – or one of them!

KENNEDY: – I've actually made money. I bought a house when I was twenty-four, got a 90 per cent mortgage, sold it in the last of the boom years, made a killing and invested.

GERTIE: And lost?

KENNEDY: No. I'm ashamed to admit it, but I invested wisely.

GERTIE: Good Lor! But how did you know? From where? I mean . . . what . . . ?

KENNEDY: I have this gift. I can make money reproduce itself. I've always had it. Since school days. I traded. In anything. Buy from one boy and sell to another. No one knew. I always had money and no one knew how. Used to think I stole.

Sometimes when I close my eyes the language of finance floats before me. I feel as though I'm engaged with something supremely wicked, like being with a marvellous whore. Everything is possible. 'Dividend.' 'Charge account.' 'Money supply.' 'White knight.' 'Opening price.' 'Elastic currency.' 'Liquidity.' 'Open-mouth operations.' 'Risk capital.' 'Placing.' 'Overnight money.' 'Order.' 'Tender.' 'Yield.' A world vibrating with challenge, stimulating the imagination, releasing energies. To buy with one hand and sell with the other, to know what to buy and when to sell, to judge what the market needs, the price it can take.

And other times when I close my eyes the language of poetry floats before me.

> *And on the pedestal these words appear:*
> *'My name is Ozymandias, king of kings:*
> *Look on my works, ye Mighty, and despair!'*
> *Nothing beside remains. Round the decay*
> *Of that colossal wreck, boundless and bare*
> *The lone and level sands stretch far away.*

I'm a torn man, Gertie – artist or trader?

GERTIE: That's why I love you, you've got problems!

KENNEDY: Artist or mammon?

GERTIE: Go for mammon, more user-friendly.

KENNEDY: Why is it, do you suppose?

GERTIE: Why is it what do I suppose?

KENNEDY: Why is it that people want to be involved in the arts?

GERTIE: Glamour!

KENNEDY: I think it's God.

GERTIE: God?

KENNEDY: Being an artist, people feel, is like being in touch with the divine.

GERTIE: Being an artist is blood, sweat and tears.

KENNEDY: It's so difficult getting you to be serious.

GERTIE: Blood, sweat and tears is very serious.

KENNEDY: We all know about blood, sweat and tears, but when they've been spent, if you've made it come together – the novel, the painting, the symphony, the poem, the play — blessed! By God! Touched. By the divine! But money? Mammon?

GERTIE: I find money very thrilling.

KENNEDY: Me too. Thrilling. But a work of art — to assemble the beautiful parts of a work of art . . . ah!

GERTIE: Do you realize you burn when you're animated?

KENNEDY: Who got the deepest satisfaction from life, Masaccio who first gave perspective to painting, or the Medici who commissioned paintings?

GERTIE: Your eyes glow.

KENNEDY: Mozart or his patrons?

GERTIE: All fiery.

KENNEDY: Problem is — some of us have got it and some of us haven't.

GERTIE: Good God! Sam!

KENNEDY: Sam?

GERTIE: There used to be a young lad worked as a car-park attendant here. Samson Martin, he used to say that. 'Some's got it, and some ain't.'

KENNEDY: And did he have it?

GERTIE: What he had is the same as what you have — an identity crisis. Thought he was born to be a car-park attendant.

KENNEDY: Like I think I'm born to be an artist.

GERTIE: Like I don't know whether I'm coming or going.

[*Long pause.*]

KENNEDY: Eat your food.

GERTIE: Ah, food. Now, if you really want to know and understand everything about me, and you *do* want to know and understand everything about me, don't you, Mr Phillips, because that's the only way you'll get me into bed, and I respect you for it, you don't rush a girl, I can see that — so if you really want to know and understand me — watch me eat.

[*She removes the covering hood.*]

Have you ever watched me eat?

KENNEDY: I prefer listening to you.

GERTIE: Love food, hate eating it. The act of cutting things up on a plate – how do you do it without it sliding off the edge? How do you push potatoes and beans with a knife on to a fork without them falling? And when you succeed and you feel safe enough to raise them to your mouth, how do you make sure they stay there? That's my real terror, food dropping off my fork, back on to the plate, splashing the hostess's best tablecloth, or my best dress. So I lower my face to the plate, which I know is wrong, you're supposed to raise your food to your mouth, I know it, and sometimes I try, surreptitiously, which is impossible, because by this time I know everyone is looking at me, so I get embarrassed, and hover, and my face goes down and my fork comes up, a compromise, which doesn't work because my mouth is never ever where my fork imagines it is. I once pronged the back of my throat! You wouldn't think it possible, would you? An anxious face went down too far and an eager fork came up too high. Aaarrrgghh!

[*Feigns strangulation.*]

Eating is an agony with only one other person, at a dinner-table it's a nightmare.

[*Pause.*]

I'm glad you asked why I'm afflicted thus.

KENNEDY: Why are you afflicted thus, Gertrude?

GERTIE: Because, Mr Phillips, although I keep baldly asking you to impale yourself upon me I am, deep deep down where it counts, a very shy and tortured woman who feels she has to apologize for the air she breathes.

[*Pause.*]

I'm glad you asked me why I'm afflicted thus.

KENNEDY: Why are you afflicted thus, Gertrude?

GERTIE: Because, Mr Phillips, of Mum –

KENNEDY: Ah, Mum.

GERTIE: — who I idolized out of all proportion until I saw she had feet of clay and then I just stopped liking her. And when I stopped liking her I lost her. Like a bereavement. My fault, really, for making her a saint. We fall in love with images *we* make of ourselves and of other people. It's never really what we are or what they really are, is it?

KENNEDY: There must have been something lovable about her? Every mother has something lovable about them.

GERTIE: Lovable? She used to polish the window-ledges outside the house. Painted them glossy white, then polished them. [*Pause.*] Taught me to stand on my head in the kitchen. [*Pause.*] She wanted to ride a motor-bike. [*Pause.*] She wanted to travel. [*Pause.*] She loved sherbet dabs and I loved it that my mum was a friend who loved sherbet dabs . . . Lovable? Yes. She was . . .

[*Offers her back to him, a wordless request to button up her blouse.*
He does so. With her back still to him, he asks:]

KENNEDY: What would you say is the most important tenet of the craft of acting?

GERTIE: Meaning. No question. Get the meaning right and the right emotion follows.

[*She turns to him. Dressed and made up, she looks beautiful but — terrified.*]

Would you hold me, please?

[*He takes her in his arms, comfortingly.*
She clings.]

SCENE 3

GERTIE's *dining-room, weeks later. She's at breakfast in a morning-gown.*

Tea from a pot, toast and marmalade.

Radio 3 music: the lively end of the first movement of Ravel's String Quartet in F major.

Phone rings. Turns down radio before lifting receiver.

GERTIE [*listening*]: Where are you? [*listening*] Up the road? That doesn't give me much time to undress. [*listening*] Problems? *You've* got problems? [*listening*] No, no, of course I don't mind. I'll get rid of my lovers, put on Radio 3, light a candle, pretend it's midnight instead of eight thirty in the morning, and feed you. See ya.

> [*By which time the second 'bubbly' movement of the quartet has commenced. Turns up radio.*]

That's better.

> [*The music tempts her to dance. She can't resist and flows around free-style, expertly.*]

'You look like a crab, I hope you don't dance like one.'

> [*Door bell rings.*]

'Up the road'?

> [*She moves to open the door, repeating –*]

'Up the road'? 'Up the road'? 'Up the road'?

> [*She returns with* KENNEDY.]

GERTIE: 'Up the road'?

KENNEDY: Round the corner, then.

GERTIE: Didn't give me time to finish my morning dance.

KENNEDY: Morning dance?

GERTIE: I have tea, toast and marmalade, and dance every morning.

KENNEDY: I don't believe you.

GERTIE: You're quite right not to believe me. I *should* dance every morning. Come to bed with me? A quickie before we solve your problems and go to rehearsals?

KENNEDY: You're shameless.

GERTIE: Only with you. Only with you.

KENNEDY: Why do you do it?

GERTIE: Lust after you?

KENNEDY: Be sensible, Gertie.

GERTIE: At eight forty-five in the morning?

KENNEDY: Acting – why do you do it?

GERTIE: Is *that* your problem? Still agonizing between art and mammon?

KENNEDY: Crisis of identity, remember?

GERTIE: Most people are still coughing their way into the world at this time of the morning and you're agonizing between art and mammon?

KENNEDY: Did you say you'd feed me?

[*She senses something in his evasions.*]

GERTIE: Tea? Toast? Marmalade? Coffee?

[*He serves himself.*]

Don't you *ever* want to be looked after?

KENNEDY: All the men in my family hang around waiting to be looked after. I'm determined to depend on no one.

GERTIE: So why come to me with your problems?

KENNEDY: My physical being I'm in control of –

GERTIE: Don't I know it!

KENNEDY: – it's my soul that's in need. Acting – why?

GERTIE: Naked ambition.

KENNEDY: Don't believe you. That's only part of it.

GERTIE: A wish to be someone else.

KENNEDY: Don't believe you. That's only part of it.

GERTIE: Admiration, accolades, achievement.

KENNEDY: More. That's only part of it.

GERTIE: Power.

KENNEDY: Ah!

GERTIE: The power to control an audience, to manipulate them. To stir, to move, to thrill them. Come to bed!

KENNEDY: Getting believable.

GERTIE: The power to break their grip on what they imagine is reality and confront them with another reality. Come to bed!

KENNEDY: Keep going.

GERTIE: I've made audiences gasp. It's intoxicating. Like making a man come inside you.

KENNEDY: You are vivid at an early hour.

GERTIE: It's not the hour, it's my age. I can be vivid when I like. Come to bed!

KENNEDY: So acting is conquest for you?

GERTIE: Conquest, yes. Every actor is a Don Juan. Each night you seduce another audience. 'Love me,' you tell them. 'Listen to me, love me, come to bed with me.'

KENNEDY: What about the craft, the skill?

GERTIE: That's the least you expect of a professional. Like telling a carpenter he handles his tools expertly. Fine! We should hope so! But what's the chair like? Like telling a playwright he writes good dialogue. Fine! We should hope so. But has the play any substance? Come to bed!

KENNEDY: So, you don't think I should pursue acting?

GERTIE: No. I think you should pursue me.

KENNEDY: I'm trying to map out the rest of my life, Gertie. Help me.

GERTIE Come to bed, I'll help you.

[*He sighs.*]

Don't take up acting. Every morning you'll wake up thinking is this the 'use by date'.

KENNEDY: *I'm* too young for that.

GERTIE: Then try this for size – rejection.

KENNEDY: Ah, rejection.

GERTIE: That's the killer. Coping with rejection. To be turned down for a part makes you feel unworthy to be alive – could you take that? 'Too old, too young, too short, too pretty, too good, not good enough, too experienced, not experienced enough.' Still want to be an actor? If they've seen you playing Shakespeare, you don't get the Cockney part; if they see you in the Cockney part, you don't get the countess. 'Oh, you're a comedienne!' 'Oh, you're a tragedienne!' Still want to be an actor? And then there are those interviews when the director tells you, 'You could play this part with your hands tied behind your back,' and you go home elated, and a month passes and you bump into a chum in the supermarket and ask her what she's doing and she tells you, 'I'm rather excited, actually, I'm doing . . .' and she lets you know she's got the job you've been waiting a month to hear about and you suddenly feel like a cartload of cattle. Still want to be an actor?

KENNEDY: God, Gertie, you're desirable when you're angry.

GERTIE: There's women would hit you over the head for saying that but I love it. Tell me I'm desirable and I'll burn up on stage. There are two kinds of bad performance: one – due to no talent; two – due to no sex. If a good actor is having an off night, you can bet your bottom dollar her lover's gone off her. When I was desired I was dynamite in performance. Tell me I'm not desirable and I enter stage right like lead. Ambition slinks off into the wings. I'm a dead lump. D–E–A–D, dead.

KENNEDY: L–U–M–P, lump!

GERTIE: Still want to be an actor?

KENNEDY: You telling me I'm not desirable?

GERTIE: Are you crazy? In lights: 'Kennedy Phillips. Nightly turn-on.'

KENNEDY: How often do you think you get it right?

GERTIE: What are we talking about here, the bed or the boards? Laid or stage?

KENNEDY: Stage, Gertie, stage.

GERTIE: Never, probably. And it's for sure Mum's fault. Because

I thought she was God I had to get everything right for her, and because directors are also God I feel I have to get everything right for them. Terrifies me. The figure who always expects you to get it right terrifies me, so I get it wrong. And even when I get it right I'm not there. [*Beat.*] There! See what I mean? I always think I'm not there when I get it right. Perhaps it's the contrary, perhaps when I get it right I *am* there, it really *is* me getting it right. I always say I'm not there because I'm my mother saying, 'You can't *really* be that good, not Gertie Matthews from Palmers Green.'

KENNEDY: Gertie –

[*She interrupts him with a violence in sharp contrast to her levity.*]

GERTIE: I *know* what you're going to say.

[*Long pause.*]

The company is not going to renew my contract.

KENNEDY: The company is not going to renew your contract.

GERTIE: And they asked *you* to tell me?

KENNEDY: They knew we were close.

GERTIE: You? A company fucking manager? After twenty-five years on the fucking boards, taking shit from mediocrities a quarter my age, after stepping back for the young, after endless charities, prizes, accolades and thirty-five books of rave reviews, no director in that vast company has the courage to come himself and tell me personally, 'Gertie stay home'?

KENNEDY: I'm sorry, Gertie.

GERTIE: My God, Mr Phillips, you orchestrated your little errand with cunning.

KENNEDY: Delicacy.

GERTIE: 'Identity fucking crisis'! Engage my sympathy, get me shooting my mouth off imagining I was *the* authority on acting and then give me my cards.

KENNEDY: I wanted you to remember how good you are, fortify you.

GERTIE: I knew what you were *doing*, Mr Phillips. Doesn't work, though. All confidence flees.

KENNEDY: Not for ever, Gertie. You're a very special actress.

GERTIE: Rejection is rejection.

KENNEDY: They're shits.

GERTIE: Can't you hear them? Chinese whispers through the profession. 'Heard about Gertie? She's gone, dear. Can't learn the lines. Having trouble with the wordies.' What I call the Green Room Brigade.

KENNEDY: Shits!

GERTIE: Oh, go to rehearsals! Before you came I was a queen, dancing on air. Now I'm a cartload of cattle.

[*She is changed utterly. Part of a company, she was confident, full of bravado; deprived of a base, she deflates.*]

'Don't you go thinking you've got talent, Gertie, it's just God's gift.'

KENNEDY: Gertie –

GERTIE: She was a killer.

KENNEDY: Gertie –

GERTIE: A killer!

KENNEDY: Can I –

GERTIE: Power! That's what my mum was interested in, power! Over people's lives. Her sisters'. Mine. Dad's. She treated Dad like muck. Muck! He knew all about her but he adored her so she got away with it. Beyond the pale she was for him, even after she discovered drink and oh, did my mother discover drink! No stopping her manipulations then. Want to know why I dry? The killer still manipulates me from the grave. 'Don't you go thinking you've got talent, Gertie. It's just God's gift.' God? She didn't give a toss about God, except when she needed him on her side. Made people love her and trust her so's she could control them God-like and set them up against each other.

But not the clever ones. Not our friends. She was good with au pairs and chambermaids, had them eating out of her hand – they were inferior, see, she could control *them*. But not our friends. She went silent in front of *their* conversation. Anything she didn't understand intimidated her, so then she'd fuss around and do domestic and 'sensible' things and usually wreck our evenings.

I shall never forgive her betraying me to my aunts. Got me to confide in her, then went off and told them. Killer! But she had God on her side, see, so anything I did he'd tell her about anyway, whether I confided in her or not.

And why do you think she sucked sherbet dabs with me, lovable ole Mum? Not because she liked sherbet dabs, no! She sucked sherbet dabs with me like a ten-year-old in order to be my friend. Partner 'gainst Dad, see. 'Buy them at the corner shop, we'll eat them in the kitchen. Ssh! Our secret. Don't tell Daddy.' 'Let's go to the cinema. After school. Every Wednesday. Ssh! Our secret. Don't tell Daddy.' What a friend, I thought. She understood about sweets and movies on a school-day. 'Ssh! Our secret! Don't tell Daddy.' Lovable? Killer!

And all that polishing of the window-ledges, the order, the neatness. A trap! To make coming home impossible to resist. A terrifying killer-woman full of terrifying, ignorant nonsense, and I lived with that nonsense in terror for years and years till I was pock-marked with don'ts and guilts and confused messages sending me all over the place.

You know the season she hated most? Spring! A time of growing, stirrings, wild winds. Hated it! Oh, she was a dangerous woman. One of the wasted women of the world and there's nothing more dangerous than a wasted woman. Killer! 'Don't tell Daddy! Ssh! Our secret. Don't tell Daddy!' And then I discovered I loved him. She'd kept me from him. This dignified, deeply emotional, frustrated, de-balled man who only wanted to paint landscapes. Loved him! But too late. Now that's a real guilt. I earned that one. Not like the others which I had chained to me. Killer! I can't believe I allowed all her malevolent nonsense to rule my life. Killer! Killer, killer, killer!

KENNEDY: Gertie, can I say something?

GERTIE: So who can blame you for rejecting me . . .

KENNEDY: I get my holidays in two weeks' time.

GERTIE: Or the company . . .

KENNEDY: Let's go somewhere.

GERTIE: Black kid, white grandmother?

KENNEDY: Friends.

GERTIE: Why?

KENNEDY: Why what?

GERTIE: Go somewhere.

KENNEDY: To take stock.

GERTIE: Reassess talents?

KENNEDY: No, replenish spirits.

GERTIE: Re-evaluate strengths?

KENNEDY: No, recharge batteries.

GERTIE: Reconsider my life?

KENNEDY: No. Your life is considered, it's just bruised, needs to recover.

GERTIE: What did you have in mind, fella?

KENNEDY: I cut this article out of a newspaper some time ago, thinking I might need it one day. Look – Weekends for Lovers.

GERTIE: Thought you said 'friends'?

KENNEDY: No reason why friends shouldn't enjoy the same romantic settings as lovers. We'll take separate rooms and dine by candle-light. Look – Bell Hotel, Charlbury. [*reading*] 'Lies on a rail link to Paddington, but you'll need a car if you plan on exploring the surrounding towns and villages such as Woodstock, Chipping Norton, Moreton-in-marsh . . .' Or this: 'Prior's Hall in Essex, beautiful sixteenth-century timber-framed house . . .' Or how about a castle? 'Lumley Castle, County Durham . . . genuine thirteenth-century fortress.' Protect us from the barbarians.

[*But* GERTIE *is weeping. He takes her in his arms.*]

GERTIE: I tried to give up, honest I did. I didn't want to be just an actress, it didn't seem enough. Too frivolous. So I tried to give it up and find a way to make my life liveable by having a family. I so wanted a family, but I couldn't even keep an adopted son alive. No company to belong to, no family to belong to. Christ! Is there any further down to go? And it's not self-pity though I've never understood what's wrong with a little self-pity since there are so many around absolutely determined not to share any of their own . . . Oh, God! God! God! I hate crying. I absolutely hate women who cry.

[*He holds her tighter. We've seen them in this embrace before.*]

KENNEDY: We must stop meeting like this.

[*Which makes her smile. He sits her down.*]

I don't think you look ugly when you cry.

GERTIE: You don't really want to be an actor, do you?

KENNEDY: Not really.

GERTIE: Nor a company manager.

KENNEDY: Nor that.

GERTIE: So where's your crisis of identity? Give me a big crisis of identity. I need someone else's problem to think about so's I don't have to think about mine. I hate thinking about me. They say actors are self-centred and it may be true, but the last thing I want to do is think about me. Me, me, me! Me! Me! Me! Me! Me! Me! Me!

[*He clamps her mouth.*
She's on the verge of hysterics.]

KENNEDY: Come away with me to my castle in Durham and we'll talk about crisis of identity.

GERTIE: It's a unique relationship we have.

KENNEDY: All relationships are unique. Coming?

GERTIE: Can I suggest somewhere else?

SCENE 4

The beach — as Act I, Scene 5.
  No high winds. Only the sound of the sea.
  It's a gentle, sunny, warm, spring day.
  GERTIE *appears on the rock. She stands, remembering. Delivers the*
first and last line in recollection rather than performance.

GERTIE: *Blow, winds and crack your cheeks! rage! blow! . . . All*
  germens spill at once, that make ingrateful man . . .

  [*She begins to do the t'ai chi movements.*
    KENNEDY *appears below. Watches her a while.*]

KENNEDY: You made love here?
GERTIE [*continuing t'ai chi*]: No. In my dressing-room. And only
  once. A sort of sad consolation I permitted myself for losing
  an only child. Took a black boy in my arms to whiten my
  black despair. Wrap your racial sensibilities around that.
KENNEDY: I've already told you, I don't have them. My sensibilities are where intelligence resides.

  [*Pause.*]

GERTIE: It was good of you to think of a break. It's helped.
KENNEDY: What happened to Sam?
GERTIE: I bullied him to college. He became a physiotherapist.
KENNEDY: He taught you t'ai chi?
GERTIE: Yes. Used to call me Mrs Everybody, Mrs Ordinary
  Everybody. Attacked me for trying to pretend I was more
  than an actress.

  [KENNEDY *helps her to descend the rock.*]

We sat there — I drank brandy, he drank a Coke.

KENNEDY: *That* young?

> [*Long pause.*
> *The word 'young' sets off a train of thought.*]

GERTIE: Are you aware, Mr Phillips, how full the world is of lonely women? I could list you a dozen I know. Right now. All young to middle aged. Professional or capable, single, with children, full of affection, lively, bursting to give and give and give. Lonely. Not for friendship but for love.

Why should that be, do you think? I've never been able to fathom it out. Too fussy? Sexless? Too intelligent? Too demanding? Do we overwhelm? Give out the wrong smells? Do we carry years of defeat in our eyes? I suppose that would be very off-putting – defeat. Like failure – everyone stays away. And it's a killer. First rejection and then loneliness.

No, don't protest, there's a limit to occupying myself – walks, art galleries, Canadian exercises, gardening. Amnesty one day, a sick friend the next. I do it very well, even happily, making notes to myself about interesting radio programmes and books I imagine will help me make sense of this . . . this . . . I've run out of adjectives to describe 'life'. Bewildering? Miserable? Complex? I don't know. Probably all of them. It seethes with everything, this life. That's the word! 'Seething'! This 'seething' life, to make sense of this seething life. Even a tiny corner of it. But there's a limit. And after it I'm lonely. Desperately, painfully, heart-achingly lonely. I sometimes think I'm dying from lack of love. Loved by no one, touched by no one. Not even a child. If someone, somewhere, doesn't put their arms round me in *real* love one of these days I think I'm going to die.

> [*Pause.*]

See what I mean? Me me me me me! We came here to face your identity crisis.

> [*Pause.*]

428

Or was that just your excuse to get me away from my problem.

[*Pause.*]

Why is everyone unhappy?

[KENNEDY *deliberately breaks the mood.*]

KENNEDY: Funny you should ask, Miss Matthews.

[GERTIE *catches on.*]

GERTIE: Yes, Mr Phillips, why is it that everyone is unhappy?
KENNEDY: Identity crisis.

[*He executes a music-hall skip and spreads his arms.*]

Pah-poum!

[GERTIE *follows with a similar jump.*]

GERTIE: Identity crisis, Mr Phillips?
KENNEDY: Identity crisis, Miss Matthews. We all fall in love with the wrong image of ourselves.
GERTIE: You mean [*another little jump*] –?
KENNEDY: I mean [*jump*] *you* fell in love with an image of Mrs Ordinary Everybody –
GERTIE: And *you* [*jump*] fell in love with an image of Mr Divinely Touched Artist –
KENNEDY: When in fact [*jump*] I'm Mr Mammon –
GERTIE: And I'm [*jump*] Mrs Actress.

[*Pause.* GERTIE's *gaiety deflates.*]

Can we go home now?
KENNEDY: Didn't help?

[*Pause.*]

GERTIE: Could you fall in love with me, Mr Phillips?

[*No response.*]

Ah!

[*Pause.*]

It seems to me that every decision I've ever made has been the wrong one.

KENNEDY: You mean like coming here?

GERTIE: I mean like falling in love with the wrong man at the right time and the right man at the wrong time.

[*He puts his arms around her.*]

No, not like that. Not for comfort, Mr Phillips. I'm not looking for comfort.

[*She disentangles herself.*]

Come. Let's go home. We've solved your problem.

KENNEDY: Not really.

GERTIE: Kennedy, please.

KENNEDY: I still deeply, desperately, passionately yearn to be an artist.

GERTIE: Divinely touched!

KENNEDY: To illuminate the chaos.

GERTIE: Mammon. More practical. *Copes* with the chaos.

KENNEDY: My soul is elsewhere.

GERTIE: I read once that philosophers deny the existence of a soul.

KENNEDY: Fuck philosophy.

GERTIE [*bitterly*]: Fuck art!

KENNEDY [*shocked*]: Gertie!

GERTIE [*mocking*]: 'Gertie'.

KENNEDY: That's shocking.

GERTIE: 'That's shocking.'

KENNEDY: I didn't ever think I'd hear you say –

GERTIE: 'I didn't ever think I'd hear you say –'

[*By which time they've left the beach, muttering, mumbling, mocking . . .*
    A wind seems to be gathering.
    The sea sounds wilder.]

GERTIE's *flat. Some days later. Evening.*
  GERTIE *and* KENNEDY *sit in the shadows. They have simply not
bothered to put on the lights.*

GERTIE: When I close my eyes I'm filled with a passionate desire
  to do it all again – better. Infinitely better.
KENNEDY: When I close my eyes . . . the sea . . . a mango tree at
  the back of the house . . . a sugar-cane tree further down the
  road . . . children playing . . . on a beach . . . the sun . . .

  [*Pause.*]

  I should be going. Curtain comes down soon.
GERTIE: Know how I was born? One night my father *insisted.*
  Mum told me. She actually told me: 'Your father insisted.'
  I'm not the product of love but of my father's impatience.
KENNEDY: My passion is fresh bread and salmon. When I close
  my eyes . . . my grandmother carrying a basket of fresh bread
  on her head . . . salmon being sold on the beach . . . I hear
  shouting . . . a huge moon . . . the sea again . . . children
  bathing there . . .
GERTIE: Chekhov used to say, 'Work! In work is salvation.'
  [*Beat.*] He wrote comedies you know!
KENNEDY: Is that how you survive, humour?
GERTIE: You've got it. Black humour.

  [*Both recognize the sensitive area of language.*]

  You going to walk out on me?
KENNEDY: You could have said 'gallows' humour.
GERTIE: Sorry. Gallows humour.
KENNEDY: You give in too easily, Gertie. 'Black' applied to the

richest vein of humour seems pretty honourable to me. In fact I believe we should take humour to extreme ends of black irony. Perhaps I should be a stand-up comic! Of black black-satire.

[*He does a short stand-up comedian act, addressing an imaginary audience.*]

My black brothers, I say to you, I have a dream, I *have* a dream: become white! Nose-job, skin-job, hair-job, lip-job. Whatever job can be jobbed – take it. God just made a mistake. You're really white. White man, stay out of the sun in case you get mistaken for a mistake!

GERTIE: You're taking risks.

KENNEDY: And risks must be taken. I mean I'm not one of your blacks with a chip on every shoulder, you know, looking for offence round every corner. I'm one of your thoughtful blacks, your well-read blacks, your classical music blacks. How often have you heard me call you 'guy' or 'man'? When did you ever see me with a Walkman wrapped round my ears, shuffling to a thump thump thump thump?

GERTIE: You mean g'dum g'dum g'dum g'dum?

KENNEDY: You want to know my biggest shame? I can't even dance. There! My entire body is dislocated.

GERTIE [*coyly*]: I can't believe that.

KENNEDY: Well, you go g'dum g'dum g'dum g'dum and see what happens.

GERTIE: It's not really g'dum g'dum g'dum g'dum, is it? I mean, the beat of black music is a little more complicated than that, isn't it?

KENNEDY: What do I know?

GERTIE: Let's play some.

KENNEDY: You mean you've got tapes of black music?

GERTIE: Not your advanced Kiss FM stuff, but –

[*She's sorting through her tapes.*]

– some Lionel Ritchie.

[*She puts on a tape which lands in the middle of either 'Dancing on the Ceiling' or 'All Night Long'.*]

There, that beat's simple enough. Try this.

[*She demonstrates a simple movement.*
He attempts to follow but, as he warned, he seems disjointed.]

No, no, no. Like this.

[*There follows a comic scene in which* GERTIE *attempts to lead him through simple steps and he fails miserably until — suddenly — he picks up — follows — and, incredibly, flows with her.*
He's been lying. He could dance all the time but he still pretends it's the first time.]

KENNEDY: Hey! I can dance! I can dance! Watch me, mother, I'm a real black man after all. I got rhythm, man, and I can dance.

[*At which they both go into a dynamic dance routine. It's an exhilarating scene (requiring expert choreographing).*
They're puffing.
Long pause to recover.]

See! The soul of an artist!

GERTIE: Give me the Hamlet speech.

KENNEDY: Now?

GERTIE: Now!

KENNEDY: It's late, Gertie. I've got to be there for curtain down.

GERTIE: Five minutes.

KENNEDY: You want to decide my future in five minutes?

GERTIE: You want to be an actor? Give me the Hamlet speech.

[KENNEDY *rises to perform. Long silence before starting. He delivers it woodenly. It's obvious he's no actor.*]

KENNEDY:

To be, or not to be, that is the question:
Whether 'tis nobler in the mind to suffer

The slings and arrows of outrageous fortune,
Or to take arms against a sea of troubles
And by opposing end them. To die – to sleep,
No more; and by a sleep to say we end
The heart-ache and the thousand natural shocks
That flesh is heir to: 'tis a consummation
Devoutly to be wish'd. To die, to sleep;
To sleep, perchance to dream – ay, there's the rub . . .

[*He only manages to offer this first part before* GERTIE *stops him and, with surprising efficiency, assumes the role of director.*]

GERTIE: Start again. But listen to yourself – you're delivering each line the same way. You're going up and then coming down, like a line of little hills.

[*She demonstrates.*]

Forget the poetry, just for now. Forget it's the immortal Bard, just make sense of the lines. Imagine you're asking yourself a question: 'Should I live on or give up?' It's the most important question in your life. Or, to bring it nearer home: 'To be Mr Divinely Touched Artist or Mr Mammon? Mrs Ordinary Everybody or Mrs Actress?' Go!

KENNEDY:

To be, or not to be, that is the question:
Whether 'tis nobler in the mind to suffer
The slings and arrows of outrageous fortune,
Or to take arms against a sea of troubles
And by opposing end them. To die – to sleep,
No more . . .

[*Again the little hills.*
   At which she declares –]

GERTIE: Mammon!

[*She strides to her tape-recorder to rewind the song they've just danced to.*]

You're a hopeless actor. Get your image right – make money! Don't fall in love with an artistic soul you haven't got. Mammon! Don't be ashamed! Dance!

[*By which time we're back to Lionel Ritchie and they dance their dance routine again.*
   They're both high, high, high.
   Suddenly KENNEDY *looks at his watch.*]

KENNEDY: Gertie! Curtain down! I must fly! Do you realize you've shattered my sweetest dreams?

GERTIE: That's what sweet dreams are for, sweet man. Life is richer. Get the image right and you'll find life is richer. Trust me. Fly!

[*A swift kiss. Gone.*
   She takes up dancing where she left off.]

Look at me, mother! Better than the Harmer girl. Always was and always will be and I'm dancing with a black man half my age. Love, lust and absolutely no guilts whatsoever, which I hope is making you turn in your grave. [*listens*] What's that you say, what? [*listens*] I don't care if he doesn't love me, I don't care if he's the right man at the wrong time, 'cos it's spring, mother, wild, wild spring. So turn! Turn, turn, turn, turn . . .

[*Lights down.*]

dividend The amount of a company's profit which is distributed to ordinary shareholders.

charge account A loan facility that is renewed as it is repaid and which may, therefore, be used repeatedly.

money supply The quantity of money in circulation in the economy.

white knight A company subject to an unwelcome or hostile bid may invite a second bid from a friendly company as an alternative to succumbing to a takeover. That company is a 'white knight'.

opening price The price at which a security is quoted when a stock exchange, or other market, opens for business in the morning.

elastic currency The doctrine that a domestic currency should meet the needs of trade, through a stable relationship between the expansion of business activity and the expansion of credit.

liquidity In general, availability of funds to meet claims.

open-mouth operations Expression used to describe the Federal Reserve's use of public statements to induce a change in money-market conditions.

risk capital Long-term funds invested in enterprises particularly subject to risk, as in small or new ventures.

placing The sale of new shares to institutions or private individuals, as distinct from an introduction or offer for sale.

overnight money Money placed in the money market for repayment the next day.

order An instruction from a client to a broker dealer to buy or sell a security.

tender   Generally, to offer a payment as in a written offer to purchase or to offer a service in response to advertisement.

yield   The income from a security as a proportion of its current market price.

COMPLETE TEXT OF *OZYMANDIAS*
by Percy Bysshe Shelley

I met a traveller from an antique land
Who said: Two vast and trunkless legs of stone
Stand in the desert . . . Near them, on the sand,
Half sunk, a shattered visage lies, whose frown,
And wrinkled lip, and sneer of cold command,
Tell that its sculptor well those passions read
Which yet survive, stamped on these lifeless things,
The hand that mocked them and the heart that fed:
And on the pedestal these words appear:
'My name is Ozymandias, king of kings:
Look on my works, ye Mighty, and despair!'
Nothing beside remains. Round the decay
Of that colossal wreck, boundless and bare
The lone and level sands stretch far away.

READ MORE IN PENGUIN

In every corner of the world, on every subject under the sun, Penguin represents quality and variety – the very best in publishing today.

For complete information about books available from Penguin – including Puffins, Penguin Classics and Arkana – and how to order them, write to us at the appropriate address below. Please note that for copyright reasons the selection of books varies from country to country.

In the United Kingdom: Please write to *Dept. JC, Penguin Books Ltd, FREEPOST, West Drayton, Middlesex UB7 OBR*

If you have any difficulty in obtaining a title, please send your order with the correct money, plus ten per cent for postage and packaging, to *PO Box No. 11, West Drayton, Middlesex UB7 OBR*

In the United States: Please write to *Penguin USA Inc., 375 Hudson Street, New York, NY 10014*

In Canada: Please write to *Penguin Books Canada Ltd, 10 Alcorn Avenue, Suite 300, Toronto, Ontario M4V 3B2*

In Australia: Please write to *Penguin Books Australia Ltd, 487 Maroondah Highway, Ringwood, Victoria 3134*

In New Zealand: Please write to *Penguin Books (NZ) Ltd,182–190 Wairau Road, Private Bag, Takapuna, Auckland 9*

In India: Please write to *Penguin Books India Pvt Ltd, 706 Eros Apartments, 56 Nehru Place, New Delhi 110 019*

In the Netherlands: Please write to *Penguin Books Netherlands B.V., Keizersgracht 231 NL–1016 DV Amsterdam*

In Germany: Please write to *Penguin Books Deutschland GmbH, Friedrichstrasse 10–12, W–6000 Frankfurt/Main 1*

In Spain: Please write to *Penguin Books S. A., C. San Bernardo 117–6° E–28015 Madrid*

In Italy: Please write to *Penguin Italia s.r.l., Via Felice Casati 20, I–20124 Milano*

In France: Please write to *Penguin France S. A., 17 rue Lejeune, F–31000 Toulouse*

In Japan: Please write to *Penguin Books Japan, Ishikiribashi Building, 2–5–4, Suido, Bunkyo-ku, Tokyo 112*

In Greece: Please write to *Penguin Hellas Ltd, Dimocritou 3, GR–106 71 Athens*

In South Africa: Please write to *Longman Penguin Southern Africa (Pty) Ltd, Private Bag X08, Bertsham 2013*

BY THE SAME AUTHOR

'. . . Just when you think you've got him pinned down as a Jew, along
he comes with *Caritas*, a story steeped in Christian mysticism. And
when you fancy you've got him nailed as a descendant of lofty
Victorian teachers . . . he throws off the mask of Puritan self-
betterment and social responsibility with a sexy, rueful comedy *One
More Ride on the Merry-go-round* and a heart-stopping account of a
New York love affair in his play *Lady Othello*, both filled with aware-
ness of personal and sexual experience beyond the reach of politics'
– Michael Kustow in *Time Out*